REFLECTIONS OF REALISM

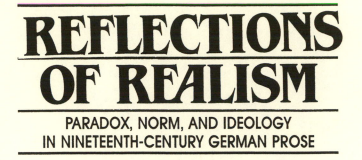

REFLECTIONS OF REALISM

PARADOX, NORM, AND IDEOLOGY
IN NINETEENTH-CENTURY GERMAN PROSE

Robert C. Holub

 Wayne State University Press   Detroit

COPYRIGHT © 1991

BY WAYNE STATE UNIVERSITY PRESS,
DETROIT, MICHIGAN 48202.
ALL RIGHTS ARE RESERVED.
NO PART OF THIS BOOK MAY
BE REPRODUCED WITHOUT FORMAL
PERMISSION.
MANUFACTURED IN THE
UNITED STATES OF AMERICA.
95 94 93 92 91   5 4 3 2 1

LIBRARY OF CONGRESS
CATALOGING-IN-PUBLICATION
DATA

Holub, Robert C.
   Reflections of realism : paradox, norm, and
ideology in nineteenth-century German
prose / Robert C. Holub.
     p.   cm.
   Includes bibliographical references and index.
   ISBN 0-8143-2291-3 (alk. paper)
   1. German fiction—19th century—History and
criticism. 2. Realism in literature. I. Title.
PT763.H68 1991
833'.70912—dc20   90-49118
                                          CIP

For Renate

CONTENTS

ACKNOWLEDGEMENTS

The idea for this book originated in an upper-division course on nineteenth-century German literature during the spring of 1983. The topic of discussion for the third week of classes was Georg Büchner's novella *Lenz*, and since I had finished with what I had prepared a day earlier than anticipated, I had to invent something for the class to look at for the final session on this work. I told the students to read carefully the passage that has come to be known as the *Kunstgespräch* (conversation on art) and expected that I would give the standard lecture on Büchner's rejection of idealism and his adherence to an early, but recognizable form of realism. I myself considered not even going over the passage again since I had read it the week before in preparation for my discussion of madness and alienation. But since I had impressed on the students the importance of paying close attention to the text, I thought I really should go through it once more. It is difficult to know why this reading produced something different for me than other readings. During the studies for my doctorate in Madison and during my professional career at Berkeley I had read the novella nearly a dozen times, but this was the first time that I noticed something peculiar in the central passage I thought I knew so well. I detected that the text did not really affirm realism as unequivocally as I had previously thought, for it was marked by a series of paradoxical and contradictory statements. Although realism was posited as an alternative to idealism, a careful reading of the *Kunstgespräch* showed me that it could be interpreted just as easily as a questioning of accepted notions of realism. During the next two classes—I extended discussion of *Lenz* for one period because of my enthusiasm—I explored with my students the way in which the *Kunstgespräch* dealt in such a sophisticated fashion with the relationship between art, specifically textual art, and reality. This set the agenda for the rest of the course. If a text apparently so familiar to me and so universally acclaimed in scholarship for its straightforward affirmation of realism proved to be more problematic than one would suspect, then perhaps other texts usually considered a part of the realist canon also exhibited some doubts about the ability of texts to reproduce an external world. These were my thoughts at the time, and during the remainder of the term I explored how realism reflects on its own poetic foundations. This was no easy chore, for it became obvious to me that most texts in the realist tradition avoid self-reflection and in most cases any reflection on the poetics that informs literary endeavor. Sometimes my attempts drew an almost total blank. But gradually during the course of the term it became clear to me that reflections on realism in realist texts were not absent but merely unforegrounded and indirect. With that realization the present project was conceived.

The conception and birth of this book was greatly facilitated by a two-year stay in Frankfurt from 1983 to 1985. It was there that I did most of the research for the project and major portions of the actual writing of the manuscript. Above all I am indebted to the Alexander von Humboldt Foundation for its generous support during this period. When I returned to Berkeley in the summer of 1985, I temporarily shelved the project and returned to it only in 1987, when I completed the first draft. For the support of the University of California during this time I am also grateful. Among the people who read the manuscript and made helpful comments are Norbert Altenhofer, Hinrich Seeba, Gail Hart, Dennis Mahoney, and Linda von Hoene. I would like to express my thanks to them and also to my students from fall semester 1988 who patiently listened to lectures derived from the manuscript and always gave encouragement and useful criticism. Even if I hadn't promised my son Alexei that I would include his name here, I would have had to mention him. His warm smile and sparkling eyes brightened my life on many a dreary day in Germany. Renate, who dislikes both dedications and official expressions of thanks, nonetheless receives both from me here. She contributed in ways too countless to enumerate.

Three chapters of this book have appeared in print in a slightly different form. The chapter on *Lenz* was published in the *Deutsche Vierteljahrsshrift* 59 (1985): 102–24; the chapter on *Romeo und Julia auf dem Dorfe* and on *Aquis submersus* appeared in *Modern Language Notes* 100 (1985): 461–97, and *Colloquia Germanica* 18 (1985): 120–39, respectively. I thank these journals and their editors for permission to include the essays with slight modifications as chapters in this volume.

NOTE ON TRANSLATIONS

For the benefit of readers who are not fluent in German, I have translated all citations, whether from primary or from secondary literature, into English. Quite a few of the German texts I used are not readily available in English editions; therefore, my references are solely to page numbers in the standard German sources. I did consult, however, English translations when they were available to me, although I sometimes found it necessary to modify translations for stylistic consistency or for reasons of accuracy. Credit is given to the English translations in the appropriate footnotes. I retained the German titles when discussing the individual works, but the first reference gives an approximate English translation. All parenthetical dates refer to the first German edition of the work under discussion.

INTRODUCTION

As ideology, literary realism does not depend
at all on the language spoken by the writer.
Language is a form, it cannot possibly be
either realistic or unrealistic . . . . There is
no antipathy between realism and myth.

> Roland Barthes,
> *Mythologies*

Literary realism has proved to be frustratingly resistant to definition. As Richard Brinkmann has shown in *Wirklichkeit
und Illusion* (*Reality and Illusion*), attempts to come to grips with this
phenomenon in the scholarship of the late nineteenth and in the first
half of the twentieth century have been uniformly unsuccessful.[1] Definitions involving such formulations as "fidelity to reality" or "close correspondence to nature" invariably end in circular argumentation. The
listing of characteristics—for example, the abundance of detailed description or the concern for formerly excluded social classes—leaves
one with a catalog that is either incomplete or so general that obviously nonrealist works would have to be included as well. Subsequent
endeavors have been equally problematic. Brinkmann's own reflections
on this issue, although provocative in their reversal of the traditional
biases, fare no better than those of his predecessors. In suggesting
that the problem of objectivity is really one of subjectivity, namely,
the increasingly problematic relationship of the subject to reality, he
leaves himself open to objections analogous to those he raises in con-

nection with prior scholarship. Critics have been quick to point out that the sampling on which his general conclusions appear to be based —Franz Grillparzer's *Der arme Spielmann* (*The Poor Fiddler*, 1847), Otto Ludwig's *Zwischen Himmel und Erde* (*Between Heaven and Earth*, 1856), and Eduard von Keyserling's *Beate und Mareile* (1903)—is both too limited and unrepresentative for such sweeping pronouncements.[2] Peter Demetz's suggestion that realism consists of a "plurality of different elements" runs into the difficulty of all such enumerations.[3] The four characteristics he delineates are ultimately so broadly defined that it is difficult to imagine what falls outside of the "syndrome" realism. Similarly the more recent attempt at a definition by Marshall Brown fails because of its amorphousness. His contention that "we consider a piece of writing to be realistic . . . whenever and insofar as we perceive silhouetting or embedding effects" remains too abstract and is potentially applicable to any literary work.[4]

Part of the difficulty, of course, results from a failure to distinguish between (and perhaps the impossibility of distinguishing between) two related phenomena. *Realism* as a general description of literature can refer to any work from the tradition. In this sense we may speak of the realism of Homer and Dante, as well as the realism of Dickens, Balzac, or Fontane. Demetz's and Brown's definitions are meant to encompass this notion of realism. But realism is also a term used to describe a particular period in literary history; the age of realism, used in this fashion, refers to the literature of the nineteenth century, especially to certain novelists in the middle and latter parts of this century. Brinkmann's discussion as well as René Wellek's notion[5] relate specifically to this historical phenomenon, which is often treated as simply a special case of intensified concern with problems of general realism. Common to the approach in both of these senses of realism is usually the attempt undertaken by critics to delineate features or qualities of individual works or eras. Whether we speak of a disturbed relationship between subject and object, silhouetting, a closed narrative structure, or simply "objective representation of contemporary social reality,"[6] we are dealing in the final analysis with textual characteristics identified in an object independent of the perceiving subject.

Perhaps a more fruitful way of dealing with the phenomenon of realism is to view it as an effect.[7] If we view realism from the vantage point of the recipient, then we shall most likely have to give up the search for a normative definition and content ourselves with tentative observations on what the effect of realism entails. For if we are serious and consequential about looking at this issue as one of reception, then we shall also have to concede that our own view of the matter is also only a partial one (in both senses of this word). Thus not only would we conclude that in theory different works, authors, or epochs could be considered realist from different historical perspectives, but also that those qualities we would currently associate with the effect of realism are products of our own historical situatedness and subject to modification by later, necessarily partial because historically conditioned, observers. Realism as a function of the reception of literature thus relativizes the entire issue.[8] Although this may be disturbing to those seeking final and definitive answers, it seems to me that the consequences of taking this position are, in practice at least, no more radical or nihilistic than most other positions. Admitting that we cannot arrive at an ultimate answer to the question of what is realism does not mean that such endeavors have no value. It simply means that, as in all such attempts, the value is both subject to alteration and established by the community of those striving to come to terms with the question.

Viewing realism as a function of reception has other consequences as well. If realism is in the eye of the beholder—or a community of beholders—we shall want to ask how a literary work makes a reader believe that it is realistic. It seems fairly evident that the relationship between text and reality is a central concern here. In general, one can say that realist works impress upon the reader that the words of the text point outside themselves to an external or nontextual world. Most often this message is implicit, although in many novels from the eighteenth century, from Defoe's *Moll Flanders* (1722) to Goethe's *Die Leiden des jungen Werther* (*The Sorrows of Young Werther*, 1774), we encounter repeated assurances of fidelity to reality. The confidentiality normally accompanying these works—they are usually made up of confessions, letters, or diaries—is a further guarantee that what is written is a reflection of something that has occurred. In texts of the nineteenth century, however, such assurances are usually delivered indirectly. Something in the style or in the manner of presentation tells the reader that the text is mirroring reality, and often scholars have assumed that a particular narrative point of view lends itself to realism more than others. Although this may be the case for French and English realism, the prose writings in Germany during the middle and latter part of the nineteenth century mitigate against such a claim. The focus once again should be not to define a quality of the work but to examine what effect this quality is apt to produce. Certain novels

15

and novellas with "subjective" or limited narrators manage very well to convince the reader that he or she is confronting a real episode or occurrence. Indeed, as we shall see in chapter five, in some cases a nonomniscient narrator may be able to effect realism (through authenticity or eyewitness accounts) better than a distant and non-involved narrative voice. What is essential, in short, is not a particular narrative technique or a particular style but, rather, that the combination of elements leads the reader to believe that the text has a mimetic relationship with the world.

Though it seems to be almost impossible to delineate universals of content or form that would define realism, it would appear to be easier to find elements that would destroy the effect of realism, at least for certain readers at certain times. A description of a trip to the moon would have seemed fantastic for readers at the turn of the century, but if such a work were written today, it would obviously not have the same effect. In certain circles the reference to miracles might be an acceptable part of reality and hence nonintrusive for the effect of realism, but for many educated readers today these references would disqualify the text in which they appear from realist literature. With regard to realist effect, elements of content appear relative to the beliefs, biases, and even age of the readership. On the other hand, as I have argued above, most stylistic elements, especially narrative perspectives, are not so much relative to variations in the readership as they are adaptable to different compositional situations. Indeed, many techniques of modern literature—for example, montage or stream-of-consciousness—also may be employed to produce a realist impact. There would appear to be at least one stylistic trait, however, that is rarely found in realist texts. The foregrounding of fictionality will almost always produce a nonrealist effect. The reason for this is simple. When a given text makes no claim to mirror or refer to an external reality but instead insists upon its nonrelationship to the world, it forfeits its potential for producing an effect of the real.

Realist texts, therefore, must stop short of foregrounding fictionality if they are to have a realist effect. Indeed, if we consider the foregrounding of fictionality to be one extreme, the texts of realism would appear to be at the other end of the spectrum. In most instances they conceal any traces of their nature as fantasy and invention: the fiction they perpetrate is that they are not fiction at all.[9] Accompanying this implicit self-denial is usually an absence of reflection on the relationship between text and reality. Works of realism, by the very fact that this relationship is not thematized, imply that it is natural, or at least that it requires no clarification. A lack of obvious self-reference, self-reflection, or self-consciousness is thus a feature frequently encountered in these works, particularly in Germany during the nineteenth century.[10] But this does not mean that such texts actually exclude self-reflection. In fact, if we examine them closely enough, we find that they quite often comment on the relationship between text and reality, but that their comments are almost always disguised or indirect. In many cases the authors of the text may even be unaware of the status and nature of these comments, and one could therefore say that they exist as an unconscious subtext suppressed by the powerful mechanisms of realist consciousness.[11] These reflections on realism and their far-reaching ramifications form the starting point for the discussions contained in this book. The thesis throughout is that in the German tradition texts that have traditionally been considered realist are most interesting and most revealing of their historical situatedness at precisely those moments when they begin to reflect upon the precarious nature of their own poetics. By reading these passages and drawing implications from them, I endeavor not only to reinterpret canonical texts but also to disclose the ideology and paradoxes informing the realist enterprise.

The ultimate purpose of my various interpretations is to show how realism functions as a normed discourse that excludes otherness. This otherness takes various forms in the works I analyze. In the novella *Lenz* (1839), the central figure reveals various inconsistencies in a realist poetics; only his madness allows him to be an outspoken advocate of such a contradictory theory. In my treatment of the nineteenth-century *Bildungsroman*, I find a subtext that preaches for self-denial and renunciation under the external veneer of self-cultivation and achievement. Keller's novella *Romeo und Julia auf dem Dorfe* (*A Village Romeo and Juliet*, 1856) represses primeval desire as illicit sexual attraction. In Storm's *Aquis submersus* (1877), literature and art are called upon to negate sensuality and affirm an "aesthetics of abnegation." In chapters six and seven, the racial dimensions of German realism are exposed. In a typically xenophobic gesture, C. F. Meyer's *Der Heilige* (*The Saint*, 1879) marginalizes the Oriental as something incomprehensible to the Central European mind. And in three "business" novels written during the last half of the nineteenth century, the contradiction in the oxymoronic designation "poetic realism" finds an uneasy resolution in the valorization of Germans over their Jewish counter-

17

parts. The norm of realism is thus defined by a series of exclusions. Although the text perpetrates the fiction that it is passively mirroring an extra-textual reality, that is, though it endeavors to produce the effect of the real, the subtext in a more active manner propagates a notion of what reality is or ought to be. No single work from the nineteenth century completely delineates this ideologically informed reality.[12] I have selected for analysis, however, those that reveal some of the most salient and pernicious features of "realist ideology" in Germany between 1830 and 1890.

The question that perhaps remains is why I choose to begin my incursion into each of these texts at the point where they contain an implicit reflection on their own realist poetics. My reasoning is twofold. First, it seems to me that these are "soft spots" in the text that are themselves produced by exclusion or repression, and that they are therefore related to the ideological exclusions that occur throughout. Since realism, as I have contended above, self-destructs by reflecting on its own fictional underpinnings, the strategies used to cover these reflections are identical to those employed to enforce its prejudiced view of the world. Indeed, often the implicit reflections on realism themselves provide an opening into an ideological space that the text itself seeks to repress. It is as if the text ruptures at those moments when it begins to discuss its own shaky foundations, revealing its aesthetic as well as its political and social biases. For this reason I also found it useful to examine briefly two works apiece from the romantic era and from early modernism. These texts provide a contrast to the unforegrounded reflexivity of the realists, and although they too are not unideological, they are less obviously normed. The second reason for looking at these texts through their implicit poetic statements is my conviction that literary and social conventions are not totally separate. Although aesthetic theories may not possess an inherent ideology, they function ideologically in a given social situation. The realism of current pulp literature, film, and TV may not have the same exclusionary function today, but the examination of how realist aesthetics implied norms in the past contributes to an understanding of how certain fictional discourses operate with disguised norms. In this sense I hope to show with the analyses presented here not only the ideology of German realism but also something of the prehistory of contemporary modes of realist representation.

18

1

BEFORE REALISM:
Romantic Irony and the Self-Conscious Text

Irony is the form of the paradox.
Paradox is everything that is at
the same time good and great.
Friedrich Schlegel,
"*Lyceum* Fragments"

What makes the realist penchant for limiting reflexivity so remarkable is that it represents an almost total negation of the poetics of the preceding generation. Before realism became the dominant style of writing toward the middle of the nineteenth century, literary texts often contained a series of reflections upon their own presuppositions, including the relationship between word and world. For the romantics about 1800 and for most of the major writers during the subsequent two decades self-reflexivity became the cardinal principle of literary practice. Irony, the multivalent notion developed by Friedrich Schlegel, captures best this essential feature of romantic theory. As various commentators have pointed out, this term has implications for both the creative act and the structure of the literary work.[1] On the one hand, it designates the freedom of the writer over her or his material as a dialectic of self-creation and self-destruction. As Schlegel states, it is "the freest of the licenses, because through it one puts oneself above oneself."[2] But it also forms the center of a work of art conceived as transcendental poetry. This aspect of this key romantic concept relates to an act of continuous upward displacement. For Schlegel irony is "a permanent parekbase"[3] likened to a model of infinity (*Epideiksis der Unendlichkeit*).[4] In both cases what is essential

19

for romanticism is a consciousness that reflects upon itself and its own activities. In contrast to the texts of realism, not only is the romantic text aware of its own status as creation, but it also foregrounds this awareness.

This paradigmatic feature of romanticism is evidenced in many of the major works that appeared around 1800. Often the early writings of Ludwig Tieck are used to illustrate how romantic irony functions since the characters in many of these works demonstrate an awareness of their own literariness. But a more intriguing and perhaps more consequential illustration of the principles of irony can be found in the *Nachtwachen von Bonaventura* (*Nightwatches of Bonaventura*) from 1804. This text, which was hardly noticed by contemporaries, was "discovered" toward the end of the nineteenth century, but until the 1960s the majority of critics concentrated on the question of authorship. The pseudonym "Bonaventura" has been identified with Schelling, Jean Paul, and several other less-known writers from the era, and until recently a new candidate for authorship was offered for consideration every few years.[5] However, this novel (if we can assign it to this genre at this point for the sake of convenience) has obviously been deemed important not merely because of the anonymity of its author but because it provides us with an insight into the techniques and tendencies of German romantic literature. In sixteen loosely connected "night watches," we meet Kreuzgang, the night watchman, who frequents cemeteries and commits various mischievous acts. During the course of the book, he also manages to inform the reader about his origins. The son of a gypsy woman and an alchemist, he was conceived at the moment when his father had conjured the devil. His mother, concerned that her satanically inspired offspring enjoy a Christian education, evidently placed him in a chest and allowed a shoemaker who had taken to searching for gold to discover him. This shoemaker named and raised him, and Kreuzgang, after a series of adventures as a satirist and a puppeteer and a period of confinement in an insane asylum, turned to the profession in which we first encounter him.

Perhaps the most obvious way in which the *Nachtwachen* exhibits a self-conscious attitude is in its relationship to the literary tradition. From the brief description I have given, it is clear that we are dealing here with a distortion of the *Bildungsroman*. Indeed, this work can be easily read as a parody of Goethe's *Wilhelm Meister* (1795–96), one of the most frequently discussed works by German romantics. The process of self-cultivation in Goethe's novel is progressive: the hero proceeds in a linear fashion, passing through various stages on his way to his goal. Though he begins as an enthusiast of the theater, he is educated to see that he must integrate himself into society in other ways and become a useful member of the larger community. Kreuzgang's progress, by contrast, is haphazard; we learn of his development in retrospective glimpses he scatters for us in several "night watches." Instead of advancing toward a goal, the logic of the novel and of the hero's narrative takes us back to his rather murky origins as godson of the devil.[6] Both works pivot on a Hamlet experience. But whereas in *Wilhelm Meister* it hastens the hero's realization that he must move on to other endeavors, in the *Nachtwachen*, in an ironic emulation of Goethe's work, Kreuzgang's departure from the madhouse and the death of his Ophelia ultimately lead him to his lonely occupation as night watchman. Witness his ironic comment from the fifteenth night watch:

> There is nothing on earth more important than the consciousness of being useful and of enjoying a steady salary—man is not simply a cosmopolitan; he is also the citizen of a state. The post of night watchman had just been vacated, and I believed myself diligent enough to occupy it with honor. The world is now very cultivated, and one is justified in demanding great talent from every single citizen. (131)[7]

Kreuzgang's integration into society as a night watchman is unmistakably an emargination, and certainly his association with night, darker powers, and madness forms a striking contrast to Meister's path to enlightenment. The controlling force in Kreuzgang's peregrinations is not a benevolent, ordered, and disciplined secret society like the *Turmgesellschaft* (Tower Society) but rather the chaos and nothingness of a world without purpose, goal, or direction.

The *Nachtwachen* is not only self-conscious of its place in the literary tradition, it is also aware of the precariousness of writing and narrative in this tradition. In contrast to both *Wilhelm Meister* and the bulk of realist prose later in the nineteenth century, we find in this romantic work frequent reflections on how a story is told. In the third night watch, Kreuzgang informs the reader that his presentation in the previous chapters is merely a repetition of how he heard about the events themselves. He makes no attempt to order events in a narrative scheme with a beginning, middle, and end (at least this is what he maintains), nor does he endow them with some meaning or import outside of their occurrence. In a sense, he is thus claiming to adhere strictly to reality; his disjointed, nonlinear style is more faithful to the world than the artificially structured narratives of more conventional writers. Indeed, later in the novel he comments—probably ironically—on his inability to construct a linear narrative: "What I wouldn't give to be able to narrate as cohesively and directly as other honest Protestant writers and authors do, who thus become great and glorious, and trade their golden ideas for golden realities" (48). This remark occurs directly after he has finished retelling in "sober prose" an autobiographical tale he had heard from a crazed Spaniard. What is unusual about this is that we hear both the original tale (fourth night watch) and Kreuzgang's version of it (fifth night watch), but there is no resemblance between the two. Indeed, the Spaniard introduces his remarks by stating that he does not want to narrate his own story in a linear fashion from one point to the next—this is too boring for him. Instead he relates his tale in the form of a marionette play with a Hanswurst; "then the whole thing becomes more plastic and more amusing" (33). Here and in other passages, the text exhibits a consciousness of narrative as a necessary fiction. Unlike the prototypical realist text, the *Nachtwachen* thematizes the necessary distortion that accompanies both the telling and the retelling of events. Text and reality exist uneasily with each other; the former does not capture or encompass the latter but, rather, forms an opaque layer through which the original can never be viewed in its pristine form.

The incongruous relationship between text and reality is reinforced in the confusion between theater and reality. At times this merely involves the motif we have already mentioned in connection with Tieck's early works: a character becomes conscious of his fictionality, thereby destroying the illusion associated with the stage. The Spaniard, for example, in relating his story has the Hanswurst speak upon the absurdity of a marionette reflecting about itself. But in this instance we see how Bonaventura goes beyond the romantic tradition of irony, how his work becomes a reflection on this self-reflexive heritage.[8] In the normal employment of this technique, a character merely comments upon his own role as character. Here, however, a character, himself the creation of a character (who is in turn the creation of an authorial name that is a creation of an unknown author) reflects upon a character reflecting about itself. The ante of self-consciousness is raised two or three levels; Schlegel's desire for a "poetry of poetry" becomes a "poetry of poetry of poetry," etc. When the Hanswurst proceeds to speak of freedom of the will and the insanity in the brain of marionettes, insisting that his is the only reasonable role in the whole farce, we begin to understand that the extreme consequence of this heightened self-reflection is a confounding of world and fiction.

This is evident in Kreuzgang's frequent musings about the necessity and unavoidability of using masks and disguises, but it is particularly striking in his confrontation with Ophelia in the asylum. Throughout the novel Kreuzgang had alluded to the topos of the earth as the stage for God's world theater, but in this episode he appears to draw literal consequences from this apparent metaphor. The woman in question was brought to the institution because she went mad while playing Ophelia's madness; in short, she remained in her role. Thus Shakespeare's reputation as a second creator is validated here in a double sense. He not only recasts reality into a play by the writing of *Hamlet* but also his play into reality by causing the insanity of the actress portraying Ophelia. Kreuzgang falls in love with the madwoman and composes letters under the name of Hamlet, in which he declares his love for her. But she cannot tell him whether she loves him since she cannot determine who she is. She wishes, therefore, to escape from the maddening conflation of role and reality, to find her way back, if possible, to her true self. Only then can she answer Kreuzgang's letters with her true feelings. She appeals to Hamlet/Kreuzgang to assist her in reading her role back (*hilf mir nur meine Rolle zurückzulesen* [118]) so that she can determine whether anything remains after the layers of fiction are stripped away. But Hamlet/Kreuzgang, who is conscious of the fictional part he is playing, contends that there is nothing other than roles: "Everything is just theater, whether the actor plays on the earth itself, or two steps higher, on the stage, or two steps lower, in the ground, where the worms take up the cue of the departed king" (119). Ophelia meanwhile has recognized that she cannot read herself backward out of the role, and therefore determines to read forward (*fortlesen*) to the "exeunt omnes" and there seek her authentic ego. When she meets with Kreuzgang in person, she believes that success is imminent—"behind the play the ego [*das Ich*] begins"—but he emphatically contradicts her: "It is nothing!" (123), and his evaluation is apparently correct. Her cry of "I love you!" is "the final speech in the play," but these are her last words in life as well; she dies after professing her love without reaching any authentic core of being. For Bonaventura there is no liberation from role-playing, masks, and disguises; even death is conceived by Kreuz-gang as "a white mask" (123). By consistently suggesting that reality is only another variant of theatrical fictions, Kreuzgang radicalizes the romantic premises that inform the writings of his contemporaries. Works of art cannot mirror events in the real world because in Bona-ventura's universe there is no essential difference between art and world. The text not only exhibits a consciousness of its own fictionality but also insists that there is nothing substantial outside this fictionality to appeal to. The literalization of the "world is a stage" metaphor thus results in a radicalization of the self-conscious ironic stance. In a gesture that one can only interpret as Fichtean, consciousness absorbs all reality into itself.[9]

This conflation of reality and fiction is not restricted to theater, however; it is also thematized with respect to written texts. In the third night watch, Kreuzgang, in a particularly pensive mood, leafs through his own "book of life" (*Lebensbuch*), which, like the *Nachtwachen* itself, is "confused and wildly written" (25). Unlike the novel in which it appears, this biography consists of both text and illustra-tions, but the origin and purpose of the book remain mysterious. The third chapter is narrated by the shoemaker who found Kreuzgang, but there is no indication that he wrote the rest of it. In fact, he himself appears on the initial woodcuts used as illustrations. The first of these depicts a shoemaker who wants to give up his profession and learn to make gold. A gypsy woman standing next to him instructs him in digging for treasures. The second woodcut portrays the same shoe-maker, obviously identified as Kreuzgang's stepfather, finding him as a child in the chest. Gradually the reader understands that this strange book contains Kreuzgang's own story. The only portion missing is his birth. We never learn what is on the first page: "On the first sheet it already looks suspicious," and page five already deals with the treas-ure hunter/shoemaker. Instead of words there are evidently "mystical signs from the Kabbala" on this page. We never know when the text becomes understandable because Kreuzgang refuses to read to us, pre-ferring instead to describe the woodcuts. What is significant about this book is that as text and illustration it equals Kreuzgang's life. He interrupts his reading, but we have no reason to assume that there is any difference between his existence in the world (of the *Nacht-wachen*'s fiction) and his existence in the text from which he reads. Indeed, a variation of this obliteration of difference is thematized in the shoemaker's brief narrative. He first asserts that the state of dreaming and waking are clearly distinguished from one another, but subsequent events belie this distinction. His dream of finding a chest actually occurs. The boundary between dream and waking, text and reality, word and world, is here impossible to ascertain. Like Novalis's hero, whose experience toward the end of the fifth chapter of *Heinrich von Ofterdingen* (1802) is the object of Bonaventura's parody here, Kreuzgang finds that the relationship between text and reality is not one of dependence and mimesis—as it must be in realism—but one of identity.

If theater and life, text and reality, are inseparable in this work, it is because the underlying poetics valorize self-reflexivity over reflection. The text continuously comments upon itself and upon its fictional status, abjuring any situation in which it would appear that it mirrors or copies something external to it. Indeed, this resistance to realism extends to the very metaphorical structure of the text. As we shall see in the following chapters, mirrors and portraits appear with great frequency in the works of realism. Usually they are associated with a system of representation in which external events are captured by the written word. In the *Nachtwachen*, by contrast, these same images are without exception employed to convey the notion of distortion. In the eighth night watch, for example, Kreuzgang broaches the theme of tragic representation: "With an iron fist the tragic poet holds the beautiful countenance of life steadily before his great concave mirror, in which it distorts itself in wild features and so to speak manifests its abysses in the furrows and wrinkles that fall in the beautiful cheeks; thus he sketches it" (66–67). Here the metaphors of mirroring and portraiture are interwoven, as they are so often, but in both cases the result of this conventionally realist imagery is a distortion of "beautiful life" rather than its preservation in art. The tenth night watch contains a related passage. Kreuzgang, like Ophelia later in the work, meditates on what would remain if all the masks were removed. His imagination tells him, however, that there would be no reflection if there were no disguise for the self: "What! Is there no I [*Ich*] in the mirror when I go before it?" (93). In contrast to the first example, a mirroring is impossible here because there exists no substantial reality to be mirrored. But what unites these two passages is their implicit denial of the mirror image. Finally, let me turn to the seventh night watch for a last illustration of this metaphor. Kreuzgang is speaking about his attempts to narrate autobiographically. Unfortunately he has always failed because, as we have witnessed, a mirror affords him no access to an authentic representation:

> I have often gone to sit before the mirror of my imagination and tried to make a satisfactory portrait of myself, but I have always lashed into the damned countenance when I finally found that it was like a picture puzzle [*Vexiergemälde*], which, viewed from three differing perspectives, portrayed a Grace, a long-tailed monkey, and from the front the devil as well. (56–57)

Here the two motifs from the previous examples are incorporated as well. The endeavor to write autobiographically is likened to a self-portrait, but the painting that results is non-unitary (*Vexiergemälde*). However, the very instability of identity, as shown by the trifurcated image, also prevents genuine self-reflection. Mirrors, perhaps the central metaphor in the theory of realism, are in the *Nachtwachen* useless for reflecting reality. When Kreuzgang eventually decides to "copy" faithfully his own physiognomy, he does it at night (57). Without light, of course, mirrors reflect nothing.

And nothing is ultimately what is associated with another, more demonic, metaphor of imitation: the echo. It is an unusual and ambiguous image in the context of the opposition that I have been outlining. It partakes of both self-reflection and exact reproduction, and is therefore a sign for both the infinite movement of self-conscious irony and an almost mechanical notion of mimetic activity. In the *Nachtwachen*, however, it also has the further association with nothingness (*Nichts*). The first time we encounter it, in the thirteenth night watch, Kreuzgang is reciting his Dithyramb on Spring while an alpenhorn sounds in the valley below. He breaks off suddenly when the horn falls silent ("the final tone and the final word faded away slowly dying") and asks the following: "Did you only write up to this word, Mother Nature? And to whose hand do you pass the quill to continue?" (107). The equation of word and tone, the written mark and the sound, is evident from this passage. Both echo "slowly dying" (107); they seem to be dependent on one another's existence. But when Kreuzgang continues to query Mother Nature on why human beings alone have consciousness—in language that very much resembles Nietzsche's essay "On the Use and Abuse of History for Life" seventy years later—he perceives only the echo of his own voice. "I hear nothing but echo, the echo of my own speech" (*Ich höre nichts, als Widerhall, Widerhall*

26

meiner eigenen Rede). We should note here that this sentence contains a certain ambiguity. Depending on punctuation and emphasis, it could mean "I hear nothing but echo" or "I hear nothing as echo." The first of these readings contains the dual function of the echo: on the one hand, reproduction of the spoken word; and on the other, reproduction of self. But the second reading throws both of these into question. If nothing is echoed, it is because there is no original voice to be copied, no ultimate referent for a possible mimetic project. Mother Nature, in eighteenth-century poetics the model for literary imitation, is conspicuously mute: "Mother, mother, why are you silent?" (107) Kreuzgang implores, seeking solace from a world outside his own consciousness. The echo that answers Kreuzgang, however, is a "sardonic voice" (*hämische Stimme*) that in exemplary undecidability originates from neither without nor within.

The ambivalence of the echo, its almost eerie resistance to origin, is a result of the demonic. In the sixteenth night watch, Kreuzgang, in a dream-like state at the cemetery, observes and listens to a poet concerned about immortality. With quill in hand the poet orchestrates thunder and the sounding of trumpets, as if it were the Judgment Day. But the dead remain resolutely asleep, merely turning over in their graves so that they will not be disturbed by the ruckus. Obviously distressed by their lack of response, the poet cries out wildly: "What? Is there then no God?" The response is an echo of the single word "God!" He concludes from this that the devil created the echo. "You can't tell if it merely mocks, or if someone is really speaking" (134). What is thematized here once again is the undecidability of echoing, but in this passage we clearly see that the forces of darkness—the very same forces that cancel all mirroring—are responsible for this ambiguity. God fails to rouse the dead, to lift them from the blackness of death into His eternal light. But it is only this light that can ensure proper and unquestionable reflection of reality. In the darkness where no origin can be seen, where, indeed, sight and the visual—the vast metaphorical reservoir for all theorists of realism from Plato to Lukács—are made impossible, the Antichrist exercises his chaotic and nihilistic hegemony. Kreuzgang recognizes this all too well at the close of the novel. Searching in the grave for his own origin, he unearths the perfectly preserved corpse of the alchemist who supposedly fathered him. But when he touches it, it turns to ashes. Even the father is ultimately only a mask, behind which nothing remains: "I scatter this handful of paternal dust in the winds and what remains is—nothing!" But to conclude the novel on this note of simple nothingness would cheat the devil of his due. Bonaventura's *Nachtwachen* is programmed to end with nothingness, but it cannot be an original nothingness; it cannot be the sign of a speech or a mark of writing to which we can attribute authorship. Rather, it must be echo: product without origin, remark without source, the symbol and (anti)-creation of Satan. "And the echo in the mortuary [*Gebeinhaus*] called a final time—*nothing!*—" (143). In a final antimimetic gesture, the echo, liberated from all dependence on an original voice, affirms itself through absolute negation.[10]

The foregrounding of an antirealist poetics in the *Nachtwachen* is significant not only because of its contrast to theories of realism but also because almost all motifs that appear in this quintessential romantic text return in inverted form later in the century. The portrait and the mirror, the use of reading and the book, the role of narrative authority, the theological grounding for imitation—all these elements recur with some frequency in the following chapters. But Bonaventura's text is also significant because it pushes romantic irony to its nihilistic limit. The extreme form of self-consciousness that permeates this work ends up calling everything into question. Ultimately it is a (self-) destructive form that consumes anything substantial; like much contemporary theory, its radical, all-consuming drive toward (self-) cancellation is intriguing but unproductive. This, of course, is precisely what Hegel meant when he harshly criticized the notion of romantic irony. In a review of Solger's works, he describes this term as "the self-conscious obstruction [*Vereitelung*] of the objective."[11] The reason for this is that it turns all positivities into their opposites. Hegel's explanation of the effects of irony in a discussion of Ernst Raupach's *Die Bekehrten* (*The Converted*, 1826) could serve as a commentary to the *Nachtwachen* as well. After stating that irony is considered by many to be the triumph and high point of artistry, he writes: "It [irony] is supposed to consist of the following: everything that promises to be beautiful, noble, and interesting later destroys itself and turns into its opposite; genuine pleasure is found in the discovery that intentions, interests, and characters amount to nothing."[12] This could be a capsule summary of Kreuzgang's nihilistic teaching. And although Hegel does not draw any conclusions about the poetic implications of this attitude, Jean Paul, in his *Vorschule der Ästhetik* (*Preschool of Aesthetics*, 1804), remarks on precisely this point. Speaking of the contemporary situation, he draws the connection between extreme self-reflexivity, the destruction of all substance, and the neglect of imitation: "It results from the lawless license of the Zeitgeist, which self-indulgently prefers to annihilate the world and the universe—only in order to empty out a free space for *play* in the nothingness—and which rips away the *bandage* from its wounds as if they were fetters, so that it must speak with disdain of imitation and the study of nature."[13] If these types of comments reflect a dominant tendency in literary and philosophical endeavor of the early nineteenth century, then the *Nachtwachen* may not be the dark side or reversal of early romanticism, as many critics have contended, but rather its most consequential application.[14]

The results of an extreme application of romantic irony do not have to lead to nihilism, however. A brief examination of textual self-consciousness in Heinrich Heine's *Ideen. Das Buch Le Grand* (*Ideas. Book Le Grand*, 1826), written a little more than two decades after the appearance of the *Nachtwachen*, shows how the emancipatory impulse that lay at the foundation of both Fichtean philosophy and romantic irony can be radicalized and extended beyond the realm of a solipsistic subject.[15] Perhaps the most imaginative of the series of *Reisebilder* (*Travel Pictures*) published from 1826 to 1831, *Ideen. Das Buch Le Grand* consists of twenty chapters of varying length. For purposes of discussion it is most conveniently divided into four sections, and this can be done most readily by looking at the narrative personae Heine employs. Throughout the work the narrator addresses a woman (Madame) whose identity is never revealed; in the first and last quarter of the work, however, the narrator himself is not clearly identifiable. At different points he assumes various guises: an Italian knight, an Indian count, a broken-hearted lover. In these sections the dominant themes are familiar from the romantic literary canon: love, death, and suicide. At the close of the fifth chapter and throughout the next quarter of the book, however, the loosely structured narration shifts focus; here the narrative persona becomes a somewhat distorted mirror of the author talking autobiographically about his youth. The major event he discusses is the invasion of the French army into the German Rhineland at the beginning of the nineteenth century. Napoleon and his drum major, Le Grand, become symbols of emancipation for a backward, anesthetized Germany unwilling to follow in the footsteps of the French Revolution. In the third quarter of the work, after the demise of Napoleon and the death of Le Grand, the narrator reflects on a variety of themes, including academic scholarship, the writing profession, and the political absurdities following the Congress of Vienna in 1815, before the work closes with the return to the dispersed romantic masks and motifs.

Quite obviously the form and themes of *Buch Le Grand* differ significantly from those of the *Nachtwachen*, yet there are surprising overlaps in their compositional techniques. Both are feigned autobiographical works in which the narrator refuses to give a linear account of his life. At times both show that they are able to compose traditional stories, especially if they are speaking of others: Kreuzgang manages to retell the mad Spaniard's tale of murder in a somewhat conventional fashion, and in the eighteenth chapter of *Buch Le Grand*, Heine, in relating "the real story that should be told in this book" (304),[16] provides the reader with a slightly stilted but fairly direct narrative about a knight who is rejected by a certain Signora Laura (304–5). For the most part, however, it is quite obvious that a non-linear compositional technique is the rule. Moreover, both texts exhibit a penchant for commenting on the writing process itself. In several passages Heine seems to outdo Kreuzgang in thematizing his own activity. We will recall that Kreuzgang regrets his inability to narrate in a straightforward fashion. In the thirteenth chapter, Heine takes up the same topic, insisting, however, that his seemingly chaotic style is really to the point: "In all previous chapters there is not a line that does not belong to the topic. I write concisely, I avoid all superfluity, often I even neglect what is necessary" (284). The fiction of speaking—Heine continuously interjects "Madame" as a form of direct address—is here abandoned for writing, but it is a writing informed by the spoken word. We are obviously supposed to understand this self-reflection on the writing process as ironic—in the classical sense of not saying what one means. But, like so much of Heine's irony, it is also meant to be taken seriously. Since Heine's project, like Kreuzgang's, has no mimetic pretensions, since it is not intended to reproduce reality objectively, but to produce one subjectively, there is no external constraint on the direction of the text. Where writing follows the associations of a mind rather than an ordered pattern imposed on it by the conventions of traditional storytelling, nothing can be out of place.

But Heine's other reflections on the writing process take a somewhat different direction. In the fourteenth chapter he writes about his career in a humorous fashion, touching on topics ranging from his reputed disrespect for religion to his sarcastic wit. Commenting on the accusation that he dissembles in his works, he assures the reader—

ironically, of course—that this is not the case: "I do not deceive
at all. I do not mince matters; I write in all innocence and simplicity
whatever comes to mind, and it is not my fault if that is something
sensible" (289). The spontaneity that Heine praises here, however, is
derived not from inspiration but from necessity. Since he lives from
his writing, he is caught in an economic nexus that exists independent
of his subjective will. "The fellow from Langhoff's printing office is
now standing in my room waiting for manuscript, and the hardly born
word wanders warm and wet to press, and what I think and feel at
this moment can already be printer's waste by noon" (290). Like Bonaventura, who tells of the suicide of a poet unable to publish his play
Der Mensch (*Man*) (eighth night watch), Heine mocks an idealist notion of literature that ignores material needs and realities of the actual
writers. Thus he too debunks the notion of immortality. Kreuzgang
discusses this topic often, always showing how futile such thoughts
are in a world without meaning and purpose. Heine's treatment of
this issue is just as derisive, although somewhat more materialistic—
and humorous. Reminded of Horace's dictum "nonum prematur in
annum," he remarks that this rule could apply only to someone kept
by a rich patron, not to an author in a free-market economy. "Ma
foi, madame, I could never survive that rule for twenty-four hours,
let alone nine years. My stomach has no understanding of immortality.
I have already thought about the matter, and I want to be only half
immortal and completely satiated" (291). Here the relationship between text and reality is not just a question of poetics. Since the literary
work is a commodity and the author its producer, the materiality of
the text, not just as marks on a page, but as pages for the market,
is affirmed as an economic reality.[17]

Heine's text is thus every bit as self-conscious as Bonaventura's,
but what makes it particularly important for our consideration is the
way in which Heine carries out his various reflections. In the course
of this work, he repeats nearly all the self-reflexive topoi we encountered in the *Nachtwachen*, but they often possess a different force than
they had in the earlier work. Perhaps the best example of this involves
the confusion between life and theater. The mottoes to chapters one,
two, and twenty are identical; each speaks of unrequited love: "She
was lovable, and he loved her. He, however, was not lovable, and she
did not love him" (247, 249, 308). Each time this motto appears,
it is said to come from an old play (*Altes Stück*), but it is obvious
that this sentence, as the description of a possible dramatic plot, is

so general and so clichéd that no specific drama is actually meant. To clarify his relationship to this motto the narrator informs "Madame" that he played the lead role and that although it is a tragedy, the hero does not die at the end. Part of this allusion to a play about unrequited love is an intertextual reference to Heine's own work. As many readers would have known at the time, the bulk of Heine's early love poetry dealt with a variation of this very theme; as many readers now know, the poems collected in the *Buch der Lieder* (*Book of Songs*, 1827) have often been associated—incorrectly in my view—with Heine's infatuation with one or both of his cousins.[18] The point here, however, is that Heine as narrator, like Kreuzgang, confounds occurrence on the stage with events in the world. Indeed, Heine also includes the topos of God as the primeval playwright: "They [writers like Goethe and Shakespeare] all learned it from the great primeval poet who in his thousand-act world tragedy knows how to drive humor to the utmost, as we see every day" (282). Both Heine and Kreuzgang thus imply that for theological or ontological reasons we are always "in character," and in this sense the boundary between stage and reality is a fiction.

Heine as narrator differs from Kreuzgang, however, in two very significant areas. First, his ironic awareness does not lead to a vortex of introspection; he does not peel off successive layers to reach a core of meaninglessness. Rather his irony consistently refers the reader back to an extratextual dimension, a world not able to be contained in or by words. Although his novella—I use this genre designation loosely here—could hardly be considered realistic by the standards accepted in the latter half of the nineteenth century, it continuously reaffirms a relationship between text and reality. The hero of the "old play" does not complete his role, but rather becomes the narrator of *Buch Le Grand*. Heine escapes the nihilism of the *Nachtwachen* not because he limits the self-conscious text or because he appeals to a transcendental authority to halt the spiraling reflexivity but because his consciousness of the precariousness of self and of the nondistinction between fiction and reality does not fall into the metaphysical trap of searching for origins and ultimate purpose. For such a search is itself futile and idealistic; one can only wind up with a nonverifiable ground or a disparaging of all grounds. By repeatedly relativizing the values, beliefs, and concepts of his era, Heine is able to maintain a connection to life and to the world.[19] His role in the tragedy is thus nontragic; he ends up celebrating the continuation of his self-conscious stance: "I live, and that is the main point" (253). Thus he breaks off from the role-playing in the initial quarter of the text to discuss the consequences of the French Revolution and to mock the provincialism of his own country. Certainly these affirmations are subject to ironic reflection as well. The "I" which survives the tragedy is textually no more substantial than the other personae; and the French invasion of Germany is itself fictionalized. Napoleon was actually in Düsseldorf at the beginning of November in 1811, not on a beautiful day in the spring, as the description suggests (274). But despite the uninterrupted fictionalization, the logic of the irony in this text is one of continued differentiation and displacement, not one of ultimate futility and nihilism.

Second, and perhaps more important, Heine's text distinguishes itself from Bonaventura with regard to the transparency of the ironic stance. If we can say that Kreuzgang pushes self-awareness to its extreme, then we could maintain that Heine makes us aware of the very process of employing irony. His technique here is what the Russian formalists have called the laying bare of the device (*obnazhenie priëma*). The continued use of a formal feature or device by one generation causes it to become a norm of literary production. When this occurs, subsequent writers may foreground this device, calling attention to it.[20] The difficulty of doing this with romantic irony is that it is itself already a reflexive structure; indeed, we have seen above that one can conceive of it as the self-consciousness of the text. It can only be foregrounded, therefore, by its own application, and the foregrounding will only be perceivable if it is drastic enough. This is precisely what Heine undertakes in the novella. Although we can never be quite sure when his seriousness ends and his irony begins, his use of stereotypical romantic motifs calls into question a tradition of reflection on fictionality that had become forced and sterile. This is seen most readily in the first and last quarters of the novella where Heine introduces a series of typical romantic personae. His abrupt switching from one to another highlights the constructed and fictional nature of literary texts, but the poses are so stylized and hackneyed that the reader becomes conscious of irony as an element of romantic ideology. One could say that in these chapters he uses masks in order to unmask irony itself. Although the *Nachtwachen*, therefore, still stands inside the romantic tradition, employing its own most powerful philosophical tool to push it to its limits, *Buch Le Grand*, from a temporal distance of two decades, ironizes even this consequential use of irony.

One might be tempted to discuss the difference between Heine and Bonaventura in terms of Hegel's distinction between irony and comedy. The former, as we have seen, destroys everything "that has value and dignity for human beings."[21] The latter, according to Hegel, cancels only those characteristics that are themselves negativities: "a negativity in and of itself, a false and contradictory phenomenon, a whim, for example, an obstinacy, a special caprice against a powerful passion, or even a supposedly tenable principle or solid maxim."[22] Since the main targets of Heine's wit are the political, social, and aesthetic absurdities of the early nineteenth century, he appears to exemplify this Hegelian notion of the comic. Certainly Heine himself would have placed his work outside the purely destructive, and especially in the 1830s he, like Hegel, is extremely critical of the romantics' "bad infinity." In works such as *Die romantische Schule* (*The Romantic School*, 1835) and *Zur Geschichte der Religion und Philosophie in Deutschland* (*Concerning the History of Religion and Philosophy in Germany*, 1834), he castigates romantic poets for their conservative and reactionary political views. Although Heine here formulates his critique largely in terms of religion—romanticism is identified with a desire to return to the Catholicism of the Middle Ages—he also criticizes stylistic and thematic elements of this movement, including "humorist irony," which is called "only a sign of our political lack of freedom."[23]

Still we cannot ignore that *Buch Le Grand* itself contains considerable ironic force, nor would we want to separate it too sharply from Bonaventura's *Nachtwachen*. At least a portion of the significance of both works, despite their different emphases, lies in their careful avoidance of a poetics of imitation or copying. Although they differ in their mood and manner, they are united in their tendency to carry irony to an extreme and in their self-conscious foregrounding of fictionality. In this sense they distinguish themselves from the realist texts that appear later in the decade. As we shall see in the following chapters, the reflexivity associated with irony and self-consciousness is not entirely eradicated from the texts of realism; rather, it appears to go underground, to hide beneath the surface of the text, as it were. For if these features were too prominent, the effect of realism would be destroyed or at least severely diminished. What we shall witness most often, therefore, in the analysis of realist works is a latent contradiction. Superficially these texts propagate a poetics called "realism." It entails in one form or another a mimetic relationship between text and reality. But at various points a reflexive moment threatens the serenity of this surface, and it is here that we often encounter, along with the repression of the self-conscious ironic stance of romanticism, other repressions and exclusions simultaneously occurring. The ruse of realism is to make readers think that they are viewing an unmediated social reality. My endeavor in the following pages is to expose this ruse and to try to see where, how, and why it is perpetrated.

2

THE PARADOXES OF REALISM:
Artistic Aporias of the *Kunstgespräch* in Büchner's *Lenz*

The marvelous logic of the mad seems to
mock that of the logicians because it
resembles it so exactly, or rather because it is
exactly the same, and because at the secret
heart of madness, at the core of so many
errors, so many absurdities, so many words
and gestures without consequence, we
discover, finally, the hidden perfection of
language.

> Michel Foucault,
> *Madness and Civilization*

When in an era God, like the sun,
goes down, shortly thereafter the world
too steps into darkness.

> Jean Paul,
> *Preschool of Aesthetics*

Few works of German literature have elicited as
much critical response as Georg Büchner's *Lenz* (1839),[1] and no other
part of this novella, with the possible exception of the opening pages,
has drawn quite as much attention as the *Kunstgespräch*, or conversation about art. Situated slightly before the midpoint of the novella,
the *Kunstgespräch* is actually more a monologue than a conversation.
It consists almost entirely of remarks by the character Lenz on themes
related to literature and the fine arts. Only at the start ("at that time

36

the idealist period was beginning; Kaufmann was one of its supporters; Lenz disagreed vehemently" [1. 86])[2] and toward the middle ("Kaufmann objected that he would find no prototype in reality for an Apollo of Belvedere or a Raphael Madonna" [1. 87]) do we find anyone engaging Lenz in actual conversation. The argumentative nature of Lenz's remarks, however, suggests that he is meeting unstated or unrecorded objections. If there is an anonymous interlocutor in this conversation, then it is almost certainly the tradition of German classicism and romanticism, the *Kunstperiode* (period of art), as Heine at about this time labeled it.[3] Kaufmann seems to represent this tradition, and the brunt of Lenz's attack, at least toward the beginning of the *Kunstgespräch*, is directed against the idealizing penchant of these movements. Still, this side of the conversation is left for the reader to infer. Although we are informed that this is a discussion at the dinner table, in the context of the novella the *Kunstgespräch* thus presents the main character's views with little debate or comment from other parties.

With some justification commentators have noted the remarkable nature of this passage. In the novella it distinguishes itself by a number of features. For one thing, it is the longest sustained speech by the central figure. In no other part of the work does Lenz utter more than a few sentences at a time, and these are not infrequently semi-coherent exclamations delivered in a state of delirium. Thematically it is the only time that the storm-and-stress playwright takes up matters pertaining to his former metier. When he first arrives in Waldbach, Oberlin refers to his career as a writer, but at that point Lenz seems to shy away from, or even to disown, his earlier work: "I beg you not to judge me by them" (1. 80). And stylistically it contains a number of features rarely or never found in other parts of the novella. Besides the relative coherence of Lenz's statements as opposed to other passages,[4] it is also the only section of the work in which Büchner slips into the present tense rather than using the subjunctive for indirect speech or the past tense for narrative reporting. Moreover, the repetition of "he said:" (*Er sagte*) twice toward the beginning of the *Kunstgespräch*, along with other stylistic and thematic considerations, gives the impression that Büchner had not quite finished with this section, and it is quite possible that he intended to rework parts of this "conversation" to make it at least uniformly direct or indirect speech. Finally, it is one of the sections for which Büchner apparently had no source either in Oberlin's journal, on which many other passages are based, or in works on or by Lenz.

But the *Kunstgespräch* also seems remarkable in the context of German poetics and aesthetic theory. Customarily it has been read as one of the earliest and strongest programs for realism in art and literature. Although the term *realism* itself is never actually mentioned—it became popular in German criticism some two decades later—the plea for authenticity in art, the call for more careful attention to detail, and the suggestion that formerly excluded social groups should become artistically preferred subjects bring Lenz's remarks into the proximity of discussions of a later era. The realism of the *Kunstgespräch*—and this will be the subject of a more detailed analysis presently—seems to anticipate central thematic and stylistic concerns of European realism. As J. M. Ritchie notes in his review of the German branch of this movement, *Lenz* "is important in the development of realism in Germany because it contains the first consistent anti-idealistic aesthetic."[5] We should not conclude from this remark, however, that Büchner was in any way part of a conscious movement to propagate realism in art and literature. Most critics note, as Stephan Kohl does, that Büchner remained an exception for a long time,[6] but this exceptional status would only seem to enhance his significance. In fact, that he was virtually neglected by the "realists" in the half-century following his death, but enthusiastically discovered by German naturalists, those "super-realists" writing during the final two decades of the century, is a credit to his genial ability to anticipate a novel mode of representation.

The unusual position of the *Kunstgespräch* both in the novella and in German letters has led most previous commentators to emphasize two questions: Given the stylistic and thematic differences, can we say that this conversation fits into the novella? And is the theory enunciated there a statement of Büchner's own aesthetic views? On the first question there has existed historically a division of opinions. In the wake of techniques developed by the New Criticism, however, there has been a marked trend toward viewing the *Kunstgespräch* as an integral part of an organic whole. Perhaps the most important spokesperson for this view has been Benno von Wiese, who locates the passage structurally as the pivotal point for the entire novella: "For everything that happens *before* this conversation shows, despite the ever more powerfully increasing threat, nonetheless the Dionysian exultation of being [*Dasein*], the essential and indestructible quality of all reality; while only *after* the conversation the falling motion into a devastated, wayward, and insubstantial mode of existence becomes unavoidable."[7] In more recent times other critics have also managed to fit this odd piece into the puzzling composition of the novella. Martin Swales, for example, makes the strong claim that the *Kunstgespräch* "clarifies the fact that madness, because it is alienated from reality, involves also an alienation from the preconditions of artistic activity."[8] It thus would point to a state of mind now foreign to Lenz and underscore the hero's estrangement and lack of creativity. John J. Parker takes almost the opposite view in integrating the conversation into the tightly knit thematic web.[9] For him there exists a concordance, rather than a contrast, between the views Lenz expresses on art and his actions in the rest of the novella. The contention here is that both are somehow informed by realism. And finally Peter K. Jansen in his examination of the "structural function" of the *Kunstgespräch* in the novella uncovers careful preparation for its insertion. The author, he claims, takes "great pains to relate it to the protagonist's experience and thus to embed it firmly in the narrative context."[10]

I have enumerated these various opinions on how the *Kunstgespräch* fits into the novella not for the usual perfunctory reasons of scholarly convention but rather to demonstrate a point about interpretation. Professional interpreters, like their exegetical predecessors with the Bible, will always be able to show how a passage fits into a context no matter how odd or out-of-place that passage at first may appear. With the *Kunstgespräch* critics should have a difficult task facing them, since close attention to the text reveals the stylistic and thematic anomalies cited above. If we would really take seriously the work as a coherent totality, then the *Kunstgespräch* would disrupt the whole in several rather obvious ways. But we have learned not to take this maxim seriously, or, perhaps more accurately, we construct a new whole into which every part invariably fits. Thus almost every reading of *Lenz* undertaken during the past three decades has found some way to integrate the *Kunstgespräch* into the novella. This curious happenstance should indicate that the question of *whether* the *Kunstgespräch* fits into the work is superfluous. The entire issue is of no significance. What we have is a text, written by Büchner, that includes a peculiar but interesting passage. It has come down to us with what we now call the *Kunstgespräch*, and a judgment on its appropriateness is irrelevant. This is so not because we cannot and do not make such judgments but because if we or someone else is skillful enough, the passage will always fit into a coherent text. The task of the interpreter thus cannot be to decide whether this passage belongs. Rather, the more significant problem is to determine how it functions, not only in the narrower context of the novella, but in Büchner's oeuvre and in the discourse of developing realism. The *Kunstgespräch* will always be read as having some sort of place in *Lenz*, even if it is only considered a disruption. My task is to show that this early and unique reflection on realism has more importance than just another piece in an interpretive puzzle.

The second most frequently asked question in the secondary literature—are these Büchner's views?—is more interesting for a historical understanding of aesthetic theory, but ultimately just as irrelevant. Most critics have blithely assumed that the passage does represent Büchner's opinions,[11] and moreover that the *Kunstgespräch* is tantamount to a cohesive program for realism in literature and art. Whereas the second of these assumptions, as I shall demonstrate below, is based on a failure to read the text closely, the first has built its foundation on some rather shaky philological reasoning. The shakiest and most important of these is that the author is using his central figure as a mouthpiece for his own ideas. This contention is in turn bolstered by registering the divergence of the *Kunstgespräch* from other parts of the novella. Because it differs from the rest of the work in style and theme, it should be attributed to Büchner rather than to Büchner's Lenz. This argument is at best highly speculative, for there is no necessary connection between stylistic or thematic anomalies and authorial intrusions. One could just as persuasively contend that the reason for the divergences is that Büchner had not finished with this section of the work or that Büchner wished for some other reason to call the reader's attention to this passage. It is merely interesting to note in passing that critics who hold the view that this break in style is an indication of the author's voice contradict the popular position mentioned above that integrates this passage into the "organic" structure of the work.

The two major pieces of external evidence most frequently cited to show that Büchner's views are contained in the *Kunstgespräch* are a passage from Büchner's letter to his parents dated 28 July 1835 and a section from a scene in *Dantons Tod* (*Danton's Death*, 1835) in which Camille and Danton make some brief remarks about theater and art. Both are of somewhat dubious value as evidence. The letter, of course, does evidence language resembling parts of the *Kunstgespräch*. Both contain an attack on idealist writers, comparing their characters to dolls or puppets, and both support as an alternative the creation of characters who seem more real. In the letter this is expressed by the phrase

"human beings of flesh and blood" (*Menschen von Fleisch und Blut*)
(2. 444), and in the conversation we read of "life, the possibility of
existence" (*Leben, Möglichkeit des Daseins*) (1. 86). The closest parallel,
however, is usually taken to be the reference to reproducing the world
as God has created it, the well-known topos of the artist as second
creator. In the novella Lenz states the following: "The good Lord has
certainly made the world as it should be, and we surely cannot piece
together (*klecksen*) anything better; our only goal should be to imitate
Him a little" (1. 86). In comparison Büchner wrote to his parents:
"If someone were to tell me that the poet must not portray the world
as it is, but as it should be, then I would answer that I do not want
to make it better than the good Lord, who certainly made the world
as it should be" (*der die Welt gewiß gemacht hat, wie sie sein soll*) (2.
444).

Now even if Büchner had been completely candid with his parents in his correspondence (which he was not; there are a number
of evasions and outright falsehoods in his letters),[12] one should still
be suspicious of the formulation here. In the first place, this statement
is embedded in a letter that is conspicuously defensive in tone. Büchner
is trying to excuse the vulgar language and actions of his main characters in *Dantons Tod*. The entire letter is more an apology for alleged
impropriety than a program for realism. But the specific connection
in which God is mentioned is peculiar as well. I do not believe that
any critic has bothered to observe that the statement is given as a
reply to hypothetical objections to the lack of idealism and morality
in the play. One can well imagine that Büchner is simply fighting fire
with fire here. The sense of his rebuttal could perhaps be paraphrased
as follows: Those self-righteous souls who find immorality on the stage
so offensive should be reminded that they are thereby offended by
the Creator as much as His imitator. Although the tone cannot be
positively determined merely from the words on the page, it is not
difficult to see it as ironic. Further support for this sort of reading
comes from the final two clauses of the sentence just cited: "who certainly made the world as it should be." We shall have occasion at another point to return to Büchner's views and doubts concerning God.
For now, however, it is sufficient to note that almost the only certainty
with respect to this disputed issue is that Büchner was at best uncertain
about God's existence and the perfection of His creation. He constantly questioned proofs for the existence of God, and Payne's discussion of the Spinozist doctrine in *Dantons Tod* should indicate that Büch-

ner was at least able to distance himself from these views.[13] That he expresses himself with apparent certainty in this letter to his parents is thus almost surely ironic. The word *gewiß* (certainly) must be read as a sign of this irony rather than of Büchner's unshakable faith in the Creator and His work. And if we read the letter in this manner, then we should emphasize the difference, rather than the similarity, between Büchner's privately held views on art and the theory he places in the mouth of his character Lenz. In the *Kunstgespräch*, as we shall see, God plays a necessary, albeit contradictory, role. In the letter to his parents, I would maintain that He is not more than an ironic rejoinder to hypothetical critics.

The passage from *Dantons Tod* is also not as unproblematic as commentators have previously assumed. Again the common features are the criticism of idealism and the plea for realism as an alternative. The marionette-like characters in the theater, the artificiality of idealism, and even the notion of the second creator—"They forget God their Creator because of his poor imitators [*Copisten*]" (1. 37)—unite Camille's speech with Lenz's, although here too we should note that the irony in Camille's reference to God contrasts with Lenz's sincerity. Once again, however, an identification of Büchner with any of his characters appears to be precipitous. Even if we grant that the author seems to have more sympathy for (read: presents in a better light) Danton and Camille, as opposed to, say, Robespierre, identifying the views of these characters with Büchner's own is hardly justified. In fact, there is good reason to note the distance between Büchner and Danton/Camille. It should not escape the attentive reader that the two characters who seem to support a clearer view of the world as it really is are precisely the characters who are unable to see it that way themselves. In a conversation with Lucile directly after his pronouncements on the travesty of idealist theater, Camille demonstrates how completely he misjudges his real situation. He is convinced that Robespierre poses no threat to him because they are old friends (1. 38). Throughout the play Danton is shown to be similarly inept in evaluating the ways of the real world. That they should be convincing spokespeople for Büchner's aesthetic of realism is, of course, still possible, but this would entail a degree of self-irony or contradiction hitherto unnoticed.[14]

Ultimately there is no way to prove conclusively that the *Kunstgespräch* represents Büchner's views.[15] We have no means at our disposal to conduct an inquiry beyond the texts, and they can afford us no certainty on this matter. But there is also no reason to try to prove this. The conversation on art, as I have noted above, is a remarkable document in its own right. In assigning the views to Büchner and regarding the *Kunstgespräch* as a coherent program for realism, critics have managed only to make it less interesting than it is. They have resolved forcibly the many contradictions in this passage by flattening out and vulgarizing what is potentially an extremely rich piece of prose. In short, previous criticism, in its zeal to assign Büchner a place under the rubric of "early realist," has been unwilling to explore the subtleties of the text. Büchner, unlike his idealist foil Schiller, does not, I would maintain, use his characters or works simply to express his own preconceived opinions on the world. Rather, in his works problems are presented and illuminated from different perspectives. Danton, unlike Posa or Tell, is not morally correct or the personification of a philosophical principle. Robespierre is not simply an evil villain. Both characters are contradictory in their actions and thoughts, and the point of the play is not to condemn one side or the other but rather to explore the complexities and problematics of human interaction during revolutions.[16] Similarly the *Kunstgespräch* is not so much a program for realism as an attempt to define an alternative to what was perceived as idealism in art, an endeavor to explore the manner in which texts refer and relate to the world outside the text. It seems fairly clear that Büchner was in some vague fashion in favor of what we now call realism, but labeling his works and aesthetics in this fashion reflects only a superficial understanding of the problems he raises. For the significance of the *Kunstgespräch* is not its avowal of realism as an aesthetic doctrine, but rather its disclosing of the paradoxes and aporias involved with the theory and practice of realist art. In the following reading close attention to detail will, it is hoped, demonstrate how this reflection on realism is able to question the precepts of this European movement in art and literature in its incipient stages.

The *Kunstgespräch* lends itself to a tripartite division. In the first section the subject is primarily literary: Lenz speaks of Shakespeare and "Göthe" as well as of his own plays *Der Hofmeister* (*The Tutor*, 1774) and *Die Soldaten* (*The Soldiers*, 1776). The topic is fidelity to life and the effect of literature. In the second section the conversation shifts gears when Lenz relates his experience in viewing the girls on a hillside. The final section is marked by the only interruption: Kaufmann, the emissary from Lenz's father, supports an idealist position and illustrates his views with examples from ancient and Renaissance

43

art. Lenz parries this objection with remarks pertaining to painting, describing two pictures in particular. Here the *Kunstgespräch* ends. Thereafter we are told only that Lenz continued in the same manner: "He continued speaking in the same manner; the others listened attentively, much was to the point, his face had flushed from talking, and often smiling, often serious, he shook his blond curls" (1. 88). In the very same paragraph, the narrator relates Kaufmann's private conversation with Lenz concerning his father's request that he return, as well as Lenz's strong reaction to this request. But nothing relating directly to art is contained in the remainder of the discussion, and the reader has to assume that this private conversation is included in the same paragraph as the *Kunstgespräch* because of Kaufmann's participation in both.

In the context of the novella, we encounter two ways in which the *Kunstgespräch* presents the reader with a paradoxical situation with respect to the real world apparently applauded by Lenz. First, as Herbert Fellmann has noted, this passage represents a veritable flight from reality.[17] Here Lenz forgets himself temporarily ("He had forgotten himself completely" [1. 88]) thus escaping for the moment the disturbing effects of the madness that otherwise characterizes his thoughts and actions. By taking up the topic of life and the possibility of existence *in art*, Lenz is able to forget his own life and existence *in the real world*, or at least in the fictionalized "real world" of the novella. Paradoxically he can thus continue his own life and existence without the danger of its termination or interruption because of his escape to the realm of art. The *Kunstgespräch* is one of the few places in the novella where Lenz seems calm, and this has led most commentators to view it solely as a temporary respite from his madness.[18] But if this passage is read as I am suggesting, then it should be seen as a further sign of Lenz's instability, not as (or as well as) a relief from his problems. One might say that it reveals another side of his insanity or, perhaps more precisely, the precariousness of a mind whose very stability depends on the elimination of a consciousness of its own presence. Discussing art and its connections with reality seems to involve a forgetting or negation of Lenz as a person—one might even think here of Flaubert's *impersonalité* and *impassibilité*—and only by thus extinguishing himself does Lenz buy a little time for existence.

The second contextual paradox entails the only two participants in the *Kunstgespräch*, Kaufmann and Lenz himself. It is evident from the few remarks made by the former that he represents a kind of reality principle. His relationship to Lenz is thus somewhat like Antonio's to Tasso in Goethe's play. In one respect Kaufmann is simply the bearer of letters from Lenz's father, a messenger of sorts from the world beyond the isolated and strangely idyllic community in and around Waldbach. But he is also an active agent in the narrative. He reproaches Lenz for not taking up an occupation, for wasting his time and life in inactivity. From this practical perspective he urges Lenz to return to the real world, to engage himself in the actual life and doings of other human beings (1. 88). His conception of art, on the other hand, stands apparently at odds with this commonsense attitude. Although we learn very little about his aesthetic proclivities, he is said to be a "supporter" (*Anhänger*) of idealism, and, as we have already seen, he defends the idealized types of ancient and Renaissance art. For him art is evidently supposed not to imitate reality but rather to posit its ideal alternative. Lenz, on the other hand, with all his commitment to a vital, realist art, refuses to acknowledge the force of the real world in his own life. In a certain way, then, both Lenz and his would-be opponent postulate a separation of art and life: the latter explicitly in his call for idealism, and the former implicitly in his de facto separation of his own life from his aesthetic convictions to adhere to reality. And it is perhaps just this recognition and acceptance of the gulf between art and life that helps to define Kaufmann's sanity, whereas the refusal to admit a difference between the two, despite its necessity, characterizes Lenz's madness and his aesthetic views. In drawing the last consequences from realism, Lenz is unable to think of art and life as separate spheres; but in identifying them so closely, he is unable to grasp the reality upon which this type of art is supposed to be based. It is perhaps appropriate, therefore, that Kaufmann's nonartistic realism textually encloses Lenz's plea for artistic realism like a pair of ironic quotation marks.

The paradoxes of the *Kunstgespräch* are not solely contextual, though. Each section of this unusual conversation contains important theoretical points that end in unresolved and possibly unresolvable contradictions. Let us start at the beginning and see how these contradictions unfold as Lenz develops his arguments. The first part as I have outlined it has been traditionally taken to be the core of a realist aesthetic theory. Here Lenz distinguishes three groups of poets: those who try to reproduce reality, but are unsuccessful; those who idealize reality; and those who manage to produce a feeling of life in their works. Lenz indicates further that the topic of a literary work is not as important as the approach to the topic: "They ought to try immersing themselves for once in the life of the most insignificant person and reproduce it, in the palpitations, the intimations, the most subtle, scarcely perceptible gestures" (1. 87). He then proceeds to cite his earlier plays *Der Hofmeister* and *Die Soldaten* as attempts to realize this theory in practice.

At this point, at the very latest, however, we should begin to ask questions. How exactly do Lenz's literary examples match up against what he outlines as the goal of literature? In what sense do *Der Hofmeister* and *Die Soldaten* reproduce these "subtle, scarcely perceptible gestures" of human existence? Where does one find the "palpitations and intimations" so essential for Lenz? These plays, after all, consist primarily of dialogue, of words meant to be read or spoken by actors playing a role, not of pantomime and elaborate stage directions. Like most theorists of realism, Lenz begins here to slip into sensual, especially visual metaphors, to speak about realism in terms of what we see. This process will culminate later in the *Kunstgespräch*, when literature is totally abandoned for the more representational art form of painting. But already in this first section we note a shift from literature, the area in which Lenz is supposedly on his home turf (*auf seinem Gebiet*), to art associated with sight or hearing. It is therefore significant that the only literary forms to which Lenz alludes are plays (works to be seen) or songs (works to be heard). His own dramas and Shakespeare's belong to the former group, whereas folk songs and presumably Goethe's poetry alone are included in the latter: "it resounds in folk songs, sometimes in Goethe" (*in den Volksliedern tönt es einem ganz, in Göthe manchmal entgegen*) (1. 87). In both forms the senses play a role they cannot play in texts meant to be read. The rest of Lenz's language also reinforces this reliance on the visual. In criticizing the idealists he remarks: "Those people cannot even *draw* a doghouse" (*die Leute können keinen Hundesstall* zeichnen). And concerning the characters created by idealists he states: "everything that I have *seen* are wooden puppets" (*alles, was ich davon* gesehen, *sind Holzpuppen*) (1. 87; my emphasis).

This was not the only time in Büchner's writings that an aesthetic view pertaining to realism is explained in terms of the visual. In *Dantons Tod* the two central illustrations are theater, discussed by Camille, and painting, brought up by Danton in response to his friend's remarks (1. 37). Moreover, in another letter Büchner wrote to his parents to apologize for the vulgarity of his first drama, he calls his play "a historical painting" (*ein geschichtliches Gemälde*),[19] thus recalling Danton's discussion of Jacques Louis David in the play itself. Büchner, of course, was not alone in using the visual to explore problems of realism. We should recall that the term became popular in France as the result of a controversy over a painting exhibition by Gustave Courbet in 1855.[20] What is significant is that the term became so easily and so facilely attached to literary works.[21] Virtually all theorists of literary realism have found it necessary to place visual terminology and comparisons with pictorial art forms at central points in their argumentation. The motivation for this dependence on the visual is not difficult to understand. Intuitively one felt (and feels) that the pictorial arts had a more natural affinity with reality and that literature should somehow be called upon to imitate with words what the painter did with brush and colors. It should be noted, however, that literature thus moves one step further away from its previous association with sound and speech. In the nineteenth century it is increasingly considered a vehicle for inducing pictorial images in the mind of the reader rather than primarily *gebundene Rede* (verse), as it had been identified in the poetics of much of the seventeenth and eighteenth centuries. Almost entirely lost is the oral dimension that dominated theory about literature throughout the centuries.[22] Indeed, we should note that the narrators of both the *Nachtwachen* and *Ideen. Das Buch Le Grand*, despite their frequent comments on writing, perpetrate the fiction that they are speaking and this connects them with the older tradition. Lenz's use of visual and auditory examples in this passage perhaps marks him as standing between two modes of thought about literary function.

The confounding of the visual, the auditory, and the literary in the *Kunstgespräch* is thus symptomatic for the problems of an incipient realism. Lenz's formulation reveals a tension between two traditions, neither of which is fully able to account for the complexities of the written word. Both traditions attempt to bring literature to life by an appeal to the senses. The earlier views count on literature to have an effect as the result of auditory stimulation; the rising nineteenth-century aesthetic tends to rely on the reproduction of something visual. In the *Kunstgespräch*, of course, one tradition is simply grafted onto the other, but common to both is the refusal to deal with literature as the dead letters printed on a page. In appealing to the senses, Lenz, like most theorists of literature, circumvents some major problems of literature in the age of the printed word, namely, how and why do we infuse literature with life, how and why do we give it a voice, and how and why do we feel compelled to construct mental images from words. These issues, ignored in the history of realism, have surfaced more recently in radical forms in theoretical debates. Nonetheless, many of the most popular discussions of literature, like Lenz's in this passage, evidence a surprising naïveté with regard to our supposed penchant to read realistically.[23]

The tension between the living word from the oral tradition and the dead letter of the text is reproduced on the metaphorical level in the *Kunstgespräch* as well. One of the most unusual comparisons Lenz chooses occurs when he is commenting on the "prosaic people" in his own plays. He expands on his thoughts as follows: "The vein of sensitivity is alike in nearly all human beings, all that varies is the thickness of the crust through which it must break. One need only have eyes and ears for it" (*Die Gefühlsader ist in fast allen Menschen gleich, nur ist die Hülle mehr oder weniger dicht, durch die sie brechen muß. Man muß nur Aug und Ohren dafür haben*) (1. 87). What Lenz means is fairly obvious. The "vein of sensitivity" (*Gefühlsader*) is an image of life and thus related to "life" (*Leben*) as well as to the images of muscles and pulses later in the conversation. Realist or anti-idealist writers have to seek out the emotional core of their characters, breaking through superficial observations. The vehicle for this thought brings with it an odd twist, however. The image of a blood vessel bursting through something meant to contain it conveys not only the sense of life but also of life's destruction. Exactly what perceptive writers are supposed to have eyes and ears for is left uncertain. Should they observe the "vein of sensitivity" before or after it has burst through its confinement? On the one hand, writers are called upon to penetrate into the life of the most unimportant people—"immerse themselves in the life of the most insignificant person" (1. 87)—discovering presumably an authentic core of human substance. On the other hand, they are supposed to observe a violent disruption of life's activities. In one case a fine and participatory role is cited, in the other the witnessing of an eruption. The realist writer, in short, must be both a relentless explorer of human life and a distanced, helpless witness of its very destruction. Not coincidentally these are also the two poles between which Lenz is seen to vacillate in the novella. The pervasiveness of life and death imagery in the *Kunstgespräch* is only an extension of its role in the world Lenz encounters and imagines. Once again, therefore, the conversation on art reveals itself to be not only an exploration of the polarities in realist art but also a continuation of Lenz's madness in the face of literary theory.

This continuity between novella and *Kunstgespräch* is perhaps most evident in connection with religious topics. It is not entirely surprising to have these issues surface so often in the rest of the novella. Oberlin is, after all, a man of the cloth, and a good deal of the source Büchner used contains references to religious matters. But that these issues should assume such a central place in the *Kunstgespräch* is more difficult to explain not because previous discussions of art contain no references to religion but because Lenz evidently wants his discussion to be different from those of the tradition. As the conversation progresses, though, Lenz slips more and more into Christian themes. At first he is content merely to insist that the writer imitate God as the original Creator. It is not without significance, however, that none of the following literary illustrations cited has a strong affinity with traditional religion. Neither Shakespeare nor Goethe nor most *Volkslieder* are known for their religiosity; a stronger argument could be made in each case for a marked antireligious or skeptical attitude. But when Lenz begins to counter Kaufmann's objections, opposing Dutch painting to southern art, he falls into a strongly religious tone. This is especially odd, since many of the most celebrated paintings from the North, paintings traditionally cited for their realism, have secular subjects. Lenz, though, selects as his examples two rather obscure works with religious motifs.

What is at issue here, however, are not merely the contradictions and inconsistencies inside the *Kunstgespräch* itself but, more importantly, the relationship between realism and religion and its ramifications for Lenz's discussion of art. Agreeing with J. P. Stern, I would contend that realism in general has the tendency to conflict with notions of transcendence and is therefore potentially at odds with Christianity, especially in its more orthodox forms.[24] Furthermore, this potential conflict between religious doctrine and aesthetic theory exists regardless of the conscious motives of the practitioners of realism. No matter what individual realists may have believed, no matter how pious they may have been as individuals, an artistic doctrine that appeals primarily to life on this earth tends to call into question traditional notions of the divinity. Like great discoveries in the natural sciences (for example, Galileo's theories on planetary motion or Darwin's theory of evolution), realism challenges conventional religious attitudes independently of the theorist's or writer's intentions. If events and agents are to be depicted for their own sake, if the tendency is toward social rather than metaphysical preoccupations, and if values are seen as rising from a human community rather than descending from a transcendent source, then large areas of religious belief are undermined by realist doctrines. It is thus not coincidental that the nineteenth century witnesses the rise of realism in theory and practice. For along with sociological and historical explanations, and the enormous advances in the natural sciences, it too challenges the underpinnings of traditional Christianity.

This potential disparity between religion and realism has far-reaching consequences for the *Kunstgespräch* and for Lenz's predicament in general. One finds in the novella a tension between an artistic theory that tends to deny transcendence and the traditional notion of the Godhead on which this theory is dependent, for Lenz predicates his doctrine of art on the existence of God as the original Creator. Only then can the writer or artist be called upon to imitate Him. If God does not exist, then presumably there is nothing and no one to imitate; there is no master plan or guide to artistic excellence. But if this is indeed so, then Lenz's experiences in the course of the novella effectively cancel his notion of realism. This is most evident in his endeavor to reawaken the dead girl in Fouday. Having heard about the girl's death, he travels to this nearby town hoping that God will bring the girl back to life and thereby provide him with a sign that He exists. But after concentrating all of his will for a long time and giving the command that the girl should arise, he receives as an answer only the echo of his own voice. This echo, as in the *Nachtwachen*, is associated with the demonic. Instead of a sign from God, he receives the mockery of Satan. Rushing out into the landscape, he feels the "triumphal song of hell" in his breast. But this theological disappointment also possesses ramifications for his aesthetics. When atheism grabs him "quite securely and calmly and firmly" (1. 94), it marks the failure of his theory of art as well. Lenz's realism thrives under the aegis of an omnipotent Creator, whom he can imitate and who guarantees that the world is worth imitating, but it collapses when its source is removed.

It would be a mistake to think, however, that the theory Lenz enunciates could be rescued simply by omitting reference to God. In *Lenz* God is not just the first Creator but also the agent that endows the world and its creatures with meaning as well as the ability to grasp

50

that meaning. Thus it is no coincidence that Lenz's most fulfilling moments occur in connection with the preparation of his sermon. In these scenes his faith is most firm and his outbursts of insanity most infrequent. For the first time since his arrival in Waldbach, we read that his nights are peaceful. He feels at ease with himself and with the Creation, which appears to have order and purpose. That his descriptions of nature directly following the sermon exhibit several similarities with his conversation on art is a further sign of the stability he achieves when his belief is strongest: "The simplest, purest character was closest to elemental nature, the more sophisticated a person's intellectual feelings and life, the duller is this elemental sense; he did not consider it to be an elevated state of being, it was not independent enough, but he believed it must be boundless ecstasy to be touched in this way by the unique life of every form" (1. 85). Common to this description and the *Kunstgespräch* are the emphasis on the harmony and simplicity of existence, the need to occupy oneself with the elementary and the ordinary, and the antipathy to intellectualizing and idealism. Only when his faith wanes does Lenz require additional signs that would guarantee a meaningful existence. With the loss of God, however, following the failure to awaken the dead girl in Fouday, reality becomes senseless and chaotic. Lenz now encounters the world as a maze of puzzling signs, and his "discovery" of Friederike's[25] death is thus appropriately accompanied by the repetition of the word "hieroglyphs." Without a transcendent source assuring a meaningful world, Lenz (and the realist artist) loses touch with reality.

God in *Lenz* is thus both a source of meaning and a mediator of this meaning to the human being. He guarantees that the subject can know the objective world. If He does not exist, however, then the artist, denied epistemological certitude, is left in a chaos of impressions. Unable to attribute certainty to any sensory input, he is also denied the possibility of realism, for realism depends upon a stable and meaningful subject-object relationship.[26] Whether we ascribe this stability and meaning to God or to another source is not really the question. What is at issue, rather, is what occurs when uncertainty is introduced into the harmonious epistemological universe. One alternative we have encountered in the texts evidencing romantic irony is a reflection on the very nature of the knowing subject. The movement of self-consciousness admits the objective world only as a means to an end (infinity, nihilism) or, as I have argued in the case of Heine, as an indirect referent. The strategy of realism, on the other hand,

51

is at once more direct and more contradictory. Although it questions the source of meaning in calling into question the traditional God as the guarantor of order and sense in the world, it simultaneously depends on this (or another equally stable) source for its meaning. This affirmation of a transcendent order coupled with its apparent negation is one of the chief paradoxes that the *Kunstgespräch* discloses.

These issues also occupied a central position in Büchner's philosophical deliberations. His notes on Descartes and Spinoza focus primarily on the question of God's existence and frequently point to inconsistencies and contradictions in the philosophers' argumentation.[27] But more important for the aesthetics of realism is Büchner's recognition that Cartesian doubt can only be overcome with illicit recourse to God. Descartes removes the uncertainty of sense perception that he originally postulates and thus bridges the gulf between subject and object only through the introduction of a transcendent mediating force. God's perfection lies at the foundation of epistemological certitude. "It is God who fills up the abyss between thinking and perceiving [*Erkennen*], between subject and object; he is the bridge between the *cogito ergo sum*, between the lonely, erratic, single self-consciousness, conscience, thought, and the external world" (2. 153). The connection with the character Lenz is obvious. The Cartesian bridge exists for him only when he believes in God and when he espouses his aesthetics of realism. As the novella progresses he becomes increasingly alone (*einsam*) and erratic (*irre*). His loss of faith involves an estrangement from the world that can be understood epistemologically as well as theologically. He forfeits not only the security afforded by the Lord as Father and Creator, but also the necessary mediation between his isolated, individual consciousness and the reality he can no longer grasp. Thus, with the onset of atheism Lenz would appear to fall into the "grave of philosophy," which, Büchner contends, Descartes "measured out with such instinctive accuracy" (2. 153). Lenz's problem is that he, unlike the philosopher, cannot use "the good Lord" as a "ladder" to crawl out again. Severed forever from the world around him, denied the epistemological stability necessary for a "normal" existence, he is a Descartes who has carried doubt to its logical extreme. "To pull himself out of the abyss of his doubt there remained for him [Descartes] only one rope, and he hung and hooked his entire system on it: God. For with the kind of doubt he had it would have been completely impossible to prove His existence" (2. 156). In the abyss, however, there is also no possibility of realist art; for with the undermining of the senses, how could a connection be established between artists as subjects and the world they purport to represent? And how could one then be certain that this represented world would in turn be known by the recipient of art? Without a mediation between subject and object, the world as it is as well as its representation are both meaningless.

Perhaps Lenz's abrupt turn to an actual experience in the second part of the *Kunstgespräch* signals a realization of the philosophical difficulties inherent in his theorizing. The dominant theme in this section of his speech is the issue of adequate portrayal of the external world. Most commentators have registered two aspects of this discussion. The first is that Lenz here recognizes an eternal beauty in the simplicity of existence. In commenting on the two girls climbing down the hillside, he remarks: "an unending beauty moving from one form to another, eternally unfolding, changing" (1. 87). And a bit farther on, he reaffirms his earlier contentions that one must become emotionally involved with the object of art, that nothing is too insignificant for the genuine artist: "One must love humanity in order to penetrate into the unique essence of each individual, no one can be too low or too ugly, only then can one understand them" (1. 87). It should be noted here in passing that the attempt to construct a consistent notion of the beautiful in these remarks, occasionally attempted by a daring critic,[28] is a rather dubious undertaking. In most instances Lenz appears to be indifferent to beauty, considering it a façade beneath which the artist must penetrate. But in the first quotation cited above, he refers to "unending beauty" and slightly before this to the "most beautiful pictures" (*die schönsten Bilder*). That beauty has a positive valence in one instance and no valence or a negative one in the other is evident, but the text, I would maintain, gives us no clues as to how to resolve this discrepancy.

The second point most often noted is slightly more important for our concerns since it relates to the notion of realism. During the past half-century, it has become a commonplace to divide realists into two camps. The first, which usually becomes labeled "naturalists," advocates an exact reproduction of reality—whatever this would mean. They supposedly remain on the surface, superficially mimicking the world around them. The second and universally preferred writers, the "high" realists, are those who purportedly penetrate to a more essential layer of reality. They recognize that their task cannot lie in simply reproducing, but rather in elucidating and interpreting, the empirical world.

Now Büchner, from remarks in this section, is to be recruited for the latter group; for his character Lenz also recognizes that the external is not as important as what lies underneath the façade: "the most insignificant face makes a deeper impression than the mere sensation of beauty, and one can let the figures emerge without copying anything into them from the outside" (1. 87). That the character Lenz as well as his creator Büchner, in his correspondence, occasionally speak like crude naturalists is conveniently overlooked.

To the extent that *Lenz* is certainly not a superficial piece of prose, it clearly belongs to "realism" by any account. But in formulating his particular brand of realism, the character Lenz does not manage to escape all contradictions arising from his demand that the artist represent the world as it really is. Once again close attention to particulars is revealing. In observing the girls he comments that one would like to be a "Medusa's head in order to transform such a group into stone" (1. 87). This image of freezing a certain grouping is reinforced then by the suggestion that the descending girls repeatedly form new pictures or images. The continuity of reality is broken up into individual segments, each of which is aesthetically sufficient unto itself: "but as they climbed down among the rocks they formed another picture. The most beautiful pictures, the richest sounds group together and dissolve" (1. 87). And in the following sentence we once again encounter the suggestion that capturing reality entails a cessation of motion, a removal of a scene from its temporal sequence. With reference to the unending beauty of the forms, Lenz states: "one surely cannot hold it [presumably "an unending beauty," although "form" is also a possible antecedent] fast and put it into museums and write it out in notes and then summon young and old and let boys and old men chatter about it and go into raptures" (1. 87). In all three cases Lenz appears to validate a photographic notion of realistic portrayal not unlike that of the naturalists a half-century later.

This attempt to describe the artist's relationship to the external world is remarkable not only as a proleptic moment in the history of aesthetics but also for the inherent contradiction in realism that it exposes. First, it should be noted that Lenz here has turned completely away from words and literature; he has moved from the art form utilizing "arbitrary signs" to those using "natural signs," to use the terms of the eighteenth century. His discussion of realism now focuses on the more immediately sensual art forms: painting, sculpture, and, to a lesser extent, music. More important, however, is the reiterated image of a stopping, halting, freezing, or petrifying of reality. One should perhaps reconstruct the situation to understand better the import of this part of the conversation for a theory of realism. While watching an actual occurrence, the girls on the hillside, Lenz considers how to transform the beauty and simplicity he observes into art. What comes to mind is the Medusa, the Gorgon of Greek mythology whose gaze turns people into stone. That Lenz alludes to this particular figure would appear to support my contention concerning the nonreflexive nature of realism. Medusa as the prototype for the realist artist can capture everything she sees, but she is unable to mirror her own glance without self-destruction. But in the context of Lenz's discussion, this image is particularly striking for another reason. By selecting this reference, Lenz has again unwittingly subverted his own precepts of realist art. In transforming living creatures into cold, lifeless objects, the Medusa accomplishes precisely the opposite of what Lenz, in other statements, seems to advocate for the true realist. She removes people from life instead of recreating life, since she "preserves" life only in a lifeless state.[29] It should also be noted that once again sight and seeing play a predominant role. The preserved reality is what is seen; our eyes are the chief guide to what is real and the chief instrument for capturing reality as art.[30] That the selection of the Medusa, whose power similarly lies in her petrifying vision, was not arbitrary is demonstrated by the repetition of similar images in the following sentences, in which the emphasis is on the slice (out) of life, the snapshot of the external world. Still, the end of this section, just prior to Kaufmann's interruption, affirms activity and vitality in artistic depiction. This is especially odd and conspicuous after the bombardment of imagery concerning the freezing of action. Nonetheless, Lenz again pleads for a "living art," disdaining portrayal of the external, "where no life, no muscles, no pulse swells and beats" (*wo einem kein Leben, keine Muskeln, kein Puls entgegen schwillt und pocht*) (1. 87).

This contradiction, however, is not merely the result of carelessness on the part of the author; nor is it an endeavor to demonstrate that Lenz is not capable of logical thought processes. Rather, I think that it is the paradoxical formulation of a chief artistic aporia with respect to realism. In order to imitate reality, it is necessary to remove essential moments of reality, since the means at the artist's disposal invariably cancel or distort the movement, the constant regrouping, indeed, often the very notion of time of which reality is composed. Capturing life in art unavoidably involves a removal of art from life because the nature of aesthetic reproduction is representation in lifeless appearances. It is no coincidence, therefore, that Lenz here continues the imagery of life and death that we witnessed earlier. The artist, in endeavoring to imitate God, ends up as his antipode: whereas the Lord supposedly breathed life into humankind, the artist, like the Medusa, must make life cease. The second creation is simultaneously the destruction of the first creation. Imitation turns into annihilation. The gulf between art and life, thematized by Kaufmann's appearance, epistemologically noted in the theological connection, is here elucidated from the perspective of its artistic paradox. Eternal change versus a total motionlessness, pulsation versus petrification, life versus death, and God versus the Medusa are the antinomic poles to which Lenz's realism is ineluctably attracted.

The final section of the *Kunstgespräch* views the relationship between life and art from the vantage point of the recipient. Thus the transformation of life into art, undertaken by the artist as God and Medusa, is reversed here, and the topic becomes the translation of art back into life, accomplished by the audience. The shift in focus is accompanied by a marked individualization or privatizing of the argument as well. Dominant in the first two sections were forms of the first person plural and of the indefinite personal pronoun *man* (one). Lenz thereby conveys the impression that realism is more than merely his personal preference. In defending himself against Kaufmann's objections, however, he retreats to a totally subjective position: "What does it matter, he answered, I must admit they make me feel quite lifeless, if I delve into myself, I may indeed feel something, but then I do most of the work. I most prefer the poet or painter who makes nature most real to me, so that I feel his portrayal, everything else disturbs me" (1. 87–88). Noteworthy in this passage is the threefold repetition of the verb *fühlen* (feel), which reinforces the subjective turn in Lenz's discussion as well. Realism is no longer based on the theological imperative of imitating God, nor on the anthropological grounds that falsifying reality is "the most disgraceful debasement of human nature" (1. 87). Rather, Lenz here seeks to justify his predilection solely on the basis of his individual response to those writers and artists who reproduce nature in the most authentic fashion.

The subjectivism that comes to dominate Lenz's argumentation ultimately and necessarily undermines his earlier notions of realism. If the criterion for realist art lies in the individual's feelings rather than in specific characteristics of the works themselves, then there can be no legitimate manner to arbitrate questions of fidelity to reality. By denying a possible bridge between the objective qualities of art and the subjective responses of the individual, Lenz has relinquished any possibility of generalizing his realist "reception aesthetics." Once again the subject-object relationship is called into question, and, as before, this questioning simultaneously questions realism itself. Lenz begins his reflections in the *Kunstgespräch* with a call for reality and life, but winds up affirming only their subjective appearance in the individual's consciousness. The endeavor to escape the lonely, erratic *cogito* proves to be just as difficult for the receiver as for the producer of art.

Discussing realist art from the perspective of the recipient[31] entails another sort of transformation as well. We have seen above that theories of literary realism invariably shift to the visual, or on occasion to one of the other senses, in order to illustrate what is meant by faithfulness to reality. In the *Kunstgespräch* we noted the move from the literary to the pictorial arts as symptomatic for such theorizing. In describing the reception of art, however, this process is reversed. The pictorial forms now become translated into their literary counterparts.[32] In Lenz's conversation this translation is anticipated in the introduction to his two exemplary paintings: "I prefer the Dutch painters to the Italians, they alone are accessible; I know of only two paintings, by Dutchmen, which gave me the same impression as the New Testament" (1. 88). The effect of pictorial art is measured against a narrative passage from the Bible. Lenz appears to ignore the lesson of Lessing's *Laokoon* (1766) in here reintroducing and reversing the Horatian apothegm *ut pictura poesis*.[33] The difference is that poetry and painting are not compared because both *portray* something—as one could infer from the previous discussion from the perspective of the artist—but rather because both involve action in a temporal sequence: both tell a story. That this renewed confounding of literature and the pictorial arts is not merely an error in this isolated sentence is confirmed by Lenz's discussion of the first of the two paintings: "the first one is, I don't know by whom, 'Christ and the Disciples at Emmaus.' When you *read* how the disciples went forth, all nature is *in those few words*" (1. 88; my emphasis). Reading the description that follows, one is not certain whether Lenz is paraphrasing the biblical account (Luke 24: 13) or attempting to interpret the painting. The same holds true for the second painting Lenz selects, except that in this case he apparently has no original narrative text on which his retelling is based. The first two sentences promise the conventional description of a painting: "A woman sits in her room holding a prayer book. Everything is cleaned up for Sunday, the sand strewn on the floor, so comfortably clean and warm" (1. 88). To this point there is no hint of narrative. Lenz is merely putting the visual image into words, although the last phrase does bring in a subjective note with the characteristic "so" phrase encountered frequently throughout the novella. In the next sentence, however, a mini-narrative develops, and it is henceforth freely mixed with the depiction of details from the painting:

> The woman was unable to go to church, and she performs her devotions at home, the window is open, she sits turned toward it, and it seems as if the sound of the bells from the village were floating over the wide, flat landscape into the window, and from the church the singing of the nearby congregation were drifting over to her, and the woman is following the text. (1. 88)

In this passage narrative features ("The woman was unable to go to church"), conjectures ("it seems as if the sound of the bells from the village were floating . . . into the window"), and simple observations ("the window is open") are thrown together without differentiation. If we did not know that Lenz was describing a painting, we might easily assume that he was telling a story. What Lenz has added to the picture is a duration in time; the woman has a past, a present, and a future. There is now a vague but definable temporal sequence of events: the inability to go to church, sitting by the window, hearing the notes, reading the text. Thus Lenz's discussion of his two favorite paintings demonstrates clearly his transfer of image into narrative. He brings the pictures to life by providing them with a history, by supplying the represented figures with meaning and purpose.

For Lenz's previously enunciated theory of realism, this reversal has some rather interesting consequences. On the one hand, the reintroduction of the literary brings the entire conversation back to its original point of departure. Lenz is again on his home territory, and not just because of his familiarity with literature. He is now also able to affirm what he could not from the perspective of the writer or artist, namely, the creative, life-giving dimension of the work of art. The receiver, by placing lifeless images into a temporal flux, resuscitates art from its frozen, motionless state. This third creation, that of the receiver, reestablishes the primacy of life over death, of reality over its pale appearance. On the other hand, however, the price that one pays for this re-creation involves the sacrifice of reality itself. Lenz's descriptions and narrations, after all, are clearly the invention of his lonely, errant consciousness, not the necessary result of an "objective" portrayal. The reestablished connection to reality is arbitrary and subjective, the product of fantasy. The thread connecting past and present, the teleological moment so often denied by Büchner the natural scientist, the story line by which reality again has coherence for the viewer —all are supplied here by the dreamlike effusions of a madman. It would seem, therefore, that life, a proximity to reality, or a sense of the real is only obtainable when the creative subject fictionalizes the artwork. Only by imposing a necessarily imaginary order on art—and on the world as well—can realism retain its pretensions of capturing reality. Once again we have reached the point of paradox: the imposition of a fictional ordering (in this case narrative) is the enabling moment for a form of art (realism) that claims to escape all fictionalizing.

And once again it is not difficult to see that this paradox has something to do with Lenz's predicament in the rest of the novella. In the very first scene, we find him endeavoring to escape from the chaos of impressions by placing his arbitrary order on the external world. His notorious desire to walk on his head can be understood not only as a sign of his madness but as an attempt to prevent it as well (1. 79). In imposing his will on nature, he here parallels the recipient of art interpreting a painting, thus making sense (in both meanings of this phrase) in and of the world. The issue of invented narrative is also thematized elsewhere in the novella. We witness both the aimless wandering of the main character as well as his search for meaning and direction, and all his peregrinations vacillate between these two poles. Part of this complex of aimlessness and goal-directedness (for Lenz the goal is often simply "rest" [*Ruhe*]), of course, relates to the religious crisis discussed above. It is significant, for example, that in a conversation with Oberlin after his atheistic experience Lenz refers to the Wandering Jew: "In you alone is the way to God. But it's all over with me! I have sinned, I'm damned for eternity, I'm the Wandering Jew" (1. 94). But Lenz's life in general is also characterized by a lack of direction or goal. In this connection it is significant that he denies his past—his plays and his familial ties—as well as a purposeful future. Lenz seems to want to live the paradox that realism presents. He needs an order to prevent chaos and create meaning, yet he denies a personal narrative that would supply that order. Indeed, Lenz's madness may be interpreted along these lines as the result of his failure to impose a consistent order on the world. Unable to find purpose

59

or meaning in a world abandoned by the ultimate ordering principle in heaven, and unable to view his own life within a traditional narrative structure, he can only end in complete indifference to the world: "he was completely indifferent" (1. 101) we read in the last paragraph of the novella. And it is certainly not coincidental that the full force of this paradox is captured at the very close of this work, in the final sentence—"So he lived on" (*So lebte er hin*)—in which both the aimlessness and purposelessness of Lenz's existence as well as an implied direction (*hin*) are paradoxically fused. Lenz does indeed live this paradox. Simultaneously affirming and rejecting meaning and purpose, he, like the theory of art he espouses, is entangled in a web of aporias from which there is no apparent escape.

The realism of the *Kunstgespräch* is thus neither a simple matter nor one without consequence. It is paradoxical both in the context of the novella and in itself, if one takes it to be a serious statement on aesthetic theory. It is far-reaching in its scope, not merely because it anticipates the artistic doctrines of a later generation, but also because it forecasts the inherent conflicts within these doctrines. For the character Lenz realism becomes both a refuge and a symptom of madness, a theoretical necessity as well as a practical impossibility. It is the chimera that he pursues and that pursues him. There is little question that the *Kunstgespräch* affirms an artistic alternative to idealism, but the novella shows more insight into the difficulties in accomplishing this alternative than the writings of the "high realists" in the latter half of the century. What separates Büchner's novella from the works of Keller, Raabe, Storm, Meyer, and Freytag, therefore, is the probing and open nature of its reflection on realism. In order to do this, it necessarily defines its status as in-between. The reflection is not hidden in a text as an implicit statement of poetic intention, but it is also not a direct expression of the author's views. An integral part of the novella and an obvious interruption, embedded in a text that simultaneously inaugurates the realist tradition and proclaims its impossibility, the conversation on art in *Lenz* expounds an artistic theory that is associated with both the madness of the main character and the sanity of his counterpart, a view of art that appears to reflect the author's intention as well as the distanced statements of a literary persona. As we shall see in the subsequent chapters, no other reflection on realism is so subtle in its implications for literary theory, so candid in its discussion of aporias, and so consequential in its exploration of paradox. Nor does any other reflection on realism refuse so completely to partake in the delineation of norms that characterizes the realist enterprise throughout the rest of the century. In this regard Büchner remains an outsider, both poetically and ideologically, to the very movement the *Kunstgespräch* so trenchantly explores.

3

THE REALIST EDUCATION:
Nausikaa and the *Bildungsroman*

Wodurch also das Individuum hier Geltung
und Wirklichkeit hat, ist die *Bildung*. Seine
wahre *ursprüngliche Natur* und Substanz ist
der Geist der *Entfremdung* des *natürlichen*
Seins.

(The individual therefore has validity and
reality here through *education*. His true
original nature and substance is the spirit of
the alienation from his *natural* being.)

Georg Wilhelm Friedrich Hegel,
Phenomenology of the Spirit

$\mathbf{I}$n the sixth book of the *Odyssey*, the god-like Odysseus, naked and dirty, lies asleep at the river in the land of the Phaiakians. In one of the most memorable episodes of the epic, he then meets the princess Nausikaa, herself of divine beauty. The latter has gone to the river, prompted by Athena, to wash fine clothes for her wedding, although it is clear that no one is betrothed to her yet. While playing ball with her servants, she comes upon the stranger on the shore. Her companions flee, but the white-armed maiden, inspired by the goddess, stays and listens to his speech. Without revealing his identity and amid profuse compliments, he entreats her for mercy and assistance. She orders clothes to be brought for him, gives him oil with which to bathe, and tells him what to do when he comes into the city. Clean and well-dressed, Odysseus later arrives at the house of Nausikaa's father, Alkinoos, and is received respectfully by him and his wife, Arete. Although he does not know his name or his ultimate destination, Alkinoos immediately agrees to help him return home. First, however, a meal is prepared, and Odysseus is shown the idyllic garden estate. The next day an assembly is called at which the Phaiaken men participate in various athletic contests. Here we first encounter the singer Demodakos, another figure identified with the immortals. At the games Odysseus, insulted and challenged by Euryalos, demonstrates his skill and prowess. Alkinoos, recognizing the nobility and excellence of the stranger, orders that gifts be given, and a reconciliation between Odysseus and Euryalos is easily accomplished. Then we encounter Nausikaa for the last time in the epic. She asks that Odysseus remember her when he arrives home; he assures her that he will honor her as he would honor a god, since she has given him life. At the feast that follows, Odysseus asks Demodakos to sing of the fall of Troy. Noticing his moans and sighs during the performance, Alkinoos suspects that his guest has some connection with the events in the song. He finally asks him to reveal his identity, where he has been, and where he is going. Beginning in the ninth book, then, Odysseus, taking over for the blind Demodakos, relates his adventures to his host and the assembled guests.

The Nausikaa episode is thus a prelude to two important compositional features, one a reflection or self-reflection, the other the introduction of a narrative device. In the figure of Demodakos, Homer is obviously presenting his mirror image. The first song he sings is some variation on the *Iliad*; it tells of the fame of the hero Odysseus, of Agamemnon, and of the conflict between the Trojans and the Achaions (8. 73–78). The singer of the *Odyssey*, in other words, sings of a singer singing; he portrays his fictionalized self. We are not only allowed a glimpse into the social function and significance of the singer in Greek society, but also are shown for perhaps the first time in Western literature a situation in which the narrator and his subject merge into one figure. Demodakos's performance, however, is curtailed when Alkinoos notes Odysseus' sighs. Soon thereafter the subject of his song and his audience are also revealed to be a single person, and for the next three books Odysseus himself assumes the function of narrator. The poet and his reflection cede to a narrative voice reflecting on himself and his adventures. By allowing Odysseus to relate his own story, Homer sacrifices omniscience in narration for authenticity and involvement. Indeed, here we encounter a significant switch from the epic

63

purview to the more private, subjective mode. The *Odyssey* combines in this manner the two major modes of narration preferred in a much later age by German realists. On the one hand, we find the distanced, "objective" overview guaranteeing a truthful account. Third-person narrative must not strive toward the obliteration of the narrator as character—witness, for example, the "subjective" tone in Raabe's narrators. But in the paradigm of realism developed around Flaubert's theoretical pronouncements and in Germany propagated by Friedrich Spielhagen, verisimilitude is enhanced by the elimination of our awareness of the narrator as person, as a presence. On the other hand, we can identify the first-person report with realist narrative since this type of narrator seems to be in a unique position to guarantee the fidelity of what has occurred. Here truth contributes to the effect of realism. Even if we ultimately discover the partiality of the narrator's account, a certain effect of realism is retained because the narrator has actually experienced what he/she has described. This is particularly true when language is presumed to be a non-distorting vehicle for relating experiences. If we assume good will on the part of the narrator—that is, the absence of irony and dissimulation—this type of account in its apparent subjectivity will be as realistic as the objectivity of the impersonal third-person.

Even if Homer had not been consistently considered the paradigm of realism for Germans in the eighteenth and nineteenth centuries, the Nausikaa episode would seem to possess a potential allure for novelists of German realism because of its reflection on epic style. And indeed, two of the most celebrated novels of the mid-nineteenth century, Adalbert Stifter's *Nachsommer* (*Indian Summer*, 1857) and Gottfried Keller's *Der grüne Heinrich* (*Green Henry*; first version 1854/55; second version 1879/80) contain an allusion to the very books of the *Odyssey* in which the hero visits with the Phaiakians.[1] In Stifter's work Nausikaa serves as one of a series of images associated with absolute beauty and thus integrates various thematic threads. In Keller's novel she is associated with Dortchen Schönfund, Heinrich's last infatuation before his own return home. Both works also seem to combine the two alternative narrative modes of realist epics. In the original version from 1854/55, Keller included both a third-person narrator, who opens and closes the novel, and a long insert with first-person narration, the so-called *Jugendgeschichte* (Story of My Youth). Stifter's text has apparently one form of narration; Heinrich Drendorf tells his story throughout in the first person, except in passages in the third volume where the Freiherr von Risach relates his own past. But as several critics have noted, this first-person narrative tends toward omniscient, "objective" narration. The conspicuous absence of reflection, the lack of psychological depth, the tendency to describe things phenomenologically, and the endeavor to present experiences exactly as they were originally perceived makes Heinrich's account resemble closely the traditional third-person report.[2] In this respect Stifter likewise combines the two Homeric modes noted above, but in each of these works, the Nausikaa experience has a significance beyond that of a mere reflection on narrative. Both *Der Nachsommer* and *Der grüne Heinrich* are customarily subsumed under the subgenre of the *Bildungsroman*, or novel of education or self-cultivation.[3] In such novels we usually find a young man coming to terms with himself and the world around him through a series of learning encounters.[4] In these two pedagogical works of the 1850s, both Heinrichs meet their own version of Nausikaa at pivotal points in their development. What is more, in each case this encounter discloses a reflection on realism in art, on the relationship of model to original. The Nausikaa allusion thus provides the occasion for an intersection of education and realism as well as for the reflection on the realist education of two heroes who, like Odysseus, linger at the home of the beautiful maiden just before their final goal.

I

In Stifter's *Nachsommer* Nausikaa is mentioned twice, both times in connection with a marble statue Risach acquired in Cumae. The statue, which depicts a young girl, has been observed by Heinrich several times before it becomes associated with aesthetic perfection. In his initial entrance into Risach's home, Heinrich must have passed by it, although it is not described until just before he retires on his first evening in the Asperhof. At this point he does not recognize or feel anything unusual:

> In the middle of the stairway where there was a landing like an enlarged area or stairwell, I could see a figure made of white marble standing on a pedestal. By a few lightning flashes that just then illuminated the room the head and shoulders of the figure glowed ruddier than it would have with just our candles;

I also saw that the landing and the stairway must get its illumination through a sky light. (6. 81)

The following day he notes only that daylight produces a gentle glow on the white marble in comparison to the light of the candles and the lightning of the previous evening (6. 87). Here he is more interested in natural phenomena than in beauty. On a subsequent visit to the Rose House (Heinrich's designation for Risach's estate) after meeting Natalie for the first time, he refers to the statue as a muse. Only in the second volume, though, does he take a closer, more contemplative look at the marble maiden. What impresses him then is the unspeakable beauty of a work of art. Here Heinrich—and his creator Stifter—are obviously continuing the German tradition of Grecophilia, which had dominated aesthetic theory from Winckelmann through Hegel.[5] Greek art, especially sculpture, is applauded for its perfection, simplicity, and harmony. At this point Heinrich suddenly thinks of that other paradigm of Greek culture, the Homeric epic: "I thought of Nausikaa as she stood at the portal of the golden hall saying to Odysseus, 'Stranger, if you reach your homeland, remember me'" (7. 74). Heinrich is alluding to the eighth book of the *Odyssey*, when the hero, having received gifts from his hostess, is preparing to enter the hall to drink with the men and to hear Demodakos's song (8. 461–62). It is Nausikaa's final appearance in the epic. In *Der Nachsommer*, however, she appears again after Heinrich and Natalie have declared their love for each other. On a winter visit to the Asperhof, Heinrich immediately seeks the marble statue, which now represents for him "antiquity in its greatness and splendor" (8. 63). Then he goes to the library, finds a copy of the *Odyssey*, and proceeds to read the Nausikaa passage. Again he identifies Alkinoos's daughter with the marble muse: "When Nausikaa came, I felt just as I had the first time I had really looked at and understood the marble statue" (8. 64–65). But as he reads farther, another association forces its way into his thoughts. He conjures up the image of his love Natalie; in his mind she becomes the "present-day Nausikaa" (*Nausikae von jetzt*), and he winds up thinking of her and reading his book simultaneously (8. 65).

The encounter with the marble statue and its association with Nausikaa and Natalie is an important element in Heinrich's progression toward self-realization. When he first met Risach, he was interested almost exclusively in science. On his initial visit to the Rose House, the book he selects for reading is Alexander von Humboldt's *Reise in die Äquinoktialländer* (*Travels in the Equinoctial Lands*, 1814/25). Herder, Lessing, Goethe, Schiller, and Homer are also included in the baron's well-stocked library, but at this point Heinrich chooses to "put them aside" (6. 56). That he notices only the marble and the reflection of light on it is consistent with his development at that time. But even as a scientist, one can perceive that he has a proclivity toward beauty, that he will be receptive toward the subtle "aesthetic education" he will obtain from his mentor Risach. In cataloguing minerals and plants, he mentions his dissatisfaction with the customary classifications: the scientific system orders things according to one of several characteristics; Heinrich prefers to retain along with this a classification based on overall perception and description (6. 27–28). The same conflict recurs when he studies animals: Heinrich proceeds "aesthetically"—at least in the classicist sense of the word—seeking the essential characteristics as the basis of his ordering.[6] Gradually he learns, however, that even his iconoclastic approach to natural phenomena is inadequate for an appreciation of beauty. His initial attempts at landscape painting, for example, are failures because he is still too much of a scientist. Since he has not yet learned to see the whole but rather concentrates too meticulously on the separate parts, he "succeeds much more in the scientific than in the artistic" (7. 31). His recognition of the beauty of the marble statue is the turning point in his transition from scientist to appreciator of art. Although there are hints of insight before this episode, the lightning that illuminates the sky that fateful evening is an obvious analog to the epiphanic flash that occurs in Heinrich's mind. From that moment on he realizes what beauty entails, or, as Risach states, he gains "possession of beauty" (7. 76), and accordingly reorders his priority with respect to science and art. He himself describes his stage-like progression in a passage found between the two Nausikaa experiences:

> Once the world was as clear as it was beautiful; I tried to learn and understand a great deal, made quite a few sketches, and took a lot of notes. Then everything became increasingly difficult; my scientific projects were not as easy to solve, they grew more complicated and constantly pointed to new questions. Then another time came; no longer did science seem the ultimate in life, it was not really important if you knew some detail or not, the world shone as if from some inner beauty, a beauty you should comprehend as an entity and not as fragmented [*die man auf*

einmal fassen soll, nicht zerstückt]; I admired it, I loved it, I tried to make it more a part of me, I longed for something great and unknown that must be there. (7. 221)

This unknown to which Heinrich here refers would seem to be the love for Natalie that is the added association in his second Nausikaa encounter. On the educational journey from science to art to fulfillment in love,[7] the marble statue of Nausikaa signals at each juncture a major advance in the hero's development.

As the epitome of artistic perfection and the centerpiece of the novel,[8] the Nausikaa-like statue is also a reflection on the artistry of the work in which it is contained and on its own pretension to realism. Important in this regard is that the recognition of beauty in the plastic arts occurs simultaneously with the allusion to a literary art form. Analogous to the "Conversation on Art" in *Lenz*, we find here a confounding of the visual and the literary. In the first "correct" encounter with the statue, Heinrich even notes that the gown tells (*erzählte*) of the pure and closed form (7. 74). In the second episode, while reading the epic, he recalls his initial viewing of the sculpture. Seeing and reading, the image and the word, are merged into one activity—or at least considered equatable. This merger, however, is merely a continuation of a long series of such associations throughout the novel. Both Risach and Heinrich's father have a passion for paintings and books, and each is accorded equal respect in their collections. When Heinrich begins his scientific expeditions, he uses two methods to record his observations: written reports and sketches. In his endeavor to communicate his experience to his father, he uses the same means. Indeed, in a sense Herr Drendorf points to the similarity between art and literature early in the novel when he advises his son on his future profession. Noting his curiosity with respect to nature, the elder Drendorf tells his son that he should be a "describer of things" or an artist, that is, someone who copies with words or images. And just prior to Heinrich's first viewing of the statue, we find that his thoughts also evidence a tendency to equate or associate the visual and the literary arts. He composes many letters and reads a great deal, but these activities evoke in him other artistic desires: "The poets, as the most noble beings that I had now encountered, reminded me again of painting" (7. 68). In a moment this process will be reversed, when the statue reminds him of the words found in the Nausikaa episode in the *Odyssey*. In both cases, though, we witness the easy transition from painting/sculpture to

68

poetry/literature, a transition that, as we have seen in our discussion of Büchner, is characteristic of the age of realism.

One of the reasons that this transition is so easily accomplished in *Der Nachsommer* has to do with the unusual theory of linguistic reference expounded in the novel. Both Heinrich and Risach, in telling their respective life stories, place emphasis on the image-like quality of words. Heinrich insists on knowing the names of the things he perceives, as if the mere word somehow captures the essence of the object (6. 23). Risach demands precision in language so that the object or activity is more accurately represented: "Indeed, the words that made an object representable to the senses were far preferable to me than those that only designated it in general. Thus, for example, it made a much greater impression on me when someone said: the Count is riding on his dappled horse, than simply he is riding on a horse" (8. 81). It does not seem to be coincidental that directly following this sentence Risach relates his endeavors at sketching various types of objects: "With a red pencil I drew deer, horsemen, dogs, flowers, but liked most of all to sketch cities where I conjured up the most wondrous figures" (8. 81). For words, like images, have a mimetic function in the world of *Der Nachsommer*, and they can therefore be interchanged without difficulty. Like Socrates, who in arguing with Kratylos, claims that a name, just like a painting, is an imitation (430d, 10), so too the heroes of Stifter's novel suggest that there is a fundamental similarity between the relationship word-thing and the relationship picture-thing. Indeed, this Platonic connection is reinforced in various passages in other parts of the text.[9] Perhaps the most significant of these occurs in the second volume when Risach is extolling poets as the "priests of the beautiful." He places poetry at the pinnacle of the hierarchy of art forms not because it is conceptual—which was the justification used by theorists from Lessing through Hegel—but because it is not bound to any material. Risach thus borrows an argument that romantic aestheticians had employed to vault music to the top of the aesthetic hierarchy. But in a strange twist, he applies the argument to poetry. His only problem is what to do about words and their referents. As different as Enlightenment and romantic aesthetics were with respect to their ranking of poetry, they at least agreed in essence that language is its material. In using a romantic argument for an Enlightenment result, Risach is forced to make words transparent vehicles rather than materials. Poets are assigned the Platonic task of mediating to us the eternally permanent things in the midst of the constant flux of life, a thought lifted quite evidently from Greek philosophy. But they do this only because the materials they use are *thoughts* and not words: "Only literature has almost no tangible material [*Stoff*] any more; its material is thought in the widest sense of the word; the word is not the material, it is only the bearer of the thought, as for example the air carries the sound to our ears. Literature is therefore the purest and highest of the art forms" (7. 35).[10] In their ordinary usage words and images both imitate things; in poetry, however, words suddenly become akin to Platonic ideas, the eternal forms of which reality itself is an imitation. In both cases, though, the visual and the literary are functionally proximate as vehicles for representing another more real or more ideal (and therefore ultimately more real) realm.

The proximity of the visual to the literary marked by the marble statue's association with Nausikaa is reinforced on the level of description as well. If words, as individual units of meaning, are likened to images, then series of words are used to constitute structures resembling paintings. The graphic arts and literature are identified with one another by the very style Stifter employs in his works. Description dominates narration. In this regard he is the most tenacious and consistent advocate of the dictum *ut pictura poesis* since Lessing's celebrated separation of painting and poetry in *Laokoon* (1766). Events are conspicuously absent in *Der Nachsommer*; one could restate the entire plot on a few pages without sacrificing any major occurrences. As even its earliest critics pointed out, the genre designation Stifter chose, *Erzählung* (story or narrative), seems inappropriate; for in this work, as in few others, almost nothing is told (*erzählt*).[11] Instead we encounter description: of nature, of furniture, of rooms, of buildings, indeed, of paintings themselves. Stifter, obviously aware of his critics' objections, even included an inner-textual defense of his *Trutz-Laokoon* (*Defiant Laokoon*), as Arno Schmidt has called his work.[12] When Risach is narrating his life history to Heinrich, he employs the same sort of digressive, epic devices that Heinrich uses in his first-person account. At one point, however, recognizing that he has been describing and thus relating "things that are not important" (8. 93), he excuses himself. But his eager listener entreats him to continue in the same manner: "'I beg you,' I rejoined, 'please continue as you are, do not withhold any images left from your younger days; they conjure up such a lovely image, they provide a perspective, it is as if a flat shadow were given a rounded life. Besides, unless your time is more strictly allotted, mine is no hindrance that you should keep something from me'" (8. 93).

70

Here Heinrich is obviously supplying the rejoinder to Stifter's critics as well. As readers, we too are supposed to experience the word-paintings that characterize his prose as enrichments of the story, as an element of depth and beauty. In connection with *Lenz* we noted the metaphoric connection between painting/sculpture and literature during the age of realism and the dependence on the visual in the history of theorizing on realism. With Stifter's novel this theory is put into practice; the metaphors are taken seriously. No other writer during the nineteenth century displays a greater concern for portrayal and description. In this context it is certainly not coincidental that from his earliest novellas (*Kondor* [*Condor*, 1840] and *Feldblumen* [*Wild Flowers*, 1841]) to his last works (*Nachkommenschaften* [*Descendants*, 1864]), Stifter chose painters as protagonists. Indeed, in *Der Nachsommer* Heinrich is also something of an artist; he takes up landscape painting, as we have seen, when he is ready to proceed beyond his limited scientific outlook. The narrators in Stifter's prose works thus vie with their artistic heroes; the former paint with words and phrases, and the latter utilize brush and palette. In this fashion the style itself, as well as the content, reiterates the realist equation of literature and the graphic arts.

From the foregoing remarks it should be obvious that mimesis plays a decisive role in the theory and the composition of *Der Nachsommer*. The terms *Nachbildung* (copy), *Abbildung* (drawing), *Urbild* (original), and even *Bild* (picture or image) recur with astonishing frequency and regularity in the many conversations on science, architecture, painting, and sculpture. The function of both science and art is to give a true and precise picture or copy of the real world, and this mimetic relationship between artwork and reality is also coded into the Nausikaa episodes. The marble statue and the literary figure achieve artistic perfection when they become identified with Natalie. The equation between the art forms of sculpture and poetry is completed by the merger of art with reality.[13] This is suggested already in Heinrich's initial epiphanic experience. In his description of the statue, he continuously refers to it as if it were a living being. It is not only beautiful, but innocent (*unschuldvoll*) as well, and it (she) seems to have lofty thoughts (*erhabene Gedanken*). The cheeks are calm and serious (*ruhig* and *ernst*), and the mouth, so finely formed, looks "as if it should say judicious words, or sing beautiful songs." Heinrich has the impression that he is in the presence of a real maiden: "I had the sensation as if I were standing by a silent living being, and almost shuddered as if the maiden could move at any moment" (7. 74). At this point the attentive reader can already sense that the statue of Nausikaa is an artistic representation of Natalie, the girl who, when she meets Heinrich, is both suggestively silent and indescribably beautiful. Only in the second Nausikaa experience does Heinrich himself recognize that Natalie is the real-life counterpart to the work of art. While reading the *Odyssey* after viewing the statue, he imagines "the beautiful image [*Bild*] of Natalie": "she was the present-day Nausikaa, so true, so simple, so without ostentation with her emotions, yet not concealing them either. Both forms merged into each other. (8. 65). It is this final merger of art and reality that completes Heinrich's *Bildung* from scientist to lover of art. Art itself, however, although it may—and perhaps should—lead one back to life, is conceived here in terms of imitation of an external world. And the epiphany of its mimetic function is reached when the difference between art and life can no longer be perceived.

Imitation is all-pervasive in *Der Nachsommer*; almost every character in the novel is involved with some sort of mimetic activity. Eustache travels through the country sketching anything that appears to him worthy of preservation. Heinrich draws first as a scientist, then for his father, and finally as an amateur artist. His first-person narrative is obviously a form of imitation as well. Even the priest who occasionally visits the Rose House occupies himself with sketching—not for artistic purposes, as we are told, but to assist his memory: he wants to plant flowers in his garden that are similar to the ones he sees on Risach's estate. Imitation is thus a natural, universal activity not necessarily restricted to the realm of aesthetics. Although it apparently culminates in artistic creation, its origins are humble. On one level it arises from our "natural" inclination to group similar items and to discover their essential characteristics. In *Der Nachsommer* this is the realm of the scientist, conceived not as inventor or experimenter but as the humble discoverer of an already given reality.[14] Heinrich's notion of science is mimetic (and thus obsolete even for the nineteenth century): his goal is to find out what is already happening in the world of nature, not to interfere with or control natural processes. Like Risach he wants to allow the things themselves to speak; the role of the scientist is thus one of a patient listener and recorder of the already and always spoken. There is no conflict between scientist and artist because both have the same task: copying and preserving reality. The latter activity simply places its emphasis more squarely on the totality of the imitated object and therefore on a classicist notion of beauty. On the other hand, art is inextricably connected with craftsmanship. In opposition to an "Aethetics of Genius" (*Genieästhetik*), *Der Nachsommer* stresses diligence and practice. Eustache's sketches are not art in the true sense of the word, but his accuracy and skill are prerequisites for the true artist. When Heinrich turns to landscape painting, his chief failing is technique. Accordingly he receives constructive criticism, applies himself, and improves his artistry. The ancient connection between crafts and art is thus preserved in the world of the novel; indeed, the latter seems to grow organically out of the former. But the ultimate source of our mimetic drive is shown to be anthropological. Art speaks to an innate proclivity for recognizing reproductions:

> We have a more inner, a sweeter feeling when we see a landscape, flowers or even a human being formed by Art than if we have these things before us in real life. What children admire is the spirit of the child that has produced so much in imitation; what we admire in Art is that a man's spirit has made an object of our love and admiration tangible, even if faulty it nevertheless imitated something that we are attempting to comprehend with our reason, something that we cannot draw into the limited circle of our love, before which the sense of awe, reverence, and humility in beholding its majesty becomes increasingly greater the more precisely we perceive it. (7. 153)

In describing a general principle of art, Risach here also seems to be alluding to Heinrich's Nausikaa experience. The art object itself does not contain value independent of the reality it imitates. Art is not autonomous in the strict sense of the word. Rather, it has value as a commemoration and reproduction of an "object of our love and reverence." Nausikaa and the marble muse are incomplete without Natalie.

The mimetic quality of art appears to be called into question only twice in the novel, and in both cases the mimetic norm is restored by Risach's gentle pedagogy. In the first instance we find Heinrich unable to appreciate paintings from the medieval period. At first he rejects these works because of their darkness and dreariness. Later he recognizes that they are beautiful and should be admired, but his own mimetic sketches for his scientific activity still interfere with his appreciation of these works. The objects portrayed seem to him to be the result of convention and not imitation. "Old paintings did not appear to me to be imitations, but to a certain extent to be valuable objects that simply exist, and in them things are found that one is used to seeing in old paintings" (7. 100). Heinrich's thoughts at this stage of his development actually seem more modern than his later views. Here he would appear to agree with E. H. Gombrich's main thesis in *Art and Illusion* that the depiction of reality in the history of painting is arbitrary and conventional.[15] Heinrich, however, "advances" to a deeper understanding of the essentially mimetic qualities of these paintings. Under the patient tutelage of Risach he comes to realize that those things he had previously considered arbitrary are actually the result of the most careful attention to detail:

> I learned the relationship of older paintings to Nature—my friend had almost exclusively older paintings. I became able to distinguish that the old masters imitated Nature more faithfully and more beautifully than the moderns, that they had an inexpressible amount of tenacity and patience in mastering natural characteristics, perhaps more, I felt, than I had myself, and perhaps more than many a contemporary disciple of Art. (7. 102)

Art that struck Heinrich—and may strike us—as nonmimetic winds up fitting the paradigm better than contemporary nineteenth-century works. Heinrich's educational progress in aesthetics, which occurs just after the first Nausikaa episode, is another step away from a purely scientific mentality. All art from the past now falls under the domain of a single mimetic principle. In maturing to this point, Heinrich cannot imagine a greater attentiveness to "the essence of nature" (7. 102) than in those painting he formerly regarded as mimetically deficient.

The second case involves the large painting worked on by Eustache's brother Roland.[16] It appears that it is some sort of abstract landscape. Although Heinrich can identify various objects—cliffs and earth—the absence of more customary natural objects—"mountains or streams or plains or forests"—makes this painting clearly an exception in the world of the novel. It is no doubt significant that it is described almost solely in negative terms. Heinrich's first remark is, "I had never seen anything like it" (8. 52), and he repeatedly emphasizes what is lacking, suggesting, of course, that these things really should be there if the painting is to be acceptable as an aesthetic representation. Risach explains the nonmimetic quality of Roland's endeavor as follows: "He has taken upon himself the task of portraying an object that he has not yet seen," Risach tells Heinrich, "he only sees it through the power of his imagination." And Roland himself then confirms the baron's report: "I had no particular point of departure, . . . I have simply developed forms as they occur in my soul. I also want to experiment with oil colors; they have always stimulated me more than water colors, and in them something powerful and fiery can be portrayed" (8. 53). That Roland's nonmimetic path is being criticized here will not escape the attentive reader. His sin is not only a lack of reverence for nature but subjectivity and passion as well, both of which are repeatedly criticized in the novel. That he is not openly rebuked is almost certainly due to Risach's pedagogical principles, whereby time and experience are called upon to cure all deviations from decorum. Risach's comment, "We shall see how successful he is" (8. 53), is surely made in this spirit, as well as the advice: "Work and choose as you see fit; your spirit will guide you" (8. 54). Alone with Heinrich, Risach reinforces his disapproval of Roland's present course with the short, but meaningful utterance: "He should travel" (8. 54). Roland is clearly on the wrong track with respect to art because he has broken the sacred aesthetic commandment of verisimilitude. His abstract, subjective, and impressionistic landscapes will be, Risach hopes, merely a stage he overcomes in his own self-cultivation.[17] Like medieval art Roland's work will inevitably be brought in line with the mimetic ideal.

With respect to literature Heinrich has an even easier time defending an all-encompassing mimetic principle. This facility is paradoxically related to the unique quality of words as the material of literature; they are read with the eyes, but, unlike pictures or pictographs, they are not direct representations of external reality. The arbitrary connection between words and things—which Risach and his ward would very likely dispute—has important ramifications for the aesthetics of the novel. It allows the young Drendorf to identify specific literary works—particularly those of Greek writers—with a vague notion of realism without stipulating precisely why they should be placed in this category. He cannot compare what he sees with the actual words, but must instead imagine what the writer saw and determine what kind of impression this made on him. He prefers the writings of Homer, Aeschylus, Sophocles, and Thucydides to those of the modern age because they saw things and events "with clear eyes," and because it seems to him that they are "more natural, more true, simpler and greater" (7. 28). Since he does not have to test this hypothesis with his vision, as he does when he views the older paintings, his evaluation with respect to the mimetic qualities of poetic works is less constrained, more "subjective," and ultimately a mere repetition of traditional notions. On the other hand, writers who, like Roland, create out of an excess of emotions are summarily discredited. In Heinrich's view they have not learned to observe and record, i.e., they have not sought to perfect their skills, depending instead on passion. They have ignored, in short, the two sources of mimetic activity outlined above: the natural sciences and the crafts. "In natural science I had gotten used to observing the characteristics of things, to value those qualities and pay homage to their essential nature. I found no qualities whatsoever among the authors of bombast [*den Dichtern des Schwulstes*]; it seemed the height of ridiculousness that someone who had learned nothing was trying to create something" (7. 28). Poets are thus constrained by the same aesthetic principles as painters. The essence of sound writing is imitation and objectivity, and for this reason Heinrich, in contrast to Aristotle, can also place historians in the same category as dramatists and epic poets: they all have in common the task of being faithful to reality and nature.

Ultimately the justification for mimesis as the central tenet for any aesthetic endeavor is rather traditional and familiar. In a passage reminiscent of the first part of Lenz's *Kunstgespräch*, Heinrich has recourse to the notion of the poet as a second creator. His objection to bombastic writers is not only that they lack scientific study and technical training but, above all, that they falsify God's creation. Their activity is not merely inept, but blasphemous as well: "They did not portray Nature as it is within and outside of man; rather they tried to make it more beautiful and tried to elicit certain effects. I turned away from them. If reality isn't sacred to them, what is? How are they capable of creating something better than God's Creation?" (7. 28). The corollary to this proposition of second creation is that no poet or artist can ever completely capture the first creation in a work of art. Those who presume to imitate reality exactly, who seek perfect mimesis, are foolish. Thus in one of his later novellas, *Nachkommenschaften*, Stifter gently mocks the painter Friedrich Roderer for trying to create a picture that would be identical with nature. Doomed to failure in his mimetic enterprise, Roderer eventually gives up his profession to marry and start a family. Heinrich had learned this elementary lesson in his early development. His first attempts at artistic landscapes are accompanied by the recognition that "no one can produce things, namely landscapes, in their full essence" (7. 33). Imitation is essential, but perfection in creation belongs to God alone. In a work of art, Risach tells Heinrich, the result should be similar to what the Creator has made: "and this is really Art; it participates to a lesser or greater extent in Creation and imitates it" (7. 152). True art, the baron concludes, is thus necessarily limited; it is "the approximation of the divine" (*die Annährung zu den Göttlichen*) (7. 154), not divine creation itself. And in this sense it is also an act of reverence. In the harmonious universe of *Der Nachsommer* art is a "branch of religion" (7. 153), and its priests are the poets and painters who humbly represent what God has already created.

Heinrich's education is thus simultaneously an initiation.[18] At the altar of the marble muse, envisioning Nausikaa and her earthly incarnation Natalie, he takes the rites of the religion of pious mimesis. He had, of course, been preparing for admission to this cult for a long time. His own natural inclinations, combined with the masterful guidance of Risach, bring him to full maturity. By the close of the novel, when he himself undertakes the mimetic task of recounting his development, his *Bildung* has been completed. In learning about imitation, however, it is obvious that Heinrich performs an act of imitation as well. While he and others are continuously preoccupied with creating copies (*Nachbildungen*, *Abbilder*) of originals (*Urbilder*), while the Rose House idyll is almost obsessed with paintings and sketches (*Bilder*, *Abbildungen*), Heinrich is educating himself in accordance with an original as well. He finds in Risach, and later in his own father, the perfect model (*Vorbild*) for his own self-cultivation (*Bildung*). His life, like the artists' paintings and sculptures and the poets' writings, is thoroughly informed by mimesis. In two senses *Vor-Bilder* is the correct designation for Heinrich's models. Not only do these men precede him temporally—Risach and Herr Drendorf are older men—but they also appear in front of (*vor*) him, presenting themselves as paradigms for proper behavior and thought. Heinrich's account, the text of *Der Nachsommer*, is thus more than a simple imitation of reality. It is an imitation of an imitation, and as such partakes of a complex mimetic nature in which theme (mimesis in art, imitation in education), style (description as the dominant mode of presentation), and composition (autobiography as imitation of one's own life) reinforce one another. The only time Heinrich apparently surpasses his primary model Risach is when he marries the woman he loves, something that was denied to his mentor. Appearances here may be deceiving, however, for in a sense Risach possessed the original here as well. He had long ago acquired the marble muse, the image of Nausikaa and the symbol of perfection and beauty. In taking possession of Natalie—and Heinrich expresses it in precisely these terms (7. 287)—the hero may look forward to a more fulfilling existence, but he does not by any means escape the mimetic complex that determines his exemplary *Bildung*.

II

The allusions to Nausikaa in *Der grüne Heinrich* are of a somewhat different nature. They begin with a speech made by Römer, the mad painter from whom Heinrich learns the fundamental techniques of painting. Römer advises his pupil to read Homer, and he teaches him to appreciate the artistry of the epic, as well as the appropriateness of each detail and action. His reference to the Nausikaa episode occurs in a passage that deserves to be quoted in full despite its length:

> Nowadays people are always demanding something exquisite, interesting, and piquant, and in their stupidity they do not even know that there can be nothing more exquisite, piquant, and eternally new than a Homeric conception in its simple classicism! I would not wish for you, dear Lee, ever to learn from experience exactly the exquisite piquant truth in the situation of Odysseus, when he appears naked and covered with mud before Nausikaa and her playmates! Do you want to know how it turns out? Let us stick to this example! Suppose you are wandering about in a strange land, cut off from your native country and from all that is dear to you, and you have seen a great deal and gone through a great deal, are full of care and anxiety, are, in short, utterly wretched and forsaken; then, at night, you will inevitably dream that you are approaching your native land. You see it gleaming and shining in the loveliest colors; beloved shapes, gracious and graceful, advance to meet you; then all at once you discover that you are wandering about ragged, naked, and covered with dust; an unspeakable shame and anguish seizes you, you try to cover yourself, to hide, and you wake up bathed in sweat. This is, as long as there are human beings, the dream of the miserable man, who has been tossed about; and thus Homer has drawn this situation from the deepest and most permanent elements in humanity. (5. 23–24)

On one level this passage simply foreshadows future events. Römer's prediction comes true in two ways. In a shabby state Heinrich meets a couple from his hometown. They report on his mother's difficulties and encourage him to return home. The same night he has a strange sequence of dreams, "just as Römer had once told him" (19. 150). In each he is on his way home and meets various people he had known in his childhood. Before entering his mother's house, he suddenly becomes afraid and tries to leave the city. He awakens in "his actual misery" happy to be freed from what had turned into a nightmare. But Römer's prediction of a Nausikaa experience also becomes a reality for Heinrich. On his actual journey home, covered with mud and dirt, he encounters Dortchen Schönfund, the adopted daughter of a rich count. Like Nausikaa, she is the beautiful maiden who takes the nineteenth-century Odysseus into her castle. There he is fed, clothed, and treated with honor and respect, just like his predecessor. He even follows the pattern of relating his life story. In the first version of *Der grüne Heinrich*, the count discovers the *Jugendgeschichte* in Heinrich's belongings, dries the wet pages, and decides to read it. Odysseus's oral tale is here transformed into a more modern written form. Later Heinrich supplements his manuscript, recounting what has occurred to him in more recent times, thus completing the parallel with the ancient hero. More important perhaps is that this Nausikaa experience, like young Drendorf's encounter with the marble muse, signals an important step in Heinrich's education. For the first time he encounters a mentor. The count, an aristocrat of spirit as well as of birth, provides Heinrich with the opportunity to cultivate himself—and to fall in love with his adopted daughter. At the count's castle Heinrich Lee, enthralled by his own Nausikaa, has found his version of the Rose House.

Besides presaging later events, however, Römer's speech shows us an important difference between the general perception of the world in *Der grüne Heinrich* and in *Der Nachsommer* and, by extension, two different conceptions of realism. In interpreting the Nausikaa episode, Römer does not emphasize the accuracy of detail or the correspondence to a possible occurrence, but rather a state of mind. For him the significance of the meeting between the homesick hero and the beautiful maiden lies in its archetypical quality. It presents us with truth insofar as this state of mind is something essentially human, something that recurs in subsequent epochs with slightly altered features. This is the reason he can predict that Heinrich will have a Nausikaa experience as well. Römer is evidently here speaking for Keller, who, as we shall see in the following chapter, postulated that certain

Urfabel (primeval fables) repeat themselves throughout history in different guises. The Nausikaa episode thus points us to an anthropologically based psychological constant rather than to an external analog to aesthetic perfection. In contrast to Heinrich Drendorf, Heinrich Lee does not encounter Nausikaa as an object of aesthetic contemplation, as a literary reality corresponding to the marble muse and Natalie. Rather, he finds in her a reflection of himself. What is important for him is not the recognition of art but the realization of his archetypical predicament. This is the reason that Nausikaa is presented by Römer and experienced initially by Heinrich as a dream. It is also the reason that no actual Nausikaa figure must appear in Heinrich's series of dreams: if the maiden herself is a symbol for a certain psychic state, it is sufficient that the psychology, not the figure, reappear. We should also note that this explanation casts light on the fairy-tale atmosphere surrounding the count's castle. More than one critic has commented on the novel's departure from "realism" in these chapters. If we regard the Nausikaa experience as a psychological reality, then this departure is only apparent. Dortchen and her father may remain unreal or unrealistic for us as literary figures; we may even be tempted to treat the entire story at the castle as another in the sequence of Heinrich's dreams, as a creation of his overactive fantasy. But at the same time, we could nonetheless maintain that this episode is "realistic," that Nausikaa points us to another approach to realism, namely, to a psychological realism. Indeed, this may be what Keller was aiming at throughout the novel. Although the events and characters most often strike the reader as real, the dominant focus of attention is Heinrich's mind and its development. The realism to which the Nausikaa episode refers us in *Der Nachsommer* is external and characterized by "epic objectivity"; Drendorf is without psychological depth despite his first-person narrative. By contrast, the encounter with Nausikaa in *Der grüne Heinrich* shows why this work has to be considered a novel of primarily psychological realism. Even in the first version, before Keller had rewritten the work entirely as a first-person narrative, all events are significant only to the extent that they form Heinrich's mental state or reveal the inner workings (and neuroses) of his psyche.

Despite the differences in the significance of the Nausikaa episode and in the notion of realism it reveals, the dominant artistic principle in *Der grüne Heinrich* is also mimetic. This is signaled by two familiar topoi: the equation of painting and poetry, and the thesis of the artist as a second creator. The first of these appears relatively early in the first version of the novel.[19] We are told that Heinrich as a young man was able to distinguish the truly beautiful in nature from that which is merely painterly (*das wahre Schöne von dem Bloß Malerischen* [16. 44]).[20] For the narrator a painterly understanding is a limitation; the beautiful and the poetic (*das Dichterische*) are more general and more advanced ways of comprehending nature for both painter and writer: "In this way of comprehending Nature, he went beyond the painterly understanding and arrived back at the generally poetic, which lies in every human being from the beginning; and this also showed him something beautiful where the painter failed" (16. 44–45). Painting is not an incorrect way to capture the world, it is simply not complete. The suggestion is that all art forms have to be subsumed under a larger category that is genuinely mimetic because it captures essences and not just appearances. Later in the novel a similar aesthetic theory is discussed. But in this occurrence it is clear that Heinrich means to encompass more than works of art with his categories. In subsuming everything worthwhile under the rubric "poetic," he suggests a departure from the purely aesthetic realm of German classicism:

> Without knowing when or how, I had fallen into the habit of calling everything in life and art that I judged to be useful, good, and beautiful, poetical, and even the objects of my chosen profession, colors as well as shapes, I called, not painterly, but always poetic, and the same with all human events that stirred and stimulated me. This was, I think, quite in order, for it is the same law that makes things poetic, or makes the reflection of their being worthwhile. (5. 7)

Heinrich goes on to reject the fantastic in art: "the incomprehensible and impossible, the unbelievable and extravagant"; these all fall outside the poetic, which is likened to the vital and reasonable (*Lebendiges, Vernünftiges*). Although there are significant differences in emphasis, Heinrich's discussion of the poetic comes close to notions encountered in Stifter's—and, as we shall see later, in Freytag's—work. The association of the useful, the good, and the beautiful, the reduction of excellence to a single aesthetic principle—"the same law" (*das gleiche Gesetz*)— is perhaps not so different from Stifter's notorious "gentle law" (*sanftes Gesetz*) from the preface to *Bunte Steine* (*Stones of Many Colors*, 1853); the call for stillness amid movement (*Ruhe und Stille in der Bewegung*), a tenet to which both authors subscribe (*GH* 5. 7; *NS* 7. 90–95), and the rejection of subjectivism and the fantastic: all these features are common to the aesthetic theory found in the two novels of education.[21] For Heinrich Lee the poetic thus becomes a central notion for life and art; painting and writing, the two creative activities he (like Drendorf) undertakes within the novel, are thereby brought into proximity, and obeying the "same law," are both subsumed under the general tenet of "reflection" (*Widerspiegelung*).

Heinrich's discussion of the artist as a second creator differs slightly from what we have witnessed previously in Büchner's *Lenz* and Stifter's *Nachsommer*. In these two works artistic creation was legitimized because it imitated an original. Artistic activity becomes an act of piety; deviation from mimetic principles is heretical. In *Der grüne Heinrich*, authored by the agnostic Keller, the logic of this argument is reversed. The hero uses the illustration of human creativity to prove that God exists: "I believed that everything that men accomplished had its importance solely in the fact that they had been able to accomplish it and that it was the work of reason and free will; and therefore Nature, to which I was being referred, could also only have a value for me if I might regard it as the work of a mind that was sympathetic with mine, and foreseeing" (4. 110–11). The analogy between God as the Creator of nature and man as the creator of art is retained here, but the source of certainty is no longer located in the Supreme Being but rather in the realm of human activity. Heinrich can become a second creator only by postulating an original whom he can imitate. In a Feuerbachian fashion he thus finds it necessary to invent an omnipotent Creator. Indeed, a good deal of the novel is occupied with various discussions of related theological issues, and not until he meets Dortchen/Nausikaa toward the end of his travels does he finally become converted to an enlightened, materialist position similar to Feuerbach's.[22] At this earlier point in the novel, however, when he is trying to induce God from the fact of human creativity, we also encounter a note of healthy skepticism. His argument is challenged by a young atheist schoolteacher known as the "philosopher." Seeing a flower, Heinrich lauds its symmetry, its perfection, and its beauty, concluding that it must have been conceived by some sort of mind: "And how lovely and beautiful it is, a poem, a work of art, a witticism, a colorful and fragrant jest!" (4. 111). The teacher concurs with the evaluation, but questions the logic: "Whether it has been made or not! Why don't you ask it! It says nothing, it does not have the time for it because it has to blossom and can't bother about your doubts! For all these are doubts that you are voicing, doubts about God and contemptible doubts about Nature, and it makes me sick just to listen to a doubter, a sentimental doubter! O dear!" (4. 111). The "philosopher" understands that Heinrich's proof for the existence of God is merely a smokescreen for his doubt, that an initial creation is in no way deducible from nature and the analogy of human activity. Although Heinrich does not yet understand or accept this position, he knows that he has been defeated. The ramification of his defeat is a recognition on the reader's part that there is no reason to subscribe to the argument of the artist as pious copier. If imitation is to be retained, it must have a materialist basis; the traditional theological justification collapses, as Lenz found out as well, with the disappearance of the original Creator.

Another, more political, reason for the necessity of mimetic art is suggested later in the first version of the novel. In one of the dreams that constitute what we have called Heinrich's psychological Nausikaa experience, the hero is riding a golden horse on his way home. Arriving at the old wooden bridge, he suddenly discovers that it has transformed itself into a two-story marble palace spanning the river. In this building he finds the walls decorated with frescoes that depict the history and activities of his native land.[23] What is most significant about these paintings for Heinrich is that they are comprehensible to the people and simultaneously of high artistic quality: "They were also understood by all the people who went back and forth on the bridge; and though they were pleasing for the connoisseurs because of their excellent robust style, they were not unenjoyable for those with less expertise due to their artistic qualities" (19. 163). Heinrich observes further and sees that the people on the bridge are the same as those painted on the walls. While some of the painted figures leave the frescoes to take their place in real life—or at least in the "real life" of Heinrich's dream—people from the bridge march into the paintings and become figures in artistic creations (19. 163; 5. 125). This strange scene recalls young Drendorf's momentary confusion of Natalie, Nausikaa, and the marble muse; for in both cases there is a merging of reality and artistic representation in the hero's mind, a momentary inability to distinguish between the original and the derivative. In *Der grüne Heinrich*, however, it seems that two additional factors are involved. The first concerns the daily activities of a people as themes for these paintings. Heinrich appears to be affirming popular art or people's art. Mimesis is justified then not as piety to the deity, but as respect for the collectivity in which the artist or writer creates. But mimesis is also bound here to self-reflection. The easy exchange between painted figure and people suggests a mirror-like structure in which the observer (Heinrich) cannot distinguish the actual thing from its reflection. Likewise the people themselves seem to appreciate this art only insofar as they see themselves in it. Here we are drawn from a manifesto for popular art back to the psychological realism of the novel. Just as the people validate an art in which they recognize themselves, so too Heinrich's story is of value because he "finds" himself in it. This reflection on realism, applied to its hero, amounts to an affirmation once again of psychological reflection. It is not by chance that the entire sequence described above occurs in a dream, that is, within the confines of Heinrich's mind. Even in postulating a popular basis for mimesis, Heinrich cannot escape his own subjectivity.

And indeed, the repeated fall into subjective fantasies,[24] thematized most often in Heinrich's inability to imitate appropriate models, gives us a clue to the aesthetic and pedagogical lesson of the novel. Time and again the hero begins his work with the intention of sticking to an original only to fail because he cannot reconcile creativity and free will with mimesis. The "drive to imitation" (16. 246) and the "imitating hand" (3. 223) are consistently diverted from their path. Heinrich's first real training in painting does not even involve direct contact with a natural object; Habersaat has him copy landscapes from postcards. When he finally turns from the "proper models" to "nature itself" (4. 64), he frequently chooses to ignore what he sees. He reasons that his omissions, additions, or mistakes do not really make a difference; nature could have looked the way he is depicting it. Römer, who himself is more familiar with convention than imitation, raises no objections, but Heinrich's uncle, a naturalist of sorts, immediately detects his nephew's distortions. "As a person acquainted with the land and the forest and possessing a sense for realism, he found the mistake quickly and easily, despite his lack of knowledge in matters of art" (4. 69). Under Römer's tutelage he does not fare much better; here he learns to copy only his teacher's Italian landscapes. By the time he arrives in Munich, it appears that he is no longer capable of adhering to the mimetic principles he espouses. His somewhat rambunctious friend Ferdinand Lys, who in the first version of the novel is dubbed a "realist" (18. 124), pinpoints the problem: he believes in God and the spiritual world; that is, he cannot be faithful to nature because he is not enough of a materialist. Here we encounter the ultimate reversal of the second-creator topos. In imitating God one does not copy an original Creator; rather, in an arbitrary and irresponsible fashion one "brings forth the world out of nothing" (5. 175). Heinrich's problem is that he shuns the "diligence of real life," replacing it with a faith in the miraculous. His landscapes become allegorical rather than realist. Like Roland in *Der Nachsommer*, he is painting with his mind, not with his eye.

The culmination of this development occurs when Heinrich relinquishes all claims to mimetic representation. After beginning work on a rather large painting of a withered spruce tree, he loses interest and allows his mind to wander. Absorbed in daydreams he scribbles on the paper and finds that his scrawlings have formed patterns resembling an enormous gray spider web. Not totally displeased with the results, he continues to work on his labyrinthine, "senseless mosaic" (5. 300) during the next few weeks. Fidelity to nature has been again sacrificed for subjective impressionism. His "colossal scrawling" (5. 300–301) is apt to remind us of Roland's "monstrous painting" in *Der Nachsommer*. Both are inordinately large projects that tend toward abstract art. In each case mimesis, the principle lauded throughout the respective novels as essential for excellence in art, is violated; and in both instances the subjectivity of the artist is apparently unconstrained by the laws of the external world. In *Der Nachsommer*, as we have seen, Risach supplies the gentle criticism of Roland's extravagance. In *Der grüne Heinrich* the hero's sober painter friend Oskar Erikson performs a similar function. When he sees Heinrich' latest artistic enterprise, he holds a lengthy ironic speech about this "pioneering" direction in the visual arts: "You have made a quick decision and thrown out everything objective, of worthless content. These diligent cross-hatchings are hatchings in the abstract, floating in the perfect freedom of the beautiful; this is diligence, purposefulness, clarity itself, in the most stimulating abstraction" (5. 302).

It is interesting to note that almost everything Erikson says here could be taken quite seriously by the modern reader. The reduction of the beautiful to formal principles, the renunciation of all mimetic representation, and the reliance on abstraction are hardly shocking propositions in twentieth-century art. For the mid-nineteenth century, however, they were surely unacceptable. When Erikson adds a few words of "criticism," the reader cannot mistake the irony. Recognizing the remnants of the original design, the withering spruce tree, he mockingly scolds his friend for his inconsistency: "But in this way it connects itself again with abominable reality, with trees that have grown and have rings that record their age! No, dear Henry, no! You must not stop here! Your strokes, appearing now in the form of stars, now in winding curves, now serpentine, now radiating, form a pattern still far too material, reminiscent of wallpaper or printed cotton. Away with it!" (5. 303–4). After this ironic tirade, which goes on for another page or so, Erikson announces that he will give up painting: "Let this babble be my touching farewell to art! From now on we shall put such things behind us and devote ourselves to a well-directed life!" (5. 305). He also reports that Lys has reached a similar decision and will dedicate himself to public office. And for Heinrich this turn from mimesis marks an implicit departure from art as well. Aside from two small paintings he finishes for the count, the colossal scrawling is his last artistic venture. He likewise plunges into other activities—first studies at the university, then the long journey home. Unable to conform to the mimetic principle in imitating life, he is compelled, like his friends, to participate in life once again.[25]

With respect to mimesis Heinrich's career as a painter is a total failure. Only at the count's castle, in the fairy-tale atmosphere in which he has his Nausikaa and "Rose House" experience, does he receive recognition for artistic achievement. Here, in the unreal world, his paintings are applauded for capturing the real. And here, for really the first time in the novel, he finds a teacher and model, a *Vor-Bild* for his *Bildung*. What interrupts his stay with the Count and Dortchen, though, is the principle that has informed the narrative from the start: psychological reality. The maternal bond, the complex Oedipal relationship that manifests itself repeatedly in the text (and in Keller's own relationship with his mother) finally precipitates his departure from his nineteenth-century Nausikaa.[26] In leaving he follows another model, the archetypical home-comer Odysseus, who, like Heinrich, paused to gather strength before making the final journey. When Heinrich completes his travels, however, he is greeted not by a faithful wife and son, but by a dead (first version) or dying (second version) mother. In the second version Heinrich buries his mother and enters the civil service, thus emulating his friend Lys, that strange fellow-painter who was likewise obsessed with self-representation. In each of the Dutchman's works, one figure bore an uncanny resemblance to its painter. In the original novel Heinrich is left without model or directions (*ohne Vorbild noch Vorschriften* [17. 137]).[27] No image or written plan precedes him or is in front of him except his own writings, which in a Narcissus-like fashion merely reflect back upon him.[28] Having fatally wounded Lys in a duel, he once again follows his dark alter ego (as well as his biological father), this time into death. In contrast to Drendorf, whose mimetic education culminates in the attainment of Natalie, Heinrich Lee, a failure at realistic representation throughout, renounces the beautiful orphan Dortchen, but thereby remains faithful to a more compelling mythic and psychological paradigm.

III

Nausikaa, reincarnated in Natalie and Dortchen, thus performs several important functions in each of these novels. Implicitly a reflection on realistic techniques, she provides a convenient focus for the themes of imitation and education so central for both works. Still, the allusion to Nausikaa seems odd and a bit out of place. In the *Odyssey* the hero was an older man who encountered a much younger woman. There was no question on his part concerning his return home. His stay on the island of the Phaiakians is clearly for him only another in a long series of episodes and trials. And it was not even the most lengthy of these; he lingered much longer at Circe's enchanted palace. The two Heinrichs, by contrast, are young men for whom Nausikaa's home could be (or is) their goal. What seems to be missing or overlooked in the reference to Nausikaa is the potential ethical conflict, latent at least in the ancient epic. We should recall, for example, that Nausikaa is awakened by Athena, who hints at her imminent marriage; she is ordered to wash clothes at the river because they are needed for her wedding. When she asks her father for permission to take the cart to the river, she omits any mention of marriage, but we are told that he "knew all" and understood what her words meant. After Odysseus has bathed and dressed, the hint of a bond between him and Nausikaa is again mentioned. Astounded by his magnificent appearance, she tells her maids that she would like to have a man like this one for her husband. Indeed, she expresses the hope that he will remain and find favor on the island. When she gives him instructions not to follow her directly, she also alludes to marriage. Although she tells him that she would not want people to talk about them as a betrothed couple, from her previous remarks and from the entire logic of the situation the reader or listener has no trouble understanding that nothing could be more to her liking (*Odyssey* 6. 25–32, 65–66, 244–45, 276–85). Yet from this promising beginning, nothing develops. Odysseus remains apparently unattracted to the maiden who "saved his life": his mind seems to be set only on his return. Nausikaa appears one more time, to ask that Odysseus not forget her; but we learn nothing of her fate. We can only guess at her feelings when she speaks to the hero for the last time. Even though we are supplied with only these hazy details, however, the situation is quite suggestive. A handsome hero, naked on a beach, meets a beautiful princess. She is expecting to meet a husband; he wants assistance for his journey. In the attraction between Odysseus and Nausikaa, as it would have been seen in the nineteenth century, is there not an implicit ethical conflict? In both *Der Nachsommer* and *Der grüne Heinrich*, each of which is concerned throughout with questions of proper conduct, is it not odd that Nausikaa is selected as a pivotal allusion and that then its ethical ramifications are ignored?

In most of the post-Homeric tradition, in fact, writers felt that there was a problem here and that something had to be done about it. Many authors who dealt with the theme assuaged their moral conscience by making a simple substitution: they allowed Odysseus' son Telemachus to stand in for his father and marry the maiden, thus picking up the loose thread by tying an acceptable nuptial knot. Goethe, however, who in the late 1780s toyed with the idea of a Nausikaa drama, espied in this constellation something far more powerful. Although he completed only a little more than 150 lines of a planned tragedy, from various sources, chiefly *Die italienische Reise* (*The Italian Journey*, 1816–17) in the section "Aus der Erinnerung" ("From My Memoirs"), we can reconstruct fairly accurately what the main course of the play would have been. As in the *Odyssey*, Odysseus would conceal his identity. But in Goethe's tragedy he would also leave some doubt about his marital status and future plans, thus fueling Nausikaa's hopes. She, in turn, conceived as a beautiful princess who has rejected all previous suitors, was to exhibit an obvious partiality for the stranger. When she finally declares her affection for Odysseus, thus compromising herself, and he reveals his intention to sail for Ithaca, a tragic course of events ensues. A marriage between Nausikaa and Telemachus, the ethical cover-up solution, is unacceptable to the resolute heroine. As Goethe himself wrote, "the girl can do nothing else but seek death in the fifth act." The guilt for this suicide is shared by Odysseus in Goethe's conception—he is "half guilty, half innocent"— but the focus of the play is clearly Nausikaa. Goethe therefore conceived of the drama as an ethical conflict. His outline is faithful to Homer's epic, extending at various points what is already strongly suggested. The tragic end, which is apt to recall Dido's death in the *Aeneid*,[29] seems to be the logical outcome of the situation and characters involved.[30]

It is likely that both Keller and Stifter were familiar with Goethe's remarks on Nausikaa—and perhaps even with the fragment itself.[31] Evidently Stifter even contemplated writing his own Nausikaa tragedy; although nothing ever came of the plan, he alluded to it in several letters at just about the time he was completing *Der Nachsommer*.[32] The tragic scenario that Goethe developed, however, was obviously unsuited for integration into either *Bildungsroman*. For one thing, this would have entailed the introduction of an ethical tension for which neither novel was prepared. The prevarication of the hero concerning his availability and the compromising of the Nausikaa figure do not fit into the scheme of either work. In *Der Nachsommer* Natalie's perfection makes any tragedy impossible. Indeed, she appears at times to be less of a character than a symbol for absolute beauty and goodness. Dortchen, although more developed as a character, is too willful, too independent, and too Feuerbachian to figure as a tragic heroine. In the first version Heinrich's abrupt death closes the work and leaves her fate an open question. We learn only that he firmly clutched the paper on which she had written the "Poem of Hope" until the end. In the revised edition Dortchen winds up being the count's niece, and she marries an aristocrat. The count informs Heinrich that she was partial toward him and that she could have been his if he had not delayed, but there is again no hint of the tragic in her fate. Undoubtedly the difference between Goethe's conception and that of the two novels has to do with the divergence in perspective. In the fragmentary drama Nausikaa was to be the central figure; Odysseus invades her world, only to abandon it and her in the final act. In the novels everything is presented from the viewpoint and for the edification of the hero. Nausikaa is an episode in his development, and in both cases this experience is integrated into the hero's process of self-cultivation. For the novelists the appropriateness of Nausikaa does not lie in the heroine's ethical conflict, nor in her tragic demise, but rather in Odysseus's plight. Stifter and Keller are as faithful to the epic as Goethe was, and they are perhaps just as concerned with ethics. But they realize their adaptation by shifting the emphasis from the female tragedy to the male renunciation of pleasure. In their works the educational value of the Nausikaa encounter entails not only the notions of beauty, fulfillment, and spirit (*Geist*), but also an ethics of abnegation and ultimately the denial of self.

These contentions may seem inapposite for *Der Nachsommer*. After all, Heinrich does marry Natalie in the final chapter and indicates that he has thereby attained all that he could ever want in life. In his own mind he has no doubt about his future happiness, no matter what professional activity he will later pursue. In contrast to his predecessor Odysseus, it would appear that he does not have to renounce Nausikaa at all. But the issue of renunciation is more complex in the novel. Heinrich may obtain Natalie, but the other central figure in the work, Freiherr von Risach, was forced to relinquish his claim to Mathilde. As a young man his love seemed as pure and absolute as Heinrich's. When Mathilde's parents refused him permission to carry on his relationship with her, however, he accepted their judgment without the protest Mathilde deemed appropriate. She interpreted his acquiescence, therefore, as a breach of faith, as a proof that his love is not what it must be, and their relationship was thus terminated. Only later, after both have married and lost their spouses, do the former lovers find a partial reconciliation. They live on estates that allow them to see each other often, and Risach assumes the educational responsibilities for Mathilde's son and his namesake, Gustav. But neither enjoyed the fulfillment of the "summer" of life; both have to content themselves with an "Indian Summer." And it is this mood that pervades the novel and colors Heinrich's relationship with Natalie as well. The young Drendorf meets, falls in love, and marries within the confines of the "post-summer" world of the Rose House. In emulating his mentor, he too enters the realm of renunciation, even though his life presents itself superficially in the guise of fulfillment. For no matter how we may judge as modern readers, there is no suggestion that Risach should have acted differently. Quite the contrary, his actions and thoughts are vindicated throughout, whereas Mathilde committed, as she herself admits, a "serious mistake" (8. 165).[33] By imitating his model, Heinrich must also partake of the renunciation of pleasure and self which Risach has practiced so stoically in his own relationship and which he now preaches to his willing pupil. The realist education turns Heinrich's potential summer with Nausikaa into an Indian summer.

Mathilde reproached Risach essentially for his lack of passion. She argued that he should have defied her parents and declared his undiminished love for her. Risach countered by contending that his renunciation, his reserve, was much more difficult. He concurred with her parents' view that their relationship should be broken for a time until both of the parties had reached maturity.[34] Implicit in his argument, therefore, is the denial of momentary gratification, of easy pleasure and of emotional reactions. The novel shows us, however, that it is not Risach's lack of passion but Mathilde's plea for passion that destroys their chance for a "summer" together.[35] And this is precisely the lesson Heinrich must learn in preparation for his attachment to Natalie. He comes to Risach well prepared for this school of renunciation, of course. We learn that already in his youth he shunned the "mere enjoyment" that most of his schoolmates pursued (6. 18). The pleasures that he experienced in his home, he informs the reader, were always "of a serious kind" (6. 18). The elder Drendorf, who, as we have seen, is a carbon copy of Risach, would undoubtedly be judged today as unnecessarily harsh and repressive. He did not allow his children to go to the theater, even to see plays of a more ennobling variety, because he feared the arousal of their emotions: "He said that the imagination in children becomes overwrought and overstimulated. They are subject to a variety of feelings that the excitement could turn into desires, or even passions" (6. 206). This polemic against passion is then continued and augmented by the owner of the Asperhof. An "excess of wishes and desires," Risach tells Heinrich, prevents us from perceiving the "innocence of things" (6. 235). Passions should not be used as a criterion for evaluating the importance of an object.[36] Here Risach is evidently adopting a principle from Kant's *Kritik der Urteilskraft* (*Critique of Judgment*, 1790) and extending it to apply to all our interactions. Natural science can only be pursued without interest, i.e., aesthetically. Later in the novel, in what must be read as a justification for his behavior with Mathilde years before, he expounds upon this anti-passionate position. Following Socrates in the *Phaidon*— and scores of philosophers in the intervening centuries—Risach separates body and spirit; the former is the realm of the passions and contains nothing noble; the latter, if properly nurtured and trained, can be employed to attain the highest goal: passionless love.

> When we here exclude all things that concern or satisfy the body or the animal nature of man, and designate as passion the continuous desire of these things to the exclusion of everything else— for this reason there is nothing more incorrect than to speak of noble passions—and when we designate as the objects of

our highest aspiration only the most noble quality of man: then we might perhaps not be incorrect to name all striving toward such objects with one single name: love. (7. 356)

Love and passion are thus placed at opposite poles, as far from one another as possible. Like scientific observation love is brought into the proximity of the object of art, which is also to be grasped without interest and desire. That Natalie resembles a marble statue and a fictional princess is totally appropriate, since she is to be appreciated and "possessed" like a work of art. Indeed, the lifelessness and coldness of the marble, often used by previous writers to signal a lack of passion, suggest, apparently against Stifter's intention, the sterility and frigidity of the love she and Heinrich share. Risach's aesthetic and realist education therefore conveys a twofold renunciatory message. Having been taught that love is a function of a Kantian aesthetic attitude, Heinrich must accordingly deny his nature, his body, his desires. And in emulating Risach, who has been at pains to defend his own passionless actions of an earlier vintage, he partakes in a structure of renunciation identical to that of his mentor.[37]

It is precisely in this point that *Der Nachsommer*, despite its classicist pretensions, departs from the pedagogical thought of its predecessors during the Age of Goethe. To demonstrate this a brief comparison with one of the chief documents of this earlier period, Schiller's *Über die Ästhetische Erziehung des Menschen* (*On the Aesthetic Education of Man*, 1795), is instructive. Both Schiller's essay and Stifter's novel are obviously responding to recent historical events; the former to the French Revolution, the latter to the revolutions of 1848, especially to the events in and around Vienna.[38] Both authors were basically freedom-loving democrats who had themselves suffered under the old order, but who were first disappointed and then shocked by what they perceived as excesses of the revolutionary masses. In a sense both works are thus responses to these excesses, attempts to come to terms with political problems within a larger, more philosophical framework. Each arrives at an apparently similar conclusion: an aesthetic education can serve to correct revolutionary abuses, to eliminate the abhorrent outbursts of base emotions and deeds.[39] Risach's homily against passion has its origin in the reaction against revolutionary violence; on the political level it implies a program of moderation. But Schiller and Stifter part company on two essential issues. For Schiller there is no question that the principles he is espousing are universal. Like Kant, he believes that aesthetic judgment involves at least a potential *sensus communis*; an "aesthetic education" is something everyone in the human species could and should enjoy. Even his frequently quoted remark about the existence of the "state of beautiful appearance" in small, exclusive circles is prefaced by a more general claim: "In accord with necessity it [the state of beautiful appearance] exists in every finely tuned soul."[40] For Stifter the exclusivity of Risach's pedagogy is never in doubt. From various comments he makes concerning his servants (6. 143–44) and the decline of appreciation for art (6. 311–12), and from Heinrich's observations on Viennese society, it is obvious that only a select few are candidates for the enlightened path. Accordingly the Rose House is an isolated estate that Risach buys after retiring from public service; that is, the aesthetic education is a retreat from politics rather than a preparation for political activity. And Heinrich is one of only a handful of visitors who has extended contact with Risach. He and Gustav are really the only ones who will ever be educated in the Rose House at all. More important for the theme of renunciation, however, is the authors' disparate treatment of the pedagogical impact of art. Schiller conceives of aesthetics as a realm of harmony or compromises between opposing forces or instincts. Although he too would repress "raw, lawless drives,"[41] his theory endeavors to reconcile natural, sensual inclinations with reason and understanding. Aesthetics, the play-drive (*Spieltrieb*), the beautiful appearance—these terms are mediators in Schiller's essay, not (or perhaps as well as) absolutes. In contrast, Stifter's aesthetic program, as we have seen, is based on a nondialectical, repressive scheme. The body, passion, and desires are evils; beauty, love, and pure science must remain uncontaminated and are thus severed from contact with this world. Indeed, although Stifter evidently felt himself to be a continuator of the educational spirit of Weimar classicism, the Manichaean framework he employs and his implicit praise of passionless old age bring him closer to Cato in Cicero's *De senectute*[42] than to Schiller in the *Ästhetische Erziehung*. The instruction Heinrich receives from Risach does not prepare him for a summer of fulfilled life but for an autumn of renunciation.[43]

The spirit of self-denial that pervades *Der Nachsommer* ultimately calls into question Risach's realist education. But it also suggests that there is a basic inhumanity informing the thoughts and actions of the main figures. That the characters appear more like marionettes than people, that every female or male character seems interchangeable, and that we encounter a total absence of individuality are surely more than stylistic quirks or compositional necessities.[44] Although Stifter's defenders over the past 130 years have claimed he has been misunderstood, it is difficult to escape the conclusion that amid all the talk of plants, rocks, animals, and art one thing is consistently missing: a concern for the human being.[45] In the case of *Der Nachsommer*, this neglect of human subjectivity is not to be understood as a harbinger of poststructuralist decentering or as a precocious Foucaultian proclamation of the death of man.[46] Rather, it seems to reflect an inability or unwillingness to face up to the complexity and variety of human nature and activities. As a young man we read that Heinrich feels sympathy for the boards made from a tree and for an elk shot in a hunt; in the latter passage he even states his antipathy for the humans (*Menschen*, not *Männer*) who made a feast from their booty: "Only the men who had shot the animal were repulsive to me" (6. 34). Yet there is no suggestion that meat is not included at the simple repasts at the Rose House, or that he opposes the slaughter of animals for food. When he visits a factory, he carefully takes note of all the processes involved in production, but there is never a mention of the workers who labor there (6. 25–26). In these occurrences he appears to confirm an opinion he hears later from Risach. When Heinrich asks him if Gustav learns about history, he is told that this is the last subject he will take up. The natural sciences are much more comprehensible than the "sciences of humans," since we are unable to become "facts" for ourselves. "The facts of humanity—indeed, the facts of our own inner being—are, as I have already said once, kept secret, or at least clouded, by passion and selfishness" (6. 238). We can surely appreciate parts of Risach's message in our ecologically minded age. Humans have indeed abused the earth, and should learn that they must live in harmony with their environment or else perish. But Risach's lesson is not merely ecological; it borders on the misanthropic. Only if we would become facts that could be examined and studied through a scientific procedure, only when we become objects for each other,[47] only when, drained of passion and drives, we begin to resemble the aesthetic automatons of *Der Nachsommer*, does the human species reach the apex of Risach's natural order. In a paradoxical gesture *Der Nachsommer*, in imitating a classicist and humanist paradigm, winds up teaching precisely the opposite of its purported model.[48] Heinrich's education, culminating in his marriage to Natalie/Nausikaa, thus climaxes not in his fulfillment but in a renunciation of individuality and humanity.[49]

Heinrich Lee's renunciation is much simpler to chart as an element of plot. Dortchen and her father clearly correspond to Nausikaa and Alkinoos; Heinrich, like Odysseus, finds refuge there before continuing his homeward journey. In leaving Dortchen behind, the woman who represents all women for him, he renounces a possible fulfillment in life, not by remaining faithful to the social convention of marriage, but by avoiding marriage altogether. When he arrives home and buries his mother, he hesitates, as we have seen, to write to his faithful and expectant Nausikaa, who becomes now perhaps more of a Penelope figure. It is here, however, as the parallel with the literary model begins to break down, that we can start to glimpse the import of Heinrich's renunciation. Once again we must search for meaning in the realm of the character's psychology, for Heinrich's self-denial belongs to the huge complex of guilt that has been central to his actions and motives throughout the novel. Above all, it is related to his ambivalence toward his mother, for whom Dortchen is a rival.[50] His feelings toward her are captured very well in fact by the German word *Schuld*, which means both guilt and debt. Heinrich is indebted to his mother not only for his life but also for the money she sends to him. Indeed, the complex of debt and guilt is closely interwoven. The mother's various sacrifices for her son, her gradual impoverishment, endured for her son's sake, induce feelings of guilt. This guilt, however, can also easily turn into resentment, and it is quite easy to read Heinrich's unspoken love for Dortchen as a punishment for his mother. Although he knows that his mother dreams of his return, he spites her by finding another woman and postponing his journey. If we interpret the novel in this fashion, one could say that Heinrich sets up a constellation in which the outcome will necessarily be renunciation. He places himself in a double bind; there is no possible correct and psychologically satisfying course of action open to him. The longer he stays, the more guilt accumulates in him for neglecting his mother; if he leaves, then he renounces potential marital (and sexual) bliss. That he ultimately chooses the latter course of action is consistent with his development throughout. For Heinrich has learned, it seems, to place himself in self-defeating situations and to select self-defeating alternatives. As we have seen with respect to his painting, he pursues a career for which he has neither the requisite talent nor the inclination to conform to accepted mimetic standards. He allows himself to reach such a degree of poverty that he has to call upon his mother to rescue him, and he repeatedly falls in love with women who are unattainable because of either his inexplicable reserve in pursuing a relationship or their obvious inaccessibility. The Nausikaa episode is thus the culmination of a series of renunciations and failures that Heinrich Lee seems to bring upon himself. His sudden demise in the first version of the novel and his sacrifice of fulfillment in the second merely carry this mechanism one step further: self-denial turns into the denial of his vital self.

The source of this self-denial is similar to Drendorf's: an extensive education in repressing passion. Like the realist text, the characters in the realist novels of education must not succumb to excess. This can be demonstrated most easily if we look at Lee's relationships with women throughout the novel. Except for minor encounters—with the actress in his youth or with the proletarian Hulda, added in the revised version—they are arranged in pairs. The second book is obviously dominated by his affairs with Judith and Anna. The former, a young widow who functions partly as a mother and partly as seductress, and the latter, the innocent daughter of a village schoolmaster, are not entirely free from literary clichés. In Heinrich's presentation, at least, they assume the familiar roles accorded to women in the literary tradition. Judith represents passion, sensuality, perhaps even sexuality; she is the Lorelei, Venus, and Eve. Indeed, these references to the temptress, especially to the biblical one, are reinforced at various points. After she threatens to take the young Heinrich to bed with her, he feels as if he has been "pushed out of a beautiful garden" (4.234). Later, to reinforce the allusion, Keller has her offer to share an apple with the hero (5. 39). Anna, by contrast, embodies purity, chasteness, and wholesomeness. She is the fair white lady for whom the green knight is willing to sacrifice everything. As Heinrich tells Judith: "Do you understand? For Anna I would like to endure everything and obey her every whim; I would like to become an upright and honest man, clean and pure through and through, so that she could see through me like a crystal; I would want to do nothing without thinking of her and live with her soul in all eternity, even if I would not see her any more from this day onward!" (4. 230–31). In light of this antinomic structure, it is not surprising that he is torn in his relationship with the two women, unable to settle on either. He does manage to kiss each of them and thus find an outlet for his passion, but his indecision proves fatal. Both abandon him: Anna in death becomes the angel to which Heinrich had stylized her in life, and Judith, in emigrating to America, leaves the young man who was unable to make a commitment.

In the third book, however, these two literary clichés return in the guise of Rosalie and Agnes. Like her predecessor, Rosalie is also a sensuous widow, and Agnes, whose name even resembles Anna's, is likewise the retiring daughter of a single parent. At the carnival, which is the central episode in this book, the former dresses appropriately as Venus, the goddess of love, whereas the latter appears as the chaste Diana.[51] What is significant about Heinrich's relationship with these women, though, is that he is not involved with them personally. Erikson and Lys, his painter friends and alter egos (neither of them are very successful as painters either), shield him, as it were, from direct contact with these imitations of Judith and Anna. Heinrich thus goes to the carnival alone dressed as a fool. He learns to repress his own desires, one might say, by placing his friends between himself and a possible romantic attachment. Indeed, Lys appears to function in this part of the novel as something of a lightning rod for Heinrich's sensuality.[52] In the first version we read of his predilection for painting beautiful naked women, and in both versions Heinrich comments on the album in which Lys has illustrated the history of his many love affairs. That Heinrich comes into conflict with Lys over his shabby treatment of Agnes points to the hero's own struggle with his sensuality. Whereas he approaches Agnes with diffidence, Lys treats her—rather callously, as we see it through Heinrich's eyes—as simply another woman. When Heinrich wins the duel with his friend—eventually leading to Lys's death in the first version, but removing him from Heinrich's life in both—he simultaneously succeeds in repressing his own desires. Indeed, no one is able to recognize this better than Lys himself. In the initial version he clearly diagnoses his friend's problem, commenting with reference to Agnes: "Just know that if you felt even a slight spark of passion, then you would, and would have to, do everything you could to remove your ward from my power and make her yours. But you have never known true passion, neither in my sense of the word, nor in yours" (18. 238). What follows in the first version is Lys's interpretation of Heinrich's *Jugendgeschichte* as it pertains to Judith and Anna. In the revised edition, because of compositional necessities, the exegesis is reworked as an insightful character analysis: "If you ever get caught between two women, you will probably run after both of them, if you like them both; that is easier than deciding for one of them!" (5. 274). But in both texts he then continues with a defense of sensuality. I cite here the more forceful first version:

> Just know further, as far as I am concerned every real man has to immediately love every acceptable woman; whether it be for a short time, a long time, or forever, the difference depends only on external circumstances. The eye is the originator, the mediator, or the destroyer of love; I can resolve to be faithful, but the eye makes no resolutions: it obeys and submits to the chains of the eternal laws of nature. (18. 238–39)

Here Lys has formulated his prosensual position in terms that make it easier for the moralistic Heinrich to reject. The hero can thus ignore his friend's advice that he attend to his own repression of passion and, by ridding himself of this personification of sensuality, take one more step on the path of abnegation.

By the time we reach the third set of pairs in the final book, Heinrich therefore has already completed the essential course of studies in his realist education. Unlike Drendorf he accomplishes this without models or direct instruction. His self-cultivation is gained through experience and manifested in his psyche. The final conflict between women is appropriately a confirmation of his previous education rather than a temptation to conscious passion. In Dortchen and his mother, in Nausikaa and Penelope, we find the somewhat distorted but nonetheless recognizable return of Anna and Judith. The mother, like Judith and Rosalie, is a widow, and although she does not resemble Venus, she exerts a certain magnetic power over her son. Dortchen, whom most commentators have erroneously dubbed a synthesis of the sensual and the spiritual,[53] clearly resembles Agnes and Anna. That Heinrich never declares his love for her, as he never did for Agnes, is only one sign of their literary kinship. In imagery used to describe them and in their personalities, the three are closely related. What is significant here, however, is that the hero repeats a familiar pattern of splitting himself, hesitating, and hence attaining neither of his loves. In the first version Heinrich fears that he cannot bring "an undivided heart" (19. 249) back to his mother after he has met Dortchen. But as we have witnessed above, in playing out his renunciatory role in the Nausikaa drama, he ends up sacrificing both women. Not that he could seriously have possessed either of them. His mother, under the Oedipus taboo and then in death, can never be a conscious object of passion. And Dortchen, who significantly assumes the part of Arete rather than Nausikaa in the playful scene she directs in the second version (6. 207), is located in a romantic never-never land in which Heinrich, on the last leg of a realist educational journey, cannot remain. Even if she were not, her very name hints that she could never be his. *Dortchen ist nicht Hierchen!*[54] Heinrich jokingly puns when she leaves to visit a friend (19. 285). But this is precisely his dilemma. The Nausikaa figure, who prefers to play her mother and thus further remove herself from the wandering hero, is always over there, at a distance, inevitably separated from the nineteenth-century Odysseus. There is no danger of passion here, not only because it has been firmly repressed in the defeat of Lys, but also because its objects, progressively removed from the hero in the successive books of the novel, finally reappear at an inaccessible psychological distance.[55]

In this scheme of things Judith's return in the revised version is an epilogue, a mere supplement to the main plot.[56] In a slight reversal of roles, she herself resembles Odysseus returning home after a long, difficult journey. This reversal had perhaps been anticipated in the earlier version in a scene in which she comes from the water naked to meet Heinrich, but this passage fell to Keller's moral censor during the rewriting of the 1870s. In failing to unite with her in a marital or sexual manner, Heinrich once again renounces fulfillment. Those critics who try to read this decision only as an enlightened gesture against the restricting confines of bourgeois marriage, or who see in the platonic bond a higher form of satisfaction and spirituality, are deceiving themselves. Heinrich knows better. After accepting Judith's refusal to live with him, he begins to understand what motivated her decision: "she had seen and tasted too much of the world to count on a full and complete happiness" (6. 324). He agrees to forgo "full and complete happiness" and to live in the type of renunciatory relationship she prefers. Nor should Heinrich's governmental post be seen solely as a sign for his active, productive dedication to the community.[57] Significantly we learn nothing about what he does or about any of his experiences. The details are presumably uninteresting. Again his own comments on the matter are telling: "About a year later I was managing the chancery office of a small district that adjoined the one in which my home village was located. Here I was able to live quietly, in modest and yet diverse activities" (6. 307). The simple life of a minor civil servant in a small Swiss village is the net result of his long series of pedagogical experiences. Gone are the hopes for artistic achievement, fame, and creative expression, as well as the desire for a passionate and fulfilling romantic attachment.[58] Here we cannot help but recall another civil servant (about whose public actions we similarly learn nothing) who resigns himself to living platonically next to the woman he had once hoped to possess. If we are willing to draw this intertextual comparison,[59] we could say that Heinrich Lee also ends up imitating Gustav Freiherr von Risach, and that he thus differs from his counterpart Heinrich Drendorf only in the mode and the extent of the mimicry. Common to both young men, in any case, is a consistent pattern of self-denial and resigned contentment. Any fulfillment they appear to achieve is shrouded in melancholy. It seems that whether Heinrich obtains his Nausikaa or not, the realist education he received prepares him only for a life of renunciation.[60] In the next chapter we shall see that the repression here associated with the doctrine of realism has ramifications for other areas of psychic life as well.

4

THE DESIRES OF REALISM:
Repetition and Repression in Keller's
Romeo und Julia auf dem Dorfe

> If I were not convinced that childhood is
> already a prelude for one's entire life and up
> to its conclusion already mirrors in miniature
> the chief features of human strife, so that later
> only a few events occur whose contours are
> not already present in our minds like a dream,
> like a schema that is happily fulfilled when it
> points to something good, but that serves as
> an early warning when it points to something
> bad, then I would not occupy myself so
> voluminously with the small things of those
> times.
>
> Gottfried Keller,
Green Henry

> Sie saßen sich genüber bang
> Und sahen sich an in Schmerzen;
> O, lägen sie in tiefster Gruft,
> Und lägen Herz an Herzen!—

> (They sat across from each other troubled
> And gazed at each other in pain;
> O would that they lay in the deepest grave,
> And would lie heart on heart.)
>
> Theodor Storm,
"Geschwisterblut"
("Sibling Blood")

In the introduction I stated that realism can best be understood as an effect of the literary text rather than some quality inherent in the text. And if we accept this statement, then it would seem that one of the aspects of this effect would involve an impression of repetition. When we read a work of realism, we are told explicitly or implicitly that what we are reading is a reproduction or repetition of something that occurred prior to the writing. We are supposedly dealing with an original event, but only to the extent that it is re-presented in the text. Creativity is thus implicitly underemphasized in works of realism, if by "creative" we mean inventing something not dependent on previous occurrence. Instead, skill and organizational abilities are underscored as artistic prerequisites. Since the realist text is secondary and parasitic on a more fundamental reality, the narrator's task is one of recording, arranging, and preserving authentic existence. The guarantee that what we are reading is a repetition is simultaneously a promise of truth, for realism offers us the illusion of a window through which we gain an unobscured view of reality as well as of a mirror that faithfully reflects the world. This dual illusion is sustained by different epochs and within these epochs, by different writers in a variety of ways. As I remarked above, in the eighteenth century the fidelity of repetition is very often assured by a personal bond between author and reader. We are either told that the recorded events are true by a first-person narrator or we are presented with authentic documents (letters, diaries) by an editor. In either case we are confronted with the appeal of an individual, and we experience the text as a repetition because, and insofar as, we trust the narrator's appeal. During the age of realism, on the other hand, this personal bond gradually disappears—or at least it is taken for granted. Instead the reader encounters most often "objective" representation without personal mediation. An anonymous and apparently omniscient narrator frequently offers the reader the repeated reality without comment on its truthfulness or the narrator's reliability. Indeed, such reassurances would seem to be superfluous. For the style itself, as we shall see in this chapter, by a multitude of signals, usually conveys the message of repetition. By the middle of the nineteenth century, there is no need for the author or narrator to reassure readers that the work they are reading is a repetition. The apparent self-assurance of the text in relating its story serves instead as the stamp of its authenticity.

When we are nonetheless explicitly reminded of the repetitive nature of our reading in a mid-nineteenth-century text, it may be more than an innocent and superfluous introduction. In Gottfried Keller's *Romeo und Julia auf dem Dorfe* (*A Village Romeo and Juliet*, 1856), we find not just a single reminder of this sort but a double announcement of this story as repetition.[1] The first comes with the very title of the novella. By alluding at the outset to the celebrated Shakespearean tragedy, Keller allows the reader to anticipate the general outline of the plot, but he also signals the difference between his work and the earlier version. This is not simply an imitation of an earlier literary model but an adaptation of the Elizabethan drama, or, more precisely, an adaptation of the primeval fable (*Urfabel*) on which both Keller's and Shakespeare's tales are based. For Keller, as he wrote to the noted literary historian Hermann Hettner in 1854 just prior to the composition of *Romeo und Julia*, there is no originality or novelty in the sense of original genius: "New in the good sense of the word is only what comes out of the dialectic of the cultural movement" (*aus der Dialektik der Kulturbewegung*).[2] The title thus announces not the repetition of a Shakespearean work but rather the repetition of an archetypical theme in accord with the *Zeitgeist*. Still, as Berthold Auerbach noted in his review of *Die Leute von Seldwyla* (*The People of Seldwyla*, 1856; 1874), where the novella originally appeared, this title appears inappropriate from the perspective of realism: "It sets a mood . . . , and situates us in that literary literature [*Litteratenlitteratur*] that does not originate in life, but rather from the printed word and its memory, and this has really been overcome."[3] He suggests a change to the less pretentious "Sali und Vrenchen." But Keller, whose other titles rarely allude to the great tradition, defends his choice and feels that it is in accord with realism too: "First of all, what we ourselves write is also printed on paper and belongs, seen from this perspective, to the world of books [*zur papiernen Welt*]; and second, although Shakespeare has been printed, he is really only life itself and not a dead reminiscence."[4] In this instance, Keller apparently believes there is no conflict between poesis and mimesis, *Erfinden* (invention) and *Finden* (discovery).[5] He avoids the conflict between art and life by asserting that true art is life itself. Thus the title proclaims a threefold repetition—of Shakespeare, of the *Urfabel*, and of the *Zeitgeist*—all of which harmonize neatly with his conception of realism.

The second announcement of repetition occurs in the first paragraph, which apparently serves as a preface to the actual story. Here Keller reiterates his notion of a dialectic of culture. He reminds his readers of both the archetypal and the Shakespearean repetition ("each of those fables on which the great old works are based" [7. 85]), but assures them that his version is based on reality ("on a real occurrence" [*auf einem wirklichen Vorfall*] [7. 85]). Keller feels that there are a limited number of fables that recur in different variants and guises. The particular instance of the Romeo and Juliet motif Keller has in mind here took place in 1847. A newspaper article in the *Züricher Freitagszeitung* (*Zurich Friday Newspaper*) of 3 September 1847, under the heading "Sachsen," reported the double suicide of two young, impoverished Leipzig lovers whose families lived in enmity (7. 391).[6] It is assumed that Keller's novella is based on this "real event," which he takes to be a recurrence of the basic elements of the Romeo and Juliet legend. Realism, therefore, is both the result of the actual occurrence, the real-life events that inform the newspaper story, and the fact that reality itself, what Keller calls *Menschenleben* (human life) (7. 85), necessarily repeats itself throughout time.

This introductory message to the reader may not be quite as simple as it appears, however.[7] It is a passage that Keller reworked for the separate printing of the novella in 1875,[8] and the changes that he made—according to Keller the original version was "miserably stylized" (*miserabel stilisiert*)[9]—may reflect more than mere formal improvements. In the original, Keller seeks to deny that his novella is "an idle invention": "To tell this story too would be an idle invention if it were not based on a true occurrence" (*Auch diese Geschichte zu erzählen würde eine müßige Erfindung sein, wenn sie nicht auf einem wahren Vorfall beruhte*) (7. 394). The revised version substitutes "imitation" (*Nachahmung*) for "invention" (*Erfindung*). Keller apparently anticipated with this change Alexander von Villers's criticism of the first formulation, which appeared a few years later in 1881. Villers maintained that Keller's sentence from 1855 was illogical: "To say this story would be an invention if it were not based on a true occurrence amounts to about as much as saying this tree would be a frog except that we are dealing with a horse, that is, it is pure nonsense."[10] Keller's revision meets this objection by making "imitation" (*Nachahmung*) clearly refer back to the title. His novella is not simply an imitation but an adaptation based on a real event. Still, it is curious that the two words in question here, "invention" (*Erfindung*) and "imitation" (*Nachahmung*), which are putatively antonyms, especially as they relate to poetics, can be exchanged by Keller so easily. In the first version he defends himself against "idle invention," and in the second against "idle imitation," but both cases involve the same ultimate piece of evidence, the real event: reality serves as his defense against idleness.

The second significant change Keller made in this sentence, the substitution of *wirklich* (real) for *wahr* (true), is not very important for the sense of Keller's defense, but it is revealing in the context of a reflection about realism. The interchangeability of "true" and "real" points to one of the most fundamental tenets of nineteenth-century literature. Writers had always promised to deliver the "truth," but it was not until the age of realism that it became so closely associated with the real. Aristotle, we should recall, thought drama more suitable than history as a vehicle for conveying truth, although it was evident to him that the latter deals with actual events but the former does not. Likewise, the aesthetics of German idealism, although it too often hailed the "real," did not associate it with actual occurrences. It is thus false to see realism prefigured in writers such as Schiller or Friedrich Schlegel, whose notion of truth in art has little to do with capturing empirical reality.[11] This is evidently not the case by the time we arrive at the middle of the nineteenth century. For Keller the truth value of an artistic work can be measured by its reality as an event, or at least by the reality of its constituent elements. This does not mean, of course, that there is no room for invention in his works, but rather that the reality of an occurrence serves as the guarantee for truth. The frame of reference here, like that of the natural sciences, is immanent, rather than transcendental; our ability to grasp reality, by observation and experience, simultaneously gives us access to truth.

The final changes occur in the second sentence of this short prefatory paragraph. Besides excluding the gratuitous comparison between the number of fables and the number of metals, Keller rephrases the latter part of the sentence as follows:

Original: "they [fables] occur again and again anew with changed conditions and in the most peculiar guises" (*sie ereignen sich immer wieder aufs neue mit veränderten Umständen und in der wunderlichsten Verkleidung*) (7. 394).

Revision: "but they are constantly appearing in new form and compel the hand to preserve them" (*aber stets treten sie in neuem Gewand wieder in die Erscheinung und zwingen alsdann die Hand, sie festzuhalten*) (7. 85).

105

Here Keller has not only reformulated the thought of the reccurrence of these fables in different guises—in which he himself employs a different guise (*Gewand* for *Verkleidung*)—but also added another strange justification for writing the novella. For in the revision, the notion of compulsion is introduced. The hand of the writer is forced to grasp these fables. The word *Hand* thereby has a dual function. It signifies, in the first place, the handwriting, the text of the piece of literature that captures the current and appropriate variation of the *Urfabel*. But this metaphor also has a literal dimension. One encounters the rather unusual image of a hand trying to hold fast a fable that has appeared (*in die Erscheinung treten*) in a new disguise. This phrasing creates the impression, therefore, not only of compulsion but of an urgency and a deception. It is as if the writer is forced to grasp something that is never quite the original, something that always escapes him, because it is protean, and because it is only the appearance of a more fundamental essence. The fables compel the writer to grasp them, revealing themselves not only as powerful in some undefined sense but potentially as elusive as well.[12]

It is a curious fact worth noting here that this introductory statement occupied more of Keller's correspondence about the novella than any other single passage—with the possible exception of the satirical barbs included at the close of the first version and omitted in the second. Most of his comments were in response to criticism, since friend and foe alike seem to wonder at its very inclusion. Auerbach, for example, considered it entirely unnecessary: "That is, to put it simply, a petit-bourgeois convention [*ein Philisterzopf*]. What are all these assurances about fidelity to reality?"[13] Villers, who appears to disagree with Auerbach about the evaluation of the work on every other point, concurs with him here, calling it "something entirely superfluous."[14] Yet Keller, at various times and with a variety of reasons, is bent on defending it. In a letter to Auerbach in response to his review, Keller gives the following justification:

> If I had made no remark concerning the actual occurrence of the anecdote and concerning the similarity with the Shakespearean theme, then they would have accused me of a farfetched and stupid repetition [*einer gesuchten und dämlichen Wiederholung beschuldigt*], whereas, with that short note placed in the front, the story receives a justified point [*die Geschichte dadurch eine berechtigte Pointe erhielt*]; for those who would not have thought once

about *Romeo and Juliet*—and there are many such people since people read rather thoughtlessly nowadays—would have then considered the matter much too crass and fantastic [*kraß und abenteuerlich*].[15]

Keller appears to be arguing at cross-purposes here. On the one hand, he states that he feared the accusation of a farfetched and foolish repetition (presumably of Shakespeare) and sought to preclude this with the title and introduction. On the other hand, he justifies the choice of the title on the presumed nonrecognition of the original fable by the readership. It is difficult to understand how he could be reproached for imitating Shakespeare if the similarity with *Romeo and Juliet* would not have occurred to his inattentive reader. Moreover, Keller indicates that the title needs to be included to make the novella more palatable, more literary. He thus appears to negate his earlier statement in the same letter to Auerbach concerning the reality and authenticity of Shakespeare. For now Shakespeare is being used as a means to make the actual event less "crass and fantastic" for the audience. It is a protection against reality rather than reality itself.

Almost twenty years later, on the occasion of a separate printing of *Romeo und Julia auf dem Dorfe*, Keller turns to this point again. Writing to Ferdinand Weibert on 29 August 1875, he argues for the preservation of the introduction as follows:

> Concerning the opening of the story, it cannot very well be omitted since the title, which now can no longer be changed, needs a few words of explanation. Namely, it is important for me to say that the main motif really occurred again because only this justifies the entire work. This whimsical thought is probably not found in any aesthetics, but there is something true in it. In this way my little piece [*Werklein*] is not an imitation.[16]

Keller now defends the reference to the real event as a counterweight to the title. His novella is not an "imitation" (of Shakespeare) because it is based on reality. Here, in contrast to his letter to Auerbach, reality becomes the antidote for the overdose of the literary. But Keller goes even further when he claims that the entire work is only justified because it refers to an actual occurrence. Shakespeare, once called "life itself" (*das Leben selbst*), is evidently a mere pre-text for something else. He is used only as a façade for the real thing, the double suicide in 1847 near Leipzig. The title is presented as something that potentially diverts us from reality, and now this diversion is portrayed as unfortunate ("the title, which can now no longer be changed"), rather than necessary.

What makes the inclusion of the twice-asserted repetition even more unusual is that in both cases the reproduction is not very close to the alleged originals.[17] In connection with Shakespeare's *Romeo and Juliet*, as we have just seen, Keller himself recognized that his novella resembled it only in the barest outline. Robin Clouser, who has written the most complete account of the similarities to date, is able to note a number of less obvious connections, but her argument is unconvincing at several points, for example, when she attempts to link the Friar to the Black Fiddler.[18] Indeed, the episode with Friar Laurence and the sleeping potion, which leads to the *separate* suicides of the Shakespearean lovers, based on a deception and an undelivered message, seems to have been an essential element in the plot from its very inception.[19] That it finds no place in Keller's novella only underscores its distance from the actual *Urfabel*. But Keller also makes little effort to repeat the account he had read in the *Freitagszeitung*. In the novella there is no real issue made of parental consent for a marriage. The suicides occur in September, rather than on 15 August, and the method of suicide is not a shot through the head but drowning. These differences, of course, are due to what one usually calls poetic license, and I am not criticizing Keller for altering either the Shakespearean plot or the newspaper account. What is at issue here is, rather, why it was so important for Keller to insist on the repetitive nature of the novella. I have argued that from the perspective of nineteenth-century realism such a claim is superfluous, and Keller's contemporaries found it equally obtrusive. Furthermore, Keller's insistence on its inclusion—with confusing and contradictory justifications—and his "stylistic" changes suggest the possibility of motives other than the ones readers are usually offered. Could it be that the avowal of realism as repeated reality actually diverts the reader from the "original" event? Could the compulsion forcing Keller to capture the fable have a different source than he is willing, or perhaps able, to identify?

One way to approach these questions is to examine two issues that have occupied commentary on the novella since its appearance: the motivation for the double suicide and the nature of the bond between the two protagonists. When Walter Silz discussed the first of these issues in 1935, he was able to note rather widespread dissatisfaction with the tragic conclusion.[20] This dissatisfaction originates, no doubt, in the feeling that the ending is somewhat arbitrary. Hegel seems to have anticipated such objections when he wrote in his *Aesthetics*: "There is no reason to prefer misfortune, simply because it is misfortune, over a happy ending except for a certain fashionable sensitivity that revels in pain and sorrow and finds it more interesting than painless situations, which it considers mundane."[21] According to this view, there should be no tragic ending when there is no necessity for the tragedy other than individual and subjective predispositions. With reference to Hamlet, Hegel laconically observes: "The sandbank of finitude does not satisfy him" (*Die Sandbank der Endlichkeit genügt ihm nicht*).[22] This conclusion, which Hegel mentions in the context of Shakespeare's *Romeo and Juliet* as well, could be just as valid for Keller's later adaptation. That critics have nonetheless produced arguments for the precision and consequentiality of the motivation[23] may only speak for the Hegelian view—in an indirect fashion. For if the motivation had been as clear and precise as is often claimed, it would have been difficult for such strenuous objections to arise, and unnecessary to prove how well motivated the actions are. One could easily suspect that the zeal to demonstrate the necessity of the suicides results from a perceived arbitrariness that must be eliminated if Keller's status as a realist is to be preserved. For traditionally the realist writer is supposed to be one whose characters are convincingly motivated, leaving the reader with no doubt as to why things happen as they do.

That there is a great deal of doubt and ambiguity—although not necessarily a lack of realism—surrounding Sali's and Vrenchen's motives can be demonstrated by examining the three reasons most often given for their inability to remain happy and together. The first is their social status, or in the words of the novella, "the misery and hopelessness of his [Sali's] origins" (7. 175). Second is the more abstract but related issue of honor and the values emanating from the bourgeois world.[24] Keller may have thought this the most important reason, since it is rather obtrusively emphasized by the narrator, possibly because it also fits well with the social criticism of the novella.[25] In any case, critics have been particularly fond of citing the following sentence, which refers specifically to Sali's thoughts, in this connection:

> The feeling that they could be happy in the middle-class world only in an entirely honorable and irreproachable marriage was just as alive in him as it was in Vrenchen, and in both of these forlorn souls it was the last flame of that honor which had for-

109

merly shone in their houses, and which their fathers, each feeling himself secure, had blown out and destroyed by an inconspicuous mistake, when they so thoughtlessly appropriated the land of a missing man, thinking to magnify this honor by increasing their property, and believing themselves safe in doing so. (7. 176)

The third reason is Sali's role in the mental derangement of Vrenchen's father.[26] This seems to be the major obstacle for Vrenchen in particular, since she mentions it twice. It is also stated by the narrator as part of Sali's thoughts just prior to the sentence quoted above.

Now there is no doubt that all three of these reasons contribute to the motivation for the actions of the main characters. But there is also something suspicious about the manner in which they are presented to the reader. The narrator's long and rambling discussion of the matter, part of which I have just cited, is particularly suspect. In a realist novella one might expect that such narrative interruptions would be superfluous; the reasons should be obvious from the characters' previous actions and utterances. Thus although we are evidently supposed to be persuaded by the narrator's argument, since it is the voice of authority, its very inclusion should make us wary. Actually there are two arguments stated in the passage in question, or, more precisely, one stated argument and one strongly implied. The stated argument is that Sali and Vrenchen, who still remember a respectable way of life, cannot imagine joining together without the possibility of achieving this mode of existence themselves. "They wanted so badly to be content and happy, but only on a sound and respectable basis, and this appeared to be unattainable" (7. 177). The strength of this desire for respectability can also be discerned in Vrenchen's fantasy about winning the lottery and buying the biggest house in Seldwyla. The implied argument is that somehow the transgressions of their fathers play a role in keeping them apart. When Keller writes, "sometimes fate teaches us a lesson" (*zuweilen stellt das Schicksal ein Exempel auf*) (7. 176), the reader, especially one familiar with Shakespeare's play, can hardly escape the conclusion that fate is involved with these "star-cross'd lovers" as well. Indeed, Keller is unusually lavish in his references to fate. Both the star symbolism at the outset and the Heine quotation that concludes the initial scene (7. 96) point to a predetermined course of action. Fate, however, is hardly a reason in the usual sense of the word, but that the narrator alludes to such justifications here is nonetheless significant, signaling perhaps the shaky ground on which the "realistic" motivation stands. The feeling of honor so deeply imprinted on the souls of the young lovers is difficult to square with some of their prior and subsequent actions. Certainly lying to the next-door neighbor is not honorable or, in a bourgeois sense, respectable, even if it is supposed to be a harmless jest. But neither is selling a watch to buy shoes for dancing, or pretending to be married when one is not, or spending the entire evening mingling with a bunch of social outcasts. And who could imagine anything more offensive to the official middle-class code of ethics than engaging in illicit sexual intercourse, stealing a boat, and then committing suicide? The "last flame" of respectability, which supposedly burns in Sali and Vrenchen, must be only a faint flickering. Almost every action they undertake on their final day, whether it is before or after they have determined to take their own lives, violates accepted bourgeois standards.

The other two reasons also evidence some rather obvious deficiencies. Lack of social status could have proved a barrier, and according to one recent critic, it may have prevented a marriage on legal grounds alone in mid-nineteenth-century Zurich.[27] But this is never really offered as a central reason, neither by the characters themselves nor by the narrator, although it is rather curious—and typically contradictory—that Vrenchen's fabricated story about Sali winning the lottery seems to obliterate instantly all other obstacles (7. 153–56). That Sali struck Vrenchen's father, causing his insanity and subsequent institutionalization, proves to be likewise a rather flimsy excuse for keeping the two lovers apart. Like the parallel action in Shakespeare's tragedy, Romeo's slaying of Tybalt, it hardly dampens the ardor of the two lovers. It does not prevent them from sleeping together as soon as Marti has been taken to the asylum, nor does it deter them from spending a single, happy day with each other, culminating in the consummation of their feigned marriage. If we believe Vrenchen, who reasons at times more like the local clergyman than a passionate young girl in love, then her concern is long-range: she fears that Sali's blow and its consequences will be "a bad foundation" (*ein schlechter Grundstein*) (7. 144) for matrimony. Yet when the Black Fiddler later suggests that they join his carefree entourage, she does not bring up her father but rather returns to the shaky ground of bourgeois morality. Her reasoning at this point has to seem strange and strained even to the most generous reader. After witnessing a couple having a spat over the woman's unfaithfulness, she states: "I don't want to be where things like that go on; because I never want to be unfaithful to you, even though I would be willing to endure everything else to have you" (7. 178–79). Does Vrenchen really believe that in her fairy-tale world described earlier to the credulous neighbor there would be no temptation or adultery? Or, more properly, is the reader supposed to believe that she believes this? And are we to think that the girl whose will seems so firm and whose love seems so strong fears the potentially bad influence of these outcasts on her resolve? Is she giving us a variation on Emilia Galotti's "warm blood" (*warmes Blut*)—which seems equally unconvincing in the context of Lessing's play? If this is indeed the only reason she can muster for not being happy with her Sali— and she indicates that she could possibly bear everything else—then it seems rather obvious that she is searching for pretexts. She is yearning to leave the "sandbank of finitude" for the river of eternal oblivion.

The flip side of these three reasons that Sali and Vrenchen must remain apart is, of course, their love for each other. That it is an unusual kind of love hardly needs to be emphasized. The very fact that it contributes to the demise of the two lovers signals that it is of no ordinary variety. Most commentators have chosen to view it as noble and ennobling, characterized by uncompromising and ideal features. Gerhard Kaiser, whose essay on *Romeo und Julia* contains the most perceptive analysis to date, is typical of most critics when he describes the lovers in terms of absoluteness and ideality:

> The young lovers carry in themselves the unconditionality of an ideal that is at odds with the world and society and is ahead of its time, similar to the relationship between a regulative idea and empirical reality. Their absoluteness causes the lovers to fall out of reality into death and destroys retroactively the last ties to their environment, whose weakness had opened up this situation to these young people. Their ideality thus carries with it not only their own death; as a provocation to achieve perfection, it simultaneously casts a death shadow in their contemporary world.[28]

This account, attractive as it may appear at first glance, tells only one half of the story, for the implied opposition between the ideals of the lovers and their empirical reality is merely one way of viewing the events. One should also note that the ideals are *based* on social reality; indeed, if we give any credence at all to Vrenchen's lottery yarn and the narrator's harping on "honor" (*Ehre*), then we can also say that the manner in which Sali and Vrenchen look at a relationship is quite in harmony with their social milieu. The only thing that is "at odds with the world and society" is their ability to achieve the social and ethical sanctions they deem necessary for a happy existence. It is also a bit misleading to resort to a term like "absoluteness" for the lovers. Although it is true that their unwillingness to compromise certain preconceived notions contributes to their tragic end, it is also true that absoluteness in love could imply just the opposite course of action. If their love had truly represented the highest value for them, then they might have been determined, as their literary predecessors were, to rescue their love at all costs—even if they had to transgress social, moral, religious, and familial codes. It seems to me, therefore, that one could just as readily argue that they are not "absolute" enough; if they were, they would have sought another route—any route—in lieu of suicide. Kaiser and others, in short, may be thinking more of the Shakespearean model than Keller's realist adaptation.

For if we now turn to the depiction of the relationship in *Romeo und Julia auf dem Dorfe*, we find some rather odd and mysterious passages, which critics usually have chosen to ignore. Leaving aside the initial encounter as small children for the moment, we note that Sali and Vrenchen meet briefly on the day following the auction of the middle field. Significantly the scene is characterized by its deviation from the norms of everyday life, by a general wildness and pleasure that is later found only in the paradise garden (*Paradiesgärtchen*). "For, since it was a special and, in a sense, wild task [*gleichsam wilde Arbeit*], requiring no rules and no care, it was regarded as a pleasure [*eine Lust*]. The wild stuff [*Das wilde Zeug*], dried by the sun, was piled up and burned with great glee, so that the smoke spread far and wide, and the young people ran about as if possessed [*wie besessen*]" (7. 100). In attendance at this "festival of joy" (*Freudenfest*) are the two children, who seem magnetically attracted to one another: "but whenever Sali got separated from Vrenchen, he would immediately try to rejoin her, and she likewise, smiling happily all the time, would contrive to slip away to him; and to both creatures [*Kreaturen*] it seemed as if this glorious day must not and could not end" (7. 100). There is evidently already some elementary attraction between them, and the reference to them as "creatures" appropriately situates it in the instinctual and animal parts of their being. But neither knows exactly what is happening, and this element of the inexplicable accompanies their relationship until the very end. Their love is here and throughout portrayed as a force beyond the control of the two lovers. It is something that takes hold of them and causes them to undertake actions almost against their conscious, socially conditioned will. Thus when they are chased from the field by their angry fathers, we are significantly told: "and they understood now just as little about their sadness as they did before about their happiness" (7. 101). A vague sort of desire, whose origin and nature remain undisclosed, has already begun to exert its influence over their actions and emotions.

When they meet again as adolescents, the dominant feeling is shame and embarrassment, especially on Vrenchen's part. Before their brief meeting on the bridge at the cloudburst, they notice each other from afar with their respective fathers. Vrenchen hardly dares to remove her eyes from the ground. Ostensibly she is ashamed of her appearance, her father, and her actions in helping him fishing, since all of these point to her abject poverty; but the repetition of this feeling in the narration still seems peculiar. We are told that she walked behind her father "looking down at the ground in shame" (*vor Scham in die Erde sehend*). She had previously tied up her dress so that it would not get wet, but when she sees Sali, she lets it down in shame (*schamhaft*) and is "triply troubled and tormented" (*dreifach belästigt und gequält*). Sali himself is anxious enough (*bekümmert genug*), and while Vrenchen stands there staring at the ground, "completely ashamed and confused" (*so ganz beschämt und verwirrt*), Sali observes the graceful girl, who moves "in such an embarrassed and humble fashion" (*so verlegen und demütig*) (7. 118). All this description occurs in the space of a few sentences, giving the impression that there is perhaps more to their feelings than pubescent shyness, for the emphasis on shame suggests that there may be something to be ashamed of, perhaps some sort of guilt. Presumably before their love has been kindled, or rekindled, the lovers exhibit emotions one might well associate with the acts they later commit. This otherwise fiery and resolute young woman, who later faces love and death with such determination and equanimity, seems here to be plagued by a force beyond control and comprehension. Could she and Sali have forgotten some action in their past that would account for their shame? Could their emotions now be the conditioned response to something that escapes their own will and memory?

Sali's memory, in any case, seems to be tested excessively the very next day. In a remarkable passage he reflects on his experiences at the river and endeavors to conjure up an image of his beloved.

What is odd throughout the narrator's report is the mixture of recollection and forgetting that is attributed to the young man. Sali thinks continuously about Vrenchen. He considers himself enriched, and it seems to him that he has also acquired some sort of knowledge (*Wissenschaft*) the nature of which remains typically unclear to him. On the one hand, this knowledge seems sudden and new—"as if it had fallen from the sky" (*wie vom Himmel gefallen*). On the other hand, it is something he had always known—"yet it seemed as if he had in fact always [*von jeher*] known and recognized what filled him now with such wonderful sweetness" (7. 122). This is no ordinary lover's bliss; it is characterized not only by richness but, more significantly, by "unfathomableness" (*Unergründlichkeit*). The form of his happiness may be clear and distinct (it appears "in such a clear and plain image"), but its source is shrouded in the recesses of memory. And it is, then, this very faculty that fails him as he continues to mull over the events of the previous day. The harder he thinks about Vrenchen, the more obscure her image becomes: "But in all this excited activity the object itself vanished before him almost completely; that is, he finally imagined that he did not after all know exactly what Vrenchen looked like; of course he had a general picture of her in his memory, but if he had to describe it, he would have been unable to do so" (7. 123). Not only does his memory falter but also the image that his mind presents to him seems to perplex and haunt him: "This picture was constantly before his eyes, as if it were actually standing there, and he felt the pleasant impression it made on him; and yet he only saw it as something seen but once, something one has come under the power of, but without really knowing yet what it is" (7. 123). This is a strange and contradictory description indeed. It leaves both a pleasant impression and the feeling that he is in its power; it is always there, but it seems as if he has only seen it once; he recognizes it, yet it is as if he did not yet know it. Sali's mind and memory are evidently playing tricks on him; instead of the adolescent, he sees in his mind's eye the little girl: "He remembered with great pleasure and exactly the facial features that the young girl had once had, but not the features of the girl he had seen the day before" (7. 123). The pleasure that Sali experiences in envisioning the little girl and his simultaneous inability to bring his memory up to the more recent past seem odd, especially since we have just learned that his happiness appears before him "in such a clear and plain image." But it certainly suggests that the nature of the attraction between Sali and Vrenchen may not be the simple, ideal, and innocent variety most commentators have preferred to discover.

Additional statements with this unusual tenor can be found later in the novella as well. For the sake of brevity, however, I shall cite only a few additional illustrations. After their first encounter with the Black Fiddler, the lovers talk about their love. Once again Sali brings up his feeling that the origin of desire lies at some undefined and unspecifiable point in the past: "it always seemed to me as if I would have to love you one day, and without my wanting or knowing it, you have always been on my mind" (7. 133). Vrenchen feels the same: "And you've always been on mine." In their discussion of their dreams after their first night together, they both tell of a desire that is thwarted. Vrenchen recounts her dream as follows: "I dreamed [*Es träumt mir*] that we were dancing with one another at our wedding, for long, long hours. And we were so happy, neatly dressed, and we had everything we needed. Finally we wanted very much to kiss each other, but something kept pulling us apart, and now you yourself are the one that has got in the way and destroyed us!" (7. 145). It is not difficult to see in this dream a structure of guilt.[29] Her first thoughts about the reason for their inability to kiss are appropriately vague; "something" kept them apart. As we have observed before, the obscurity of the forces acting upon them is a repeated theme. When she is more concrete, however, the ambiguity is still not completely removed. For although she claims that Sali is responsible for their frustration, it is not clear that she must be referring to his striking her father: at least, in relating her dream, she does not explicitly state this as a reason. Finally, one could note Sali's desperate queries just after the two lovers have left the Fiddler's nocturnal procession: "'We have escaped them', said Sali, 'but how do we escape ourselves? How do we avoid each other?'" (*Wie meiden wir uns?*) (7. 181). Again we are confronted with a passage that is not totally unambiguous. *Wie meiden wir uns?* can mean: How does each of us avoid the other? Or: how does each avoid him- or herself? And it can mean both. For the problem Sali and Vrenchen face, I am about to suggest, is one involving both their peculiar relationship and their identity as individuals.

A brief recapitulation and some comments are perhaps in order at this point. The motivation of the young lovers has proved to be a more thorny issue than most critics have previously granted. The three most obvious reasons for their actions all evidence flaws in logic or psychological coherence. Neither the characters nor the narrator are consistent and unambiguous in discussing the issue.[30] The nature of their love for each other is similarly marked by ambiguity. It seems that three factors are involved: an inexplicable attraction, a just as inexplicable repulsive force, and a failure to recognize or remember the source of the desire that seems to have been with them as far back as their memories can reach. Furthermore, we should note that their love is somehow asocial, since it is able to be consummated only outside accepted societal conventions. Finally, we could return to Keller's insistence on including notification of a double repetition, which does not exactly fit his work. One of the most significant deviations from both "originals" is the addition of the initial scene of the novella. Here we witness the motivation for the subsequent quarrel between the two farmers, but we also experience the intimacy of the children. In the face of this significant supplement to the basic plot and the unusual circumstances surrounding the motivation and desire of the two lovers, is it too much to suggest that somehow *Romeo und Julia auf dem Dorfe* repeats an *Urfabel* of which Keller himself remained unaware; namely, the tale of two children, once intimate with each other and later shunned by society for their love and compelled to atone for their unspeakable violation of social codes with death? Could the novella, in short, repeat the primeval structure of incest?

To suggest that incestuous feelings lurk somewhere in one of Keller's works is hardly novel, of course. Traditionally, however, the mother-son relationship has been the focus of attention.[31] In Keller's oeuvre, especially in the early works *Der grüne Heinrich* (*Green Henry*), *Pankraz, der Schmoller* (*Pankraz the Pouter*, 1856), and *Frau Regel Amrain* (1856), it is difficult to overlook the special nature of this bond. The domination of the son by the mother, the feelings of guilt evidenced by the son, and his inability to form lasting liaisons with other women have frequently been considered the result of the author's unresolved Oedipal conflict. Indeed, Keller's biography, the traditional focus of psychoanalytic criticism, seems made to order for the Freudian theorist. Adolf Muschg is possibly the most subtle commentator to view Keller from this perspective, but his study is only one in a long series of such attempts.[32] Freud himself even includes two dreams from *Der grüne Heinrich* in his *Traumdeutung* (*Interpretation of Dreams*, 1900).[33] What has attracted psychoanalytically inclined critics to Keller are some rather interesting facts about his life. The early death of his father, the hasty remarriage of his mother (ending in a separation), his own alternation between exploitation of and guilt toward his mother, his predilection for taller, inaccessible women, his bachelorhood, at times excessive drinking, the later punctiliousness in fulfilling his position as "Staatsschreiber" (cantonal secretary)—all of these biographical details contribute to a psychologically intriguing figure.[34] That his unconscious conflicts, stemming from his childhood and manifested in his later biography, would reveal themselves in his creative endeavors is a hypothesis of psychoanalytic theory that Freud initially posited in the first decade of this century in "Der Dichter und das Phantasieren" ("The Poet and Fantasizing").[35]

Freud, however, cannot be the chief support for my suggestion that incestuous structures inform this work, for it is very likely that his strong emphasis on the Oedipus complex resulted in the brother-sister relationship receiving less attention from traditional psychoanalytic quarters. Indeed, when it is considered, it is usually viewed as a variant of the mother-son relationship. Nonetheless, Freud's brief comment concerning how incestuous feelings may develop toward a sister is particularly apposite for our consideration of Keller. In his *Vorlesungen zur Einführung in die Psychoanalyse* (*Introductory Lectures to Psychoanalysis*, 1917), he observed the following: "The little boy can take his sister as a love object as a replacement for the faithless mother."[36] It is not very difficult to apply this statement to Keller's situation.[37] The mother's remarriage can be interpreted as her "betrayal" of little Gottfried, causing his substitution of his sister Regula as love object. But one need not proceed in such a schematic Freudian fashion; there are several features in Keller's relationship to his sister that seem peculiar and noteworthy in their own right. That Regula never married and, after their mother's death, assumed the maternal function in Keller's life may not have been entirely up to her.[38] It seems that Keller was extremely restrictive with his younger sister, perhaps overprotective in a manner suggesting more than normal fraternal concern. In a letter to his mother of 14 August 1851, for example, he admonishes her to pay careful attention to Regula's behavior: "frequent pleasure walks and going out, promenading in the moonlight, etc. are very reprehensible for a middle-class girl."[39] Keller is obviously playing the role of father here, but this role potentially (and psychoanalytically) overlaps with that of the absent lover. A more suggestive and literary indication of Keller's unconscious attraction to his sister can be found in the initial dream in the so-called *Traumbuch* (*Dream Book*). Among other things Keller relates how a fifteen-year-old girl attempted to seduce him. (Keller was twenty-seven at the time.) Suddenly, however, he finds himself accompanied by two girls, and he comments on their appearance as follows: "They were exactly the same, the only difference being one between a slightly younger and an older sister." These two sisters proceed to take him home and to shower him with affection, but they also warn him that "evil women" (*böse Weiber*) in the next apartment watch them and try to spoil their fun. "If one wakes up and hears us," they continue, "then we are as good as dead." There is a suggestion of more intimate relations to come, but Keller is significantly unaroused: "As one of the good children stood up, removed the sheet and very carefully folded it together, and said in the process: if we are sleepy, then we can go to bed right away and sleep soundly, a completely delightful feeling went through me, but not really a sensuous one." They are, in fact, discovered before the completion of the seduction, but Keller's feelings are far from frustration. As he wrote at the end of his recounting of the dream: "Still the remaining impression of the dream was a pleasant one, and I am glad that it broke off as it did. This dream invigorated me for many days, as if I had really experienced that adventure" (21. 64–67). The figures in this dream seem rather transparent, since they have undergone only multiplication and slight displacement. The scene appears to reflect, therefore, a desire for, or actual encounter with, Regula, prevented or threatened by the mother. And that the girls are approximately the same age as Vrenchen when she falls in love with and "marries" Sali suggests a psychoanalytic link between biography and literary work.[40]

That Regula or her literary reflection played an unusual role in Keller's writings is also rather evident. Most significant in this regard is her total absence in *Der grüne Heinrich*. Besides the omission of the hated stepfather, whose exclusion serves an obvious psychological function, Regula is the only other major person or event missing from Keller's semiautobiographical work. Indeed, it appears that Regula herself was miffed by her nonappearance in her brother's novel, for Elisabeth Keller notes her daughter's reaction in a letter to Gottfried: "Regula was naturally sensitive because there was nowhere even the mention of a sister. People could conclude from this that you would be ashamed to consider her your sister!"[41] Keller's reply is predictably odd. He denies Regula's interpretation, stating that he should be above suspicion: "I believe that at my age and with my experience I should be beyond such suspicion." What his age and experience have to do with this entire matter is not at all clear, but he continues with his justification by referring to the inner logic of the text: "I am pursuing a very specific purpose with the novel, and this will manifest itself only in the fourth volume [the fourth and final volume was still unpublished at the time] and will show why I could not use a sister."[42] What this purpose is and why it excluded a sister must remain a matter of speculation, since Keller does not elaborate here or elsewhere. Muschg has suggested that the reason for eliminating his sister is jealousy:[43] a sister would compete for the mother's affection, and her exclusion is simply part of the unconscious desire to possess the mother all alone. But one could also see the elimination of Regula as an endeavor to repress occurrences or thoughts of incest when Keller and his sister were children. Eduard Hitschmann, noting the absence of "children's love games" (*kindliche Liebesspiele*) in *Der grüne Heinrich* and their presence in several other novellas, argues that incestuous feelings account for Regula's elimination: "For the psychoanalyst this contradiction is explained by the fact that with the deletion of Regula the children's love games between brother and sister were also sacrificed to the censor, that because of shamefully concealed things the co-perpetrator herself was forgotten, indeed, had to be forgotten."[44] In a strange fashion, therefore, Regula may have stumbled upon precisely the reason for her exclusion: Keller was ashamed of his sister because she was his sister. For is it totally coincidental that in the very same letter Keller assures his mother and sister that not everything in the novel was experienced (*erlebt*), "just as many things are not true at all, for example, the love affairs"?[45] In Keller's association of the exclusion of his sister with feigned "love affairs," could we not see an unconscious substitution that substantiates the hypothesis Hitschmann offers?

An alternative explanation for Regula's absence in *Der grüne Heinrich* is that, as Keller himself wrote, a sister was simply not needed. The reason for this superfluity is perhaps the identification of sister and mother. When the mother appears, Keller means the sister too. As he wrote to his mother in a letter addressed—as always—to her alone, he is really writing to Regula as well: "And I say hello to Regula also, as my letters are always really addressed to both of you anyway."[46] In other works written during or shortly after the composition of *Der grüne Heinrich*, we can also find variations on mother-daughter identification. Perhaps most obvious and suggestive in this regard is the fragmentary drama "Theresa," whose plot is constructed around a triangle, two-thirds of which consists of a widowed mother and her daughter. In *Pankraz, der Schmoller*, besides the incestuous overtones in Ester-chen's unfaithfulness to her brother while he is on his adventure, the mother and daughter likewise act as a unit. Both are deserted unexpectedly by Pankraz and wait patiently for his return (like Keller's mother and sister); both appropriately fall asleep when he begins to describe his love, Lydia; and both exhibit a noteworthy curiosity for a repetition of the story, or at least for hearing the name of Pankraz's woman friend. Finally, in *Frau Regel Amrain und ihr Jüngster*, the mother's name, Regula, usually considered an allusion to Keller's aunt,[47] could also be taken as an amalgamation of mother and daughter. If we grant that Keller had an unresolved Oedipal complex, therefore, it would seem that his sister might be encompassed by it as well through the psychic mechanism of identification.

If Keller did repress incestuous desires toward his mother and sister, it is not surprising to find only indirect references to incest in his works. Even though some form of incest was a favorite theme in eighteenth-century literature and in romanticism,[48] it is apparent that Keller, like most realists, found it inappropriate. Nonetheless, it is not difficult to find rather obvious patterns of incest in several works besides *Der grüne Heinrich*. In *Der Schmied seines Glückes* (*The Maker of His Fortune*, 1874), John Kabys, the adopted son, takes the place of his father by sleeping with his "mother"; but in this doubly Oedipal plot, his own son winds up replacing him just as he had replaced Litumlei in his mother's bed. Jukundus and Justine in *Das verlorene Lachen* (*The Lost Smile*, 1874) are not only similar because of their names, but also because of their smiles, which match, the narrator tells us, like twins (*Zwillingsgeschwister*). And Muschg reminds us that Reinhart's engagement to Lucia in *Das Sinngedicht* (*The Epigram*, 1881) contains a twofold echo of the incest taboo: "As lover he steps into the place of a maternal omission of love, and, although he does this only symbolically and without breaking a taboo, he thus cancels the marriage of the parents. Even more, as a token of reconciliation he receives from the 'injured' clan his sister as a wife."[49] But Keller's most suggestive work for the hypothesis of a structure of incest in *Romeo und Julia* is *Dietegen* (1874), which is generally recognized as a parallel to the earlier novella. Besides their resemblance in basic plot, however, we also find a similarity in the brother-sister relationship—assuming, of course, that such a relationship is hidden somewhere in

Romeo und Julia. For Dietegen, saved from death by Küngolt, is adopted by her family as their own son and then promised to his new sister as a husband.[50]

These echoes of incest, as well as Keller's relationship to his mother and sister, would be of little relevance for an interpretation of *Romeo und Julia* if the text itself did not provide ample evidence of a structure of incest.[51] Although commentators have tended to overlook these clues, they are not really very difficult to find. In the very first scene, we encounter the remarkable similarity of Manz and Marti, a resemblance that is conspicuous because of the emphasis placed on it. Not only do the names have a similar sound, the characters' appearance and actions throughout the novella are nearly identical. The narrator does not even need to present them separately on the opening pages of the novella; a single description suffices for both. They are the same age, wear the same clothes, and plough their fields in the same manner. Even the apparent difference between them winds up being canceled. We are told that there is only one way to distinguish them: "at first sight one could have told them apart only by the fact that one wore his white cap with the peak tipping forward over his brow, whereas the other's fell back on his neck" (7. 86). But immediately the narrator reestablishes the identity: "But even this distinction alternated between them depending upon the direction in which they were plowing" (7. 86).[52] Later they both bid for the same field, and, in a self-destructive fashion, each arouses the hatred of his mirror-image. While the children are celebrating the clearing of the field, both fathers are angered and simultaneously call their children back to their homes (7. 100–101). The mischievous citizens of Seldwyla even contribute to their sameness by selling them the identical lottery ticket (7. 103). They both hire a battery of dishonest lawyers and consultants, and both wind up impoverished and forced to fish for survival. Significantly Marti imagines that they are not identical, that Manz at least has enough to eat and drink; but the narrator again lets the reader know that there is no difference here either (7. 118). Finally the end of both farmers is equally unpleasant. Marti is reduced to incoherent babbling, and Manz becomes a fence for stolen goods. It is not insignificant, therefore, that we are told that Marti, upon his arrival at the asylum, "was as happy as a child" (*freute sich wie ein Kind*) (7. 142); and when Manz hears about his adversary's plight, almost the exact phrase is used. Sali reports to Vrenchen: "Since all sorts of vagabonds come into our place, we have heard about what has been happening here, and it makes my father as happy as a child" (*worüber mein Vater sich freut wie ein kleines Kind*) (7. 143). Again there is identity in apparent dissimilarity.

This doubling of the father, like the doubling of the sister in Keller's dream, has long been recognized by psychoanalytic theory as a mechanism that provides a safe and acceptable alternative to the single figure. If Marti and Manz are considered a unit, as one parent, then the children, of course, become siblings.[53] In fact, we do not even learn which child belongs to which father until well after the first scene has closed and the "weaver" has begun to weave the fate of the two families. The first mention that Sali is Manz's son occurs just prior to the "festival of joy" on the middle field. But perhaps most important is that in viewing Manz and Marti as a unit, we can more easily account for the trauma surrounding Sali's striking of Marti with a stone. This act is more than just a child raising its hand against a grown-up; it represents a son striking his father as well.[54] This helps explain why Sali's action, the symbolic fulfillment of the first half of the Oedipus myth, is such an insurmountable barrier to the future happiness of the two lovers—and perhaps also why it momentarily allows them to come together in "marriage." The unconscious guilt resulting from this event—in Sali's case because of the blow itself, in Vrenchen's from her role as accomplice—is indeed "a bad foundation" (*ein schlechter Grundstein*) on which to build a relationship. This interpretation would be less convincing if it were not also connected with the doubling effect we have witnessed throughout the novella. For Sali's blow, undertaken "without thinking about it" (*ohne sich zu besinnen*) (7. 138), is the second time he has raised his hand against "his" father. In the struggle at the river, he is about to assist Manz in overpowering Marti, but because of Vrenchen's intervention—and she is also partially responsible for his action in the field—he turns on his own father instead. "Involuntarily he laid his hand on his own father" (7. 120). The doubling is thus structurally complete. In both instances the action is motivated by a desire connected with Vrenchen; it is explicitly described as an unconscious or instinctive reaction on Sali's part; and in both cases it is directed against the father.

Reducing the two farmers to a single father seems justified on another basis as well. The origin of the opening scene of the novella dates back to a dream from 20 September 1847, or at least to an entry from this date in Keller's diary-like *Traumbuch* (21. 80–81). The activity of plowing, the violation of the middle field, and the designation of this violation as crime (*Frevel*), all point to rather obvious sexual symbolism. That this dream or sketch then becomes associated with the newspaper story, which had appeared seventeen days before, possibly demonstrates the implicit sexuality at the source of the novella. But this image of lonesome plowing occurs in another form besides that of the *Traumbuch* and *Romeo und Julia*. In *Der grüne Heinrich*, as the hero returns to his home after his travels, he has a peculiar dream:

> . . . He gradually approached the city in which his home [*Vaterhaus*] was located, by means of wonderful paths, on the border of broad streams. . . . A countryman plowed on the bank with a golden plow pulled by milk-white oxen, under whose tread large cornflowers shot up; the furrows filled up with golden kernels, which the farmer scooped out and tossed far into the air with one hand, while he steered the plow with the other. (19. 150)

Noteworthy here is the association of the plowman with the father (*Vaterhaus*), as well as the similarities with *Romeo und Julia* (proximity to water, throwing of kernels/stones). In this passage, however, the doubling of the farmer has been eliminated, leaving the solitary figure. Once again it is not difficult to identify the farmer's activity with coitus, but as if it were still not clear enough, Keller later transforms the plowman behind the plow into a sailor on a ship, and describes the following scene: "Then he eagerly bored a hole in the bottom of the ship; then he placed the iron mouthpiece of a trumpet over the hole, sucked powerfully on it for a moment, which made it sound loudly like a battle horn; and it discharged a shining stream of water that formed the most glorious fountain in the small moving ship" (19. 151– 52). As Uwe Lemm notes in connection with this passage, the sexual symbolism is so evident here that anyone who does not totally reject the insights of psychoanalysis would have to recognize it.[55]

In *Romeo und Julia*, while the farmers plow, the children play, and it is not difficult to detect sexual overtones in their interaction as well. The majority of critics have called their actions "innocent" in this initial encounter.[56] Although this evaluation is often the consequence of inattentiveness to detail, it is not really at odds with the assertion of sexual overtones.[57] For at this point—and to a certain extent throughout the novella—the children are both sexual *and* innocent, and this is underscored in the text by the primeval and natural description of the middle field. The "green wilderness" they enter has connections with the biblical paradise, as Kaiser has noted, and we see the young lovers, as it were, before they have eaten from the tree of knowledge.[58]

Their sexual play occurs in two phases: first with the doll as object and then with each other. The doll, which is first dressed and undressed by Vrenchen, is stolen by Sali, who proceeds to toss it mercilessly into the air. Because of this mistreatment, a hole develops, which the curious lad then bores out and enlarges with his fingernails. In thus penetrating into the doll, Sali causes the filler material, described as a bran-like substance, to come out. Sali is not finished until the single leg is entirely emptied of its contents and hangs down like "a pitiful husk" (7. 92). When Vrenchen finally recovers the doll, she finds that its leg is attached to the trunk of the body "like the tail [*das Schwänz-chen*] of a salamander" (7. 92). After a short period of reconciliation, the two children then proceed to damage the doll further: "They bored hole after hole into the little martyr's body and let the stuffing run out from all sides. They carefully gathered it into a little pile on flat stone, stirred it around, and looked at it intently" (7. 93). They then fill the head with bran and a live fly, observing their "head of a prophet" (*weissagende Haupt*) while they embrace each other. In a moment of extraordinary cruelty, the children decide to bury the head with the fly inside; seized by the horror (*Grauen*) of their own deed, they remove themselves from the premises.

The sadism in the scene is rather apparent.[59] If I have refrained from direct commentary on the sexual imagery, it was only to avoid overemphasizing and overinterpreting the obvious. The constant references to penetration into the doll's body, the single leg being emptied and falling limp, and the evident mixture of fascination, curiosity, and pleasure with which the children go about their play plainly suggest a sexual dimension. This seems to be confirmed by the second half of their activities on this day. It begins with Vrenchen lying down on her back and singing, while the sun shines into her open mouth. For a moment Sali is perplexed; but when he observes Vrenchen's white teeth, he invents a game that enables him to approach her. The pretext for physical contact is counting teeth. Sali lies over Vrenchen and counts hers; then they switch places while she reciprocates. Because she is too young to know how to count, however, the game has to be extended: "and so she began all over again many times, and this game seemed more pleasing to them than everything else they had tried that day" (7. 95). Finally in exhaustion, Vrenchen falls asleep on Sali in the bright sunlight. Once again excessive commentary seems unnecessary.[60]

Let me emphasize and caution here that I am not asserting that Sali and Vrenchen are depicted as siblings incestuously involved with one another, or even that they have what we normally call sexual contact in this initial encounter. Such an interpretation contradicts the central document at our disposal, the text of the novella. Nor am I contending that Keller himself in any way had incest in his conscious mind while he was composing his celebrated adaptation. What I am suggesting is that the relationship between the two lovers resembles structures associated with incest, and that these structures may ultimately have their source in Keller's biography. The rationale for introducing such an explanation is that it has the potential of clearing up certain observed anomalies in the characters' speeches and actions. The two I have singled out as particularly important were the motivation for suicide and the nature of the love relationship. The symbolic breaking of the incest taboo, one of society's strongest prohibitions, sheds light on both the ostracism of the lovers from society and the necessity of death as a solution. The feelings of guilt and shame, the intimation that they are destined for each other, and the impression that a mysterious power is simultaneously pushing them together and pulling them apart can be explained in part by an early sexual and, if my hypothesis is correct, incestuous encounter. The reason, in short, for the noted inconsistencies in motivation and the peculiar nature of the lovers' feelings is because the actual motives and the precise nature of their desire remain unconscious and unavailable—for the characters, for Keller, and, to a large extent, for the reader as well. (The reader, after all, is supposedly reading an adaptation of Shakespeare and an imitation of reality.) Incest is a trivial and tautological hypothesis if one maintains, as some Freudians have, that every creative endeavor is informed by this desire and its prohibition.[61] But when it serves to elucidate hitherto controversial and obscure passages, then it can have a value beyond its psychoanalytic worth. The assumption of what I have labeled the structure of incest is productive for an interpretation of *Romeo und Julia* because it makes sense out of questions that are otherwise stubbornly resistant to exegesis.

One final aspect of the novella that can be illuminated by the unusual nature of the lovers' desire concerns the multivalent figure of the Black Fiddler. He is significant not only because he is superfluous for the main and subsidiary plots but also because he is Keller's most

126

obvious modification of the *Urfabel*. Several critics have noted that he is a vehicle by which the author develops social criticism, and there is little doubt that he functions on one level as the personification of the injustice of the farmers who usurped his field and prevented his integration into the community. But in connection with the young lovers he represents not vengeance but desire, and it is a desire that has its true home outside the normal social order. "Lust" is thus the word most frequently associated with this mysterious figure. He plays his fiddle, we learn, "when the farmers were merry [*lustig*] and celebrated a festival" (7. 130). In the *Paradiesgärtchen* one of his first remarks to Sali and Vrenchen is: "So have a good time" (*So macht euch nur recht lustig*) (7. 172). We are told that the people in his entourage are poor, "but they were all the merrier" (*aber sie waren um so lustiger*) (7. 174). Gradually the two lovers decide to join in the "common amusement" (*gemeinsame Lustbarkeit*) (7. 174). And, when the Fiddler tries to persuade them to join his troop, he tells them: "Think of a merry bridal bed deep in the woods" (*Denkt an das lustige Hochzeitsbett im tiefen Wald*) (7. 178), thus bringing the references to *Lust* into a more explicit sexual frame of reference. Indeed, in association with him music and dance assume an erotic function too. His almost threatening offer to the children in the field—"I'll fiddle for you if you want to dance!" (7. 131)—signals the identification of dance and desire, which is later made manifest in the *Paradiesgärtchen*.[62] Here the dance becomes a veritable orgy in which partners are arbitrarily exchanged in the moonlight. Vrenchen, obviously the more passionate of the two lovers as well as the one who seems obsessed with dancing, appears to enjoy the general merriment more than Sali. She glows "like a purple rose" and seems overjoyed no matter whom she dances with (7. 175). Finally, when the mock marriage has been completed, the frenzied procession, led by the Fiddler, dances through the surrounding countryside until it reaches the third field of the opening scene.

As an incorporation of desire, the Fiddler has the function of bringing the children together. Analogous to their desire, there is an inextricable and uncanny attraction associated with him. When they first encounter him in the middle field, he seems to exert a mysterious power over the lovers:

Sali and Vrenchen walked behind him, as quiet as mice, thinking he would turn away from the field and disappear without looking around. And this indeed seemed to be his intention, for he acted

127

as if he had not noticed them. Furthermore they were under a strange spell [*Dazu waren sie in einem seltsamen Bann*]—they did not dare leave the narrow path, but involuntarily followed the mysterious fellow until they reached the end of the field, where that iniquitous pile of stones covered the still disputed corner. (7. 130)

Later this attraction recurs, as we have just noted, when they follow the Fiddler over hill and dale like children behind the Pied Piper. Indeed, there is almost something comforting about his presence in the *Paradiesgärtchen*, and the children come to welcome being under "the special protection of the Fiddler" (7. 173). On the other hand, and again parallel to their love, the Fiddler has something forbidding and asocial about him. This is no doubt due in part to his association with the Satanic and Dionysian elements,[63] what we might call the dark side of the lovers' desire. The emphasis on blackness in both his name and appearance, the unusual nose, the fact that he has no proper name and that he possesses no baptismal certificate, as well as his obscure origins as the presumed grandson of the *Trompeter*, who likewise remains nameless, all of this brings him into the proximity of the forces of evil.[64] Moreover, when we first encounter him, he leaps upon the pile of stones, which appear "fiery-red" because of the flowers growing there (7. 130). The mysterious black figure on top of this fiery-red mass of stones is an obvious image of Satan.[65] When he then tells the children that their fathers have gone to the devil ("now they themselves have gone to the devil!" [7. 131]), implying that he has already traversed that route himself, or when he prophesies that the children will go "the way of all flesh" (7. 130), it is difficult to deny his affiliation with the underworld. Later, in the *Paradiesgärtchen*, this Satanic imagery is supplemented with Dionysian overtones. The wine at the Fiddler's foot (7. 172), the frenzied dancing, and the orgiastic atmosphere suggest a bacchanalian celebration. When he leads the procession—"as if possessed" (*wie besessen*) (7. 180)—we are told that he jumps around like a ghost and that the entire scene was "a veritable witches' mountain" (*ein wahrer Blocksberg*) (7. 180–81), thus confirming the identification between the underworld and the illicit passions of love.[66] Indeed, this intermingling of death and desire, which permeates the lovers' relationship, is embodied perfectly in their black seducer.

But Vrenchen also partakes of this dual nature. The references to her dark complexion and purple lips signal an unusually passionate constitution, which the narrator never seems tired of emphasizing. Although her innocence is often used to counter the Satanic features of the Fiddler, Sali's identification of her with witches and the devil, although they are supposed to be terms of endearment (7. 132–33), nevertheless brings her into association with the dark forces of desire.[67] But she also seems to stand closer to death. When Sali suggests that they consummate their marriage and commit suicide, Vrenchen responds immediately: "Sali, what you just said, I have had the same idea for a long time and I decided that we could die and then everything would be over" (7. 184). Indeed, this unity of death and desire found in the Fiddler and Vrenchen seems to be a strange echo of Keller's own psyche at the time. On a sheet of paper that Keller filled with variations on the name Betty (referring to Betty Tendering, with whom he was infatuated at the time), we find some rather strange doodlings. Among them are three skeletons, obvious allegories of death, one holding the traditional scythe, the other two playing fiddles.[68] That Keller's ardor for the black-haired sister-in-law of his publisher occurs precisely at the same time he was preoccupied with the Black Fiddler and his passionate ward hardly seems coincidental.

A final quality connecting the Fiddler with the lovers' desire is the association with forgetting or the inability to remember. We should recall here that several of Sali's and Vrenchen's remarks, as well as the narrator's comments, revolve around the failure to recollect something—whether it was the image of the beloved, the source of their love, or the origin of happiness. Indeed, this theme is tightly woven into the structure of the novella. In the scene with the doll, for example, Vrenchen decorates its head with the leaves of a poppy (7. 91), a traditional symbol for forgetting, oblivion, and death.[69] In fact, this is the only adornment that remains on the decapitated and fly-filled head when it is finally interred. When the Fiddler appears for the first time, he leaps onto the pile of stones, which, as we noted above, appears red because of the countless poppies growing on it. Although at this particular meeting the Fiddler tears the lovers out of their "blissful forgetfulness," in which they had meandered about "like two children" (7. 132),[70] as if to restore the stolen oblivion, Sali then forces Vrenchen's hand into the poppies (7. 134); and he succeeds partially in this restoration. Vrenchen refuses to engage in the old teeth-counting ritual from their initial encounter, but they do proceed to a new game, embracing and kissing passionately in the high corn —after Vrenchen has decorated herself with a garland of poppies (7.

134–35).[71] Wine and dance, consistently associated with the Fiddler, have the same effect, raising the passions and encouraging forgetfulness. When the Fiddler plays a tune for them, they dance into oblivion: "they danced without pause, forgetting themselves and the world in their swirling, singing, and commotion" (7. 173). But it is finally their inability to forget themselves and the world completely, captured in Sali's pathetic exclamation—"how do we escape ourselves?" (7. 181)— that leads to their demise. As long as they remained in the bacchanalian procession, they were oblivious to the world around them, its moral prohibitions, and themselves. But ultimately they are not able to escape any of these: "Sali grasped Vrenchen's arm more firmly and forced her to stand still; for he was the first to regain his senses. To silence her, he kissed her vehemently on the mouth, for she had quite forgotten herself and was wildly singing" (7. 181). Banishing forgetting means remembering who they are and, however dimly, why they cannot live in this world, for neither the Fiddler nor their love can consign to oblivion the haunting memory that follows them like a shadow from their past.

Although the exact name of this memory remains unspoken in the text, I have been suggesting that it can best be described with the word *incest*. Indeed, I have endeavored to show how throughout the novella the structure of an incestuous desire informs actions and speeches, thus explaining otherwise obscure motives and utterances. It is difficult to find a similar opinion in previous commentary on this work, except for one or two psychoanalytic studies of Keller (e.g., Hitschmann and Lemm). This does not necessarily speak against my thesis, of course; in fact, the repressed incest I am proposing could be called upon to account for the irresistible appeal of the work over the years. Nonetheless, Theodor Fontane, one of the most perceptive critics of his time, can be cited for indirect and unwitting confirmation of my hypothesis. In his observations on *Die Leute von Seldwyla* (*The People of Seldwyla*), Fontane reproaches Keller for his mixture of realism and romanticism (*Romantizismus*) in *Romeo und Julia*: "the first half is a novella that mirrors the genuine life of the people in its most minute details; the second half completely resembles a fairy tale, if it is not in fact a fairy tale."[72] Ignoring for the moment the psychic proximity of fairy tales to dreams and of dreams to unconscious desires, we could observe further that what troubles Fontane is the nature of the relationship between the two lovers. He assumes that Keller has taken the easy way out in reverting to the language of the fairy tale.

In short, according to the accepted standards of the nineteenth century, the lovers behave unrealistically: "Thus they do not speak like 'Vren-chen and Sali,' but like 'little brother and little sister' [*Brüderchen und Schwesterchen*], and there would be nothing wrong with this if the whole story were about this."[73] But what if, as I have suggested, this was after all "the whole story"? What if the realism Fontane witnesses in the first half of the novella is just a diversion from another kind of "realism" recounted in the primeval fairy tale about "little brother" and "little sister"? Then perhaps we would also be compelled, as Keller's hand was in capturing this tale, to conclude that the effect of repetition, the hallmark of realism that Keller is at such pains to emphasize, is ultimately synonymous with the repression of desire.

5

THE MEMORY OF REALISM:
The Aesthetics of Abnegation in Storm's *Aquis submersus*

Das Leben trügt—Erinnerung
Allein bleibt ewig treu;
Die bringet nur geheilten Schmerz
Und nur gesühnte Reu.

(Life deceives—memory alone remains
eternally true; it brings only healed pain and
expiated penitence.)

> Theodor Storm,
> "Nach frohen Stunden"
> ("After Happy Hours")

The magic of writing is like a cosmetic
concealing the dead under the appearance of
the living.

> Jacques Derrida,
> "Plato's Pharmacy"

With the novella *Aquis submersus* (1877), we are confronted at first with more traditional, less psychological signs of realism. Indeed, the reader of this work should have no trouble recognizing it as a realist piece of prose. Despite the intrusion of several "romantic" motifs and symbols, the narrators of both the inner story and the outer frame go out of their way to emphasize the authenticity of their accounts. To produce the effect of reality, both utilize precise description and detail. The opening of the novella is a case in point. Here we are told of a neglected garden belonging to a castle, and

132

then are led to a corner of this garden to examine the surrounding countryside. In contrast to my one-sentence summary of the initial paragraph, however, little in Storm's depiction is left indefinite. The garden is "ours" ("In our . . . 'castle garden'"); it belongs to *the* former ducal castle; the narrator speaks of his youth ("in my boyhood years" [*Knabenzeit*]). The corner of the garden is specified as northwest; and the small knoll is situated, we read, above the dried-out bed of a fish pond. The view to the west allows us to see the green of the marshes, the silvery flow of the sea, and the shadow of the coastal islands. Directing his and our gaze toward the north, the narrator calls our attention to the gray, pointed church steeple rising from the desolate countryside. The village to which this church belongs, we are told, is "one of the places of my youth" (257).[1]

Besides the apparent precision of description, there are two aspects of this opening that serve to reinforce the realistic effect. The first is the superfluity of details. The exact location of the hillock or the condition of the hedges in the garden seems to be unimportant for the story to follow. Even if we concede that the neglect of the garden, its deterioration over the years, as well as the concomitant suggestion of the decline of the aristocracy have something to do with the tale Johannes will relate later in the novella, there are too many additional facts in the opening paragraphs that appear as gratuitous details. They are communicated to the reader, not because they possess future symbolic value or some as yet undefined significance for the central narrative, but rather because they reflect and capture the reality of the narrator's experience.[2] At least, this is ostensibly what they are meant to do. The second aspect that lends this opening the air of realism is the intimacy with which the details are related. Although we are not supplied with any proper nouns—the narrator, the village, the duke, and even the coast remain anonymous—we are obviously being led into a private world and given privileged knowledge about it. The narrator emphasizes that it is "our" garden, that "we" (one or another "of the pensive people") climb the hillock to gain a view of the surroundings. Phrases such as *in meiner Knabenzeit, meiner Jugend*, or *meiner Vaterstadt* lend a further personal touch to the description.[3] We are even introduced to the private terminology used by the narrator and his friends. In the first five paragraphs, we encounter five separate instances of words inside quotation marks. The *Schloßgarten* (castle garden) retains its name even though it is evidently not much of a garden anymore and no longer belongs to a duke. The *Berg* (mountain) is modified by the qualifier *sogenannten* (so-called), signaling obviously the local exaggeration for the knoll. The *Gelehrtenschule* (lit., school for the learned) and the *Priesterkoppel* (pasture of priests) are presumably placed in quotation marks because these are the names they are called by the native population. And finally we are told that *Wasserfranzosen* (lit., water French) was the label that, in his youth, the narrator and his friend gave to the black beetles they collected at the edge of the water. The effect of these details is one of authenticity. The narrator has not only described a landscape; he has also populated it and introduced us to the language of its inhabitants. By thus confiding in us, the narrator simultaneously enhances the illusion of an extratextual reality. As long as we believe in his reality as a reliable and candid person, we will also believe that his report, as intimate and detailed as it is presented to us, represents accurately the circumstances in the real world.

The impression of realism we gain from Johannes's narration is of a slightly different, albeit related, variety. Here too we find seemingly superfluous detail in the opening paragraphs of his account. We learn that he has left his painting equipment and other luggage in the city, that birds fly overhead and quench their thirst with water, and that it had rained the previous night (265). Again there appears to be no reason for all of this information except to convey the effect of verisimilitude. Like the narrator's account, Johannes's narrative is also marked by signs of intimacy. The close of the first notebook with the mention of the baptism of his grandniece (310) and the opening of the second notebook with the mention of his nephew as addressee (311) are two obvious examples. Indeed, as the reader gradually discovers, the notebooks amount to a personal confession of guilt—at least this is Johannes's evaluation of the course of events.[4] The difference between the intimacy here and in the frame is that in the former case we are intruding into a family affair; we are eavesdroppers looking over the shoulder of someone for whom these words were likewise not intended. In the latter case we are part of the anonymous audience addressed by the nameless narrator. A second difference between the frame and Johannes's narrative involves the type of detail provided. Whereas the anonymous narrator seems to avoid the specificity of proper names, Johannes makes his account concrete by supplying the reader with precisely this sort of information. The very first sentence tells us the year (1661), the date (*am Sonntage Kantate* [on the fourth Sunday after Easter]), and the location of the narrator (*in unserm Hol-*

stenlande [in our Holstein]). In the next two paragraphs, we learn the name of his painting teacher (*Meister van der Helst*), his travel route (Amsterdam over Hamburg), and, through indirect means, his own name. This kind of specificity continues throughout the two note-books. The mention of the conflict with Sweden (266) or the flood of 1634 (317) are only two more illustrations of this concern for relat-ing the fictional account to a known reality.[5] The impact of all these details is a rather convincing impression that the fictional events actu-ally occurred—or at least could have occurred. Here we experience the effect of realism because our knowledge of these specific events, places, and people enhances the possibility that the rest of the account is real as well.

The endeavor to achieve an effect of realism is also apparent in the treatment of potentially supernatural occurrences, those "romantic" remnants so often cited as part of Storm's stock in trade.[6] These events are particularly important because they threaten to violate the reader's sense of the real. It is therefore all the more significant that they are always subject to a realistic explanation. Two means are employed to accomplish this. The first of these is to embed the supernatural in the mind of one of the characters, thus implying that its perception is the result of an obsession or paranoia. In *Aquis submersus* this technique is employed most obviously in connection with the *Urahne* (ances-tress). The eerie feeling that she is somehow playing a part in the tragedy is repeatedly suggested in the text. Storm, who seems to have harbored some rather set and peculiar notions about how heredity works, may well have considered that this ancestor's "evil" could really be transmitted genetically to later generations. Whenever the curse of the *Urahne* becomes associated with supernatural occurrences, how-ever, they are accounted for as the aberration of an individual mind. When the eyes of this dreaded ancestor are mentioned in connection with the dead child, for example, this appearance is clearly ascribed to the distraught mind of the guilt-ridden father: "it seemed to me that I was seeing the eyes of that ancestress of the family, as if she wanted to announce to me here out of the dead countenance of our child: 'My curse caught both of you after all!'" (333). The supernatural, encompassing both the eyes and the curse, certainly lends a fateful note to the novella. But by placing the most drastic manifestation of the curse in the mind of Johannes, by thus psychologizing the supernat-ural, the narration downplays the potential for an antirealistic effect. If we can attribute part of the *Urahne* motif to heredity and part to the psychology of a mind that does not totally escape seventeenth-century superstition, then we will have less difficulty integrating this facet of the story into a structure of realism.

The other technique for discrediting the supernatural involves leaving clues to a realistic explanation. The best illustration of this technique occurs in connection with the bony hand Johannes observes after departing from Katharina's room. Standing in the garden, he first sees his love's pale hand waving to him, but when he turns back to look again, he notices something quite different: "But I was nearly shocked when I glanced back along the garden path at the lowest window next to the tower; for it seemed to me as if I saw behind the window another hand; but this one threatened me with a raised finger and appeared to me colorless and bony like the hand of death" (299–300). The attentive reader is able to solve this mystery better than Johannes, who seems to be unable to discover the natural cause of this threatening gesture. The hand obviously belongs to Bas' Ursel —or at least we are led to this conclusion by various hints in the text. We have already learned from Katharina, for example, that the old woman lives downstairs: "she had her room downstairs because for a long time already the steps were too difficult for her to climb" (278). Furthermore, Johannes himself reports that Bas' Ursel is an insomniac, that she regrets living in her present quarters because she cannot keep an eye on the servants very well, and that she feels nothing ever occurs in the garden (279). It is easy from these clues to surmise that this watchful, sleepless, and distrusting old woman, who is not particularly well disposed to Johannes anyway, has observed his departure through the garden—an unusual event in this otherwise vacant area. If these clues are not sufficient, or if we have forgotten them in the intervening twenty pages, we are reminded of the connection in Dietrich's report to Johannes concerning Bas' Ursel's visit to Wulf on the day after the illicit night of passion. "I understood, Herr Johannes, nothing at all," Dietrich admits, "but then, and note this well, she held something in her bony hand in front of the eyes of the Junker, as if she were threatening him with it" (303). The repetition of the image of a threatening bony hand, a symbol of impending doom, confirms the "natural explanation" we have pieced together. When the pastor later makes a comment with the identical image—"May it [the painting of the dead child] admonish people that everything is dust in the face of the bony hand of death!" (330)—we recognize the connection with its earlier occurrences; but if we have been alert to the textual evidence, the supernatural dimension has been completely removed. Johannes's initial association of the bony hand with the *Urahne* proves to be a personal and paranoid interpretation, similar to his thought that the *Hausgespenste* (house ghost) is reaching for him when he mistakenly hurries into the rush swamp (300). At every point, then, the potentially supernatural event is brought back to reality by reference either to an abnormal psychological state or to a more plausible, realistic explanation.

Elements of content, such as those mentioned above, are thus essential for the production of the effect of realism in *Aquis submersus*. But these elements are also enhanced by certain formal structures in the novella. Chief among these is the use of a narrative frame around the central tale. This hallmark of Storm's fiction occurs in almost two-thirds of his works, and it has received a good deal of attention from those interested in formal devices. The central concern has usually been to discover links between the frame and the inner narrative, either in the form of a contrast or a comparison between the two narrators, or as implicit commentaries upon each other.[7] A further function of this formal technique, however, is to make the narration appear more authentic. As W. F. Mainland comments in this connection: "It [the frame] is a fictitious device made to overcome the idea of fiction. If the author has taken all the trouble to wrap something up, the reader will think that something must be genuine."[8] This is particularly true of the fictional manuscript that comprises the inner narrative in *Aquis submersus*. For in contrast to other framed novellas, here the "wrapper" serves as more than a mere point of departure for the telling of a tale. In this work it functions as the answer to questions posed explicitly and implicitly by the frame's narrator. Thus the realism of the frame reinforces the realism of the inner narrative, and vice versa. Johannes's notebooks continually refer to objects that we know to be "real" from the frame; the anonymous narrator is able to authenticate Johannes's account by merely lifting his glance to the painting mentioned in the manuscript. On the other hand, the text he reads explains to him the reality he has puzzled about since childhood. The mutual confirmation of authenticity situates the reader in a position from which it is difficult to doubt the truth of either part of the text. Located, as it were, between the two narrators, we have trouble distancing ourselves from the hermetically realist structure of the novella. Consequently we are more easily drawn into the deception of reality perpetrated by the exchange between frame and story.

An even more persuasive means for promoting the effect of realism, however, involves the use of recollection.[9] This formal technique of narration employs a figure who relates from memory past experiences. Often the framework for the narration supplies the illusion of an oral account: the narrator relates the recollected past to an audience, and the reader listens in on the telling.[10] Sometimes, as in *Aquis submersus*, the narrator (Johannes) recollects his experiences in written form. Storm, who was extremely fond of the simulated oral framework, especially in his early work, used one form or another of the *Erinnerungsnovelle* (novella of memory) in most of his prose. When one compares the frequency with which he employed this technique with its occurrence in the writings of other German realists, as Karl Laage has done, the results are noteworthy.[11] Laage finds that more than three-quarters of Storm's novellas rely on this method of narration. By way of contrast, the works of C. F. Meyer, Stifter, and Keller evidence recollection as a narrative device in one-third, one-fourth, and one-fifth of their fictional oeuvre, respectively. Although Laage notes a marked decrease in recollection in Storm's later writings—attributable perhaps to the introduction of more epic structures in his fiction from the mid-1870s on—it is nonetheless clear that Storm's work is unthinkable without this narrative technique.

A second aspect of recollection that contributes to the effect of realism might be best approached by reference to the obviously subjective nature of memory. At first glance, the introduction of subjectivity would seem to work against realism, and the texts we examined in the initial chapter would seem to confirm this. There we witnessed how the subjectivity of the narrative voices undermined the effect of realism by reflecting on the very fictionality of the text. By contrast, realism is usually associated with an objective portrayal of the world, or at least with the illusion of such a portrayal. The use of recollection as a formal technique apparently makes it more difficult for us to know what is really happening because our knowledge is necessarily restricted to what sticks in the mind of one individual. Because we have access to the thoughts of only the person recollecting, we can often have trouble learning the real motives and desires of others. In most cases we have to be content with the subjective assumptions and guesses of the narrator; only in rare cases, such as in Storm's *Ein Doppelgänger* (1886/87) do we ultimately have different sources of information. But the type of subjectivity inherent in recollection is only in apparent contradiction to realism; it actually contradicts only a narrow model of realism based on simplistic assumptions about third-person omniscient narrators. Hans Bracher is almost certainly correct when he observes that the subjective and the realistic in Storm's work go hand in hand. For the incompleteness, the very lack of connections, the obscurity of motives resulting from Storm's recollected accounts impress us as real *because* they make no pretense to objectivity.[12] What is essential is how the subjective narrator impresses the reader, rather than whether he or she is narrating in the first or third person. With Storm we are obviously dealing with a type of realism that has little to do with the tendency toward objectivity and totality found in the mainstream of the European movement. Here the effect of realism is produced by limitation and the concomitant authenticity of the speaking subject, rather than by the objective report of an omniscient voice. What is sacrificed in terms of "objectivity" is more than recouped in the intimacy and relative reliability of the narrative. Recollection is the formal means by which Storm overcomes or circumvents the "fiction of omniscience"[13] to create novellas that, despite and because of their restrictiveness, bear the powerful stamp of an authentic world.[14]

The structure of recollection is particularly complex in *Aquis submersus*. Each narrator relates memories from two specific periods of time. The frame's anonymous narrator, who stands presumably in the reader's present—at least that of Storm's contemporary reader—tells first of his childhood experiences in the nearby village; the first half of his account culminates in the reference to the painting of the dead boy. The second recollection, of more recent vintage, deals with the coincidental discovery of the second painting and the two notebooks, whose contents, we must presume, are then presented to us verbatim. Johannes's narrative is similarly divided into two parts and marked by the years 1661 and 1666. As an old man looking back upon his youth, he narrates the events surrounding his love affair with Katharina in the initial notebook and, in a second, his chance discovery of her and their child five years later. For the purposes of exposition, however, Storm is forced to place an additional level of memory in his account. While Johannes recalls his journey back to Herr Gerhardus's estate, he remembers a more distant past in which he was a teenage boy who had recently been adopted by his deceased father's friend (267–72). Thus we are really speaking of three time periods that Johannes recollects.[15]

In each of these recollections, as well as in those of the anonymous narrator, realism is reinforced by a variety of textual signals. We have already witnessed above how the intimacy of details from the past involves the reader in an authentic personal history. But each of the narrators also stresses repeatedly that his account is drawn from memory. While recalling his idyllic youth, the outer narrator mentions that he and his friend were allowed to do everything except climb the poplar tree. The addition of the interjected qualification, "as much as I recall" (258), is apparently without content or informational value. Like the clause "as I know now" (258), which occurs shortly afterward, its sole function is to remind the reader of the recollected nature of the narrative and hence to reemphasize the authenticity of the text. Similar phrases occur in Johannes's manuscript, for example, when he informs us of his failure to recall what Kurt says—"What Junker Kurt replied to this is no longer in my memory" (285)—or when he forgets what he himself replied to the pastor's prohibition to see Katharina, remembering only his adversary's remark: "What I myself said about this I have forgotten; but the words of the preacher burrowed themselves in my memory" (330). In each of these cases, a seemingly insignificant phrase or remark serves to notify us of the reality of the narrated events, and this is accomplished because the fiction of recollection, even when memory fails, invariably produces the effect of realism.

With these various signals of realism woven into the structure and the content of the text, it may be slightly surprising for us to encounter relatively few remarks by the artist-hero about his trade. After all, Johannes is identified rather clearly as a "realist" by virtue of his training. Several times we are reminded that he studied under Bartholomäus van der Helst (265, 307, 317), a Dutch portraitist influenced chiefly by Rembrandt and Hals. His schooling is further emphasized in a significant but isolated passage in which he comments by implication on the relationship between art and life. After discovering that he has unwittingly given his Lazarus the features of Herr Gerhardus, he wanders through the streets of Husum, observing the activities of the inhabitants: "The women of Ostenfeld with their red jackets, the girls from the island with their kerchiefs and fine silver jewelry, in between the wagons piled high with grain and on top of them the farmers in their yellow leather pants—all this certainly presented a picture for the eyes of a painter, especially when the painter, like myself, learned his trade from the Dutch" (313). Here Johannes divulges for the first and only time the realist principles on which his art is based; otherwise he is astonishingly silent about aesthetic matters.

140

Unlike the romantic artist-hero in the works of Wackenroder, Tieck, or E. T. A. Hoffmann, or the self-reflective narrators we encounter in chapter one, Johannes never enters into discourses concerning art; there is no "Kunstgespräch" in *Aquis submersus*. Instead we read about the technical and financial side of his profession. On several occasions Johannes mentions his painting equipment and its transportation (265, 280, 315, 331). Of particular importance is the lighting and setting for his portraits, which we hear about as well (282, 312). The acquisition of a frame, another practical consideration, provides him with the opportunity to visit Katharina's aunt. And finally the payment for his work as well as the various commissions he receives are also frequent topics (265, 306, 307, 311, 312). Johannes's profession is hardly distinguished from that of a banker or a shopkeeper; financial transactions and technical matters occupy his and our attention for the most part. Like Storm, whose comments on aesthetics are similarly superficial and sporadic, Johannes is perhaps best characterized by the label "bourgeois realist," which captures the anti-romantic, practical orientation of his professional activity.[16] Realism as an artistic school seems to be taken for granted by both Johannes and his creator; commentary is thus rendered superfluous. If we are going to find reflections on realism in this novella, then they will have to be sought in the indirect references to art and reality that are strewn throughout the text. Storm and Johannes will provide scant assistance in this search.[17]

More helpful than our "bourgeois realists" are the various comments on paintings, for here we can begin to understand what role art plays in the society that Johannes inhabits.[18] As far as I can tell, without exception painting has a commemorative function.[19] It serves as a reminder to the viewer, helping to recall something otherwise inaccessible. There are two variations on this theme found in the text. The first emphasizes the picture as a substitute for an absent person or object. Johannes is assigned the task of painting Katharina because she is to be married to Kurt von der Risch. "You should know," Wulf tells him, "that when a daughter from the nobility leaves home, her painting must be left behind" (275). This custom of replacing a person with a picture seems to have a middle-class variant as well. We learn later that Johannes receives a similar commission in Holland: "a merchant who was favorably disposed to me at an earlier time had reported to me that he had been waiting for me so that I might paint his portrait for his daughter, who had married and moved to The Hague" (307). Nor is this function of making a representation of something absent restricted to portraits. When Johannes first plans to marry Katharina and move away with her to more hospitable surroundings, he sketches the gables of her house and the adjoining landscape, planning to make a painting from it once he arrives in Amsterdam (301–2). In each of these cases, it is evident that realism plays an important role, if not in the production of art then at least in its intended effect. For here art is called upon to represent life, to take the place of an absent reality. The artist must be skillful and accurate enough to sustain an illusion whose function is the overcoming of a longing—either for a person or for an object. By means of a pleasant deception, art nullifies the separation between a person and a cherished possession, reminding and consoling simultaneously.

Realist art in this first variant negates space in making the absent present, but in its second variant it cancels time. It accomplishes this by virtue of its ability to capture a past moment for the present. It is thus not coincidental that the chief function of art in the novella entails the most extreme form of overcoming time, namely, in the commemoration of the dead. In these instances the deceased are infused with new life, the process of decay is halted, and nature itself is defied. The portrait gallery at the Gerhardus estate seems to have this sort of function; it keeps alive the memories of the dead for the present generation of inhabitants. The reference to the life-sized portraits (*von lebensgroßen Bildern*) (280) is a further sign of this revitalizing nature of art. The defeat of time is also reinforced by Johannes's sketch; looking at a painting of Herr Gerhardus "in the prime of his life" (*in kräftigem Mannesalter*), he endeavors to copy the features of his former patron—"but in a more youthful version" (280–81). The artist can thus even reverse the workings of time. A similar experience occurs later when Johannes studies the gallery of portraits in the pastor's church. Again the purpose of these commemorative paintings is to prolong the memory of the dead for the living by reproducing the "semblance of dust" (*Schein des Staubes*) (317), thus defying the natural process of decomposition. Indeed, Johannes's two most important commissions—the painting of his dead patron and his own drowned son—provide almost literal evidence for the ability of art to preserve the dead. "Let me try to capture the quickly decaying facial features" (274) is Johannes's reaction at the coffin of Herr Gerhardus. And when he paints his own son, he does so quickly, "as one has to paint the dead, since they will not show the same countenance again" (332). Realist art thus conquers not only separation in space but the ravages of time as well; it nullifies absence and death by re-presenting and resuscitating.

This recuperative function of art—especially its second variant—is emblematically captured in Johannes's lost masterpiece, the painting of Lazarus rising from his grave. When he receives the original commission from the wealthy distiller's wife, he tells us that the painting is meant to commemorate her dead husband (311). To this end Johannes is supposed to "resurrect" the distiller symbolically by giving Lazarus his features. Instead, however, Johannes honors his dead patron, Herr Gerhardus, by unconsciously using him as a model for the painting. The motif was not chosen by chance, of course. The distiller's wife wants her dead husband remembered in eternity. Johannes's wayward brush and guilty conscience team up to revive his patron, who seems to reproach him for his transgression against his daughter: "From the sheet the countenance of the dead man gazed at me as if in silent accusation of me, and I thought: One day he will confront you in this way for all eternity!" (313). But this biblical theme also seems to comment on art and realism in general. Christ's awakening of Lazarus from the dead, his removal of a body from the grave, his recalling of a person to life, can be seen as a reflection of Johannes's function as an artist throughout the novella. In two cases we literally find him at someone's coffin, endeavoring in a Christ-like manner to recall the dead to life. We are far from the Promethean image of the artist here, since there is never any question of original creation. Realist art does not make something new but, rather, preserves something already made. Emulating Christ the Son rather than God the Father, the artist resurrects for eternity instead of breathing in the initial breath of life. He does not create after his own image but faithfully rescues from oblivion images that are threatened by deterioration. The realist artist is Christ raising Lazarus from the dead; he is someone who recalls in the triple sense of revoking, remembering, and restoring.

The role of the artist and the function of art in *Aquis submersus* thus fit into the larger framework of recollection that is so important, as we have seen above, for producing the effect of realism. Recalling the past is not only the formal means by which the story is related but frequently a theme as well, for recollection necessarily involves the establishment of a link between the past and the present; one frequently remembers what has occurred because it bears a relationship to what is occurring or because it teaches us a lesson important for our current attitudes or behavior.[20] Thus the anonymous narrator tries

143

to break through the "mysterious silence" with which the church portrait looks upon "the living" (260); he seeks to read (*herauszulesen*) from the pastor's features the "meager message" they contain. Not until he has bridged the gap of time, recalling the past for the present, is the message complete. Indeed, the novella seems to be constructed on the tension between the transience of all earthly things and the human endeavor to overcome the ephemeral nature of reality through recollection and commemoration. Even the burning of the witch falls into this dualistic structuring principle. Her earthly demise, accentuated by her premature death, can be juxtaposed with the public spectacle so important for the pastor and the villagers. Consumed by flames, she serves as a reminder for the community; her life is in a sense prolonged beyond her physical presence on earth when, and because, she has become an example. Analogous to the pictures in the galleries, the burning of the witch is an act of commemoration meant to aid the recollection of the masses.

In order for the recollection to be effective, it must be accurate. For this reason fidelity to the original, a hallmark of realism in art, is of primary importance. If the painting is intended to replace the absent person or object, then it must resemble the real thing. All of the characters in *Aquis submersus* seem to agree at least on the mimetic function of art. The pastor, for whom commemoration and admonition are so essential in art and in religious practice, thus finds it necessary to compare Johannes's representation with the corpse of his dead son: "then with folded hands he stood there and regarded alternately the countenance on the painting and that of the tiny corpse before him, as if he were making a careful comparison" (334). He evidently wants to make sure that Johannes has faithfully captured his son's features. Indeed, Johannes himself in both his painting and his writing adheres closely to the precepts of mimesis. Like the preacher, to whom he is only apparently opposed on aesthetic issues, he values fidelity above all in art, especially since his work is primarily intended as a remembrance of things past. Even if he did not remind us of the accuracy of his written account—"and so it happened that everything had to come about as I have faithfully written down in these pages" (322)—we could assume his fidelity from his realist inclination in painting. For the sake of realism, the artist becomes a medium, a mediator between object and representation, world and sign. His own personality and wishes are reduced to nothing; he is taken up totally in faithful reproduction. At various points Johannes's creative aspirations seem to rebel against this view. Under pressure from Bas' Ursel, who notices the infatuation painted into Katharina's portrait, he justifies his work with the cliché that art entails more than the mere copy of a face (*nicht bloß die Abschrift des Gesichts*) (288). And he takes exception to Kurt's treatment of him as if he were not a living being: "as a person it seemed to him that I was not even present at all; he regarded me only like a machine by means of which a picture gets painted on the canvas" (285). Yet his own depiction of his activities as a painter seems to confirm this unflattering view. The "something" he notices in Katharina's eyes is inaccessible to him as a person: "and nonetheless it flowed through my paint brush furtively onto the canvas, so that without my being conscious of it an infatuating painting resulted" (285). We will recall that he has a similar experience when he unwittingly produces Herr Gerhardus's features on the Lazarus figure. In both cases reality becomes representation without human agency. Despite himself, Johannes therefore appears to validate the artistic biases of his adversaries—Kurt, Bas' Ursel, and the pastor. The realist artist is a mechanical producer who functions as an accurate copyist, insuring and enhancing the desired effect of recollection.

There is another, more melancholy way of looking at the reflection on realism implicit in remarks pertaining to the paintings, however, and it can be understood best by a consideration of one of the final scenes of the novella. As Johannes is painting his dead son, he continually hears noises in the adjacent room. Whenever he stops his work to listen more closely, however, the sounds seem to cease. Finally, in accord with the pastor's instructions, he lays aside brush and palette and goes into the room to eat: "As I entered, I was almost thrown back by my surprise; for Katharina stood across from me, and although she was in her black dress of mourning, she still possessed all of the magic aura, all of the happiness and love one could find in the face of a woman" (333). It is not long before he realizes his error: "what I saw here was only the image of her that I myself had formerly painted" (333). What is significant about this passage is that, first of all, Johannes's error really amounts to a self-deception. As the creator of the image he mistakenly takes for the real thing, he has unwittingly fooled himself. And not for the first time. His actions throughout the novella are marked by miscalculations and false estimations of what is permissible, what is possible, and how others will respond to him. The most obvious illustration of this occurs when he goes to Wulf directly to ask for his sister's hand in marriage. But almost all of his actions surrounding the acquisition of Katharina, from his overestimation of his physical strength while he is in Holland to the thought that he can defy social norms, turn out to be deceptions of one sort or another. He even deceives himself about his status as an artist; as the narrator informs us at the close of the novella, his hopes to be counted among the master painters of his time remain unfulfilled dreams (336). Deceived by and about his art, Johannes's notebooks are perhaps less the confession of a penitent sinner than the recollections of a man whose ability to reproduce reality is accurate to the most minute detail, but whose understanding of the workings of that reality is severely deficient. If we recall that these features are shared by Lenz in Büchner's novella, then we may want to hypothesize that they go hand in hand.

Part of Johannes's problem would seek to strike at the very root of his conception of art, for his mistaking of Katharina's portrait for her person points to the inadequacy of the realism Johannes uncritically pursues and the novella unreflectively discloses. The painting of Katharina, originally intended as a negation of separation and absence, becomes a reminder of their inevitability. In the same way the portraits of the dead not only commemorate the deceased but in their very commemorative function recall death itself.[21] Realist art is thus always characterized by this tension inherent in recollection itself. On the one hand, it preserves and brings to life; on the other hand, in this very act of preservation it emphasizes loss and absence, thus denying the very life it endeavors to prolong. In any case, the chief characteristic of realism here is that it is always pointing beyond itself to the thing it represents or pretends to represent. In painting, by virtue of its necessarily inorganic and two-dimensional quality, realism cancels itself for the sake of the real thing through which it has come into being. In literature the dead letter given voice and body by the reader directs us to something alive and meaningful. In both instances the object of art, whether painted on a canvas, composed in a manuscript, or printed in a book, is meant to be totally ignored for its own value; it always stands entirely for something else. The movement is thus not from death to life through art but, rather, from the dead signs that comprise the artwork to the elusive life they are meant to capture. Unlike the literary symbol, which is traditionally viewed as an entity unto itself while simultaneously referring us to something beyond itself, realism seems to partake of an allegorical mode. Its value is never self-contained but always bound up in its referent or message.

The allegorical nature of pictorial art that we find suggested in this scene is reflected in several other works by Storm as well. Indeed, even more than in *Aquis submersus*, art functions in other novellas solely by its ability to refer to an extra-artistic realm. In *Psyche* (1875), the only genuine *Künstlernovelle* (artist novella) in Storm's oeuvre, Franz's rescue of Maria is represented in a sculpture. Although this artwork is then admired at an exhibition, its purpose is only fulfilled when it unites the represented figures. As Franz himself remarks, it is Maria who brings his work to life.[22] One notes a similar movement from art to its fulfillment in life in *Waldwinkel* (*Corner of the Woods*, 1874) and *Eine Malerarbeit* (*A Painter's Work*, 1867/68). In the former work the painting hanging over the door to Richard's room anticipates Franziska's later escape from her idyllic prison. The two young figures wandering through the familiar landscape and the broken old man staring at them become a reality for Richard at the close of the novella.[23] Once again the painting is "realistic," but not in the sense that it is drawn from reality. Rather, its realism consists in its pointing to reality, in its reference to the world beyond art. This allegorical tendency of the pictorial reaches its climax in *Eine Malerarbeit*. Edde Brunken's two paintings, described at the beginning and the end of the novella, consist of elements included solely for their referentiality to the external world. The allegory of longing and bitterness shows Brunken's figure in the foreground at the foot of a statue of Venus. From this position he observes a young pair of lovers wandering through a beautiful garden. In the second painting, where renunciation and "contentment" are the theme, the positions of the figures are simply reversed. Now the cavalier and his sweetheart lounge at the feet of the goddess of love, and the representation of the deformed artist sits on a bench, observing the activities of the two "in merry coziness."[24] Edde has learned to place his own ego and its desires in the background, and this moral, allegorically depicted in the change in composition, is likewise the lesson he has learned in the intervening four years. Despite— or perhaps because of—his own pretensions to formal excellence, depiction in Storm's works seems to be always directing us to the represented rather than to representation. The value of a simulated reality does not lie in the simulation but in the reality itself and the message this reality is meant to convey. Realistic portrayal in the pictorial art forms is thus disclosed in these texts as an allegory that, as the etymological root of the word indicates, speaks of something else (allo + agoreuein).

The only figure in *Aquis submersus* who seems to appreciate the double nature of realistic painting, as commemoration and allegory, is the pastor. We learn of his attitude toward art in two places: in his initial encounter with Johannes at the church and at his son's coffin. Indeed, his views on art occupy more space in the novella than Johannes's. They consist in essence of three principles. First, art should accurately represent the real world. We have already seen that the pastor seems to compare the features of his dead child with Johannes's portrait, and this concern for verisimilitude accords well with his previous statements. When asked why he chose to have the image of the Virgin Mary removed from the church, he replies, "The features of the mother of the Saviour have not been handed down to us" (318). Evidently the artist in his view is not supposed to exercise his fantasy at all; like Kurt in an earlier section of the novella, the pastor seems to adhere to a view of the artist as a machine through which reality becomes recorded. If the artist has no access to the original reality, as in the case of Mary, then he would commit an aesthetic as well as a religious sin to create on his own accord. But this adherence to a stiflingly narrow definition of realism is also accompanied by an insistence that art have a moral purpose. Thus the pastor objects to having his own portrait painted because this would be an idle and vainglorious prolongation of what is meant to decay and disappear; or, as he phrases it, "It is not my intention that the semblance of dust should last after the breath of God has departed" (317). His son should be immortalized, by contrast, because *his* portrait, like the burning of the witch at the stake, can serve as a warning: "May it admonish people that everything is dust in the face of the bony hand of death!" (330). Mere commemoration is insufficient and may even be frivolous; art must also have a message. Its mode is thus doubly allegorical, first, in the sense that it always refers beyond itself to the real world, and second, because the represented object must teach a lesson in and for the real world. Finally, despite its realism, art must avoid an appeal to the senses. Just as the artist is a medium through which reality becomes represented, so too the senses are only the vehicles by which the represented reality becomes message. The pastor's apparent condemnation of art—"art has always whored with the world" (318)—can be read not only as a blanket censure but also as a factual and, from his perspective, unfortunate statement of necessity. Art has an effect through sensual stimulation and thus implicitly has to do with this world. If works of art provide only an arousal of the senses, if they are "wet nurses of sensual pleasure" (*Säugammen der Sinnenlust*) (318), then they do not fulfill their purpose. Only when the senses are subordinated to the other-worldly, only when the sensual, in other words, reminds the viewer of its own insubstantiality, does art become acceptable for the zealous preacher.

Johannes apparently misunderstands the pastor's opinions on art. He is not simply an opponent (*Widersacher*) of his noble trade; nor does he necessarily contradict himself when he insists on commemorating his son as a warning for the community. As we have seen above, he is primarily opposed to art that does not deliver the proper message. But while Johannes's misconstruing of the pastor's aesthetic views is an error without consequences, his violation of this principled position contributes to his tragic downfall. For Johannes's relationship to art is always characterized by the sensual, which the pastor repudiates, and part of his difficulty results from the ready transformation of the sensual in art to the sensuous in his relations with Katharina. When he paints her at the Gerhardus estate, we have already witnessed how he is almost hypnotized by her beauty. The result is the unconscious creation of an "infatuating picture" (*sinnberückend Bild*) (285), the same painting that later deceives his senses in the pastor's house. His sinful single night with Katharina is also the consequence of his inability to control his sensual nature. In this night of illicit love, we have the real-life counterpart to the pastor's remark about "whoring with the world." Johannes the artist gives himself over to sensuous pleasures here, thus violating the role of art sanctioned by his adversary. The same sequence of painting and sensual involvement is then reversed in the second notebook. Johannes, irresistibly attracted to the sound of Katharina's voice (326), again loses control of his senses ("but my senses aimed only at the woman" [*aber meine Sinne zieleten nur auf das Weib*] [328]) in Katharina's arms. The result of their first encounter was the creation of the child; this time their passionate involvement causes its death. To complete this structure of reversal, Johannes must confront again the painting of Katharina that he had created. Whereas his first viewing of the portrait is marked by the presence of his love and his hope for the future, his second confrontation with his own work is characterized by eternal separation and despair. In both cases, however, he is taken in by his senses, and this improper relationship to art frames, as it were, his two fundamentally "sinful" and sensual encounters with the reality portrayed in his painting.

The passionate, sensual Johannes belongs to the past, however. He is the former self recollected by an old man who has, perhaps inadvertently, adopted the system of artistic values prescribed by his quondam adversary, the pastor. His acceptance of these values in his life is demonstrated most definitively by the inscription found on the stone above the door to his house:

> Geliek as Rook un Stoof verswindt,
> Also sind ock de Minschenkind. (311)

> (Just like smoke and dust disappear, so also does every human being.)

Johannes had first noticed this apothegm on an old house, and on his travels he thought of it often. It served, in short, as a reminder for him of his former hubris. When the house was torn down, he rescued from the rubble the stone on which these words were transcribed. It is not insignificant that he here preserves an object—and as a poem of sorts, it is a work of art too—whose message is the impossibility of preserving,[25] nor that he reinforces this view, writing that the stone should be an admonition to him and to others concerning the "futility of earthly life" (*Nichtigkeit des Irdischen*) (311). This is precisely the lesson he could have learned from the pastor: the recollection of things from this world should remind us of the transience of external reality. Translated into a theory of art, this melancholy message becomes the paradox of recalling the sensual—a necessary element in art—to condemn the sensual. And from the two examples we have of his later artistic undertakings, it seems that Johannes has incorporated this paradox successfully into his own work. The first illustration is the painting hanging in the room in which Johannes wrote and the anonymous narrator reads. Although still adhering to basic tenets of realism in capturing the features of Herr Gerhardus and his drowned grandson, Johannes has learned that commemoration of the dead must be combined with a moral for the living, something this particular painting, which serves as a daily reminder to its penitent creator, accomplishes admirably. The second example, of course, is the manuscript itself, which is likewise realistic, commemorative, and admonitory. In each case realist art denies its own sensual quality by pointing to a world to which it does not belong and by proclaiming the nullity of the world to which it must belong.

This lesson concerning the relationship between art and life appears to be self-evident for the anonymous narrator, who sits in the same room—perhaps in the very chair—in which the words he reads were written. Like Johannes he showed no understanding for this aesthetics of abnegation in his youth. In recalling his childhood, in fact, he tells us that he was attracted by the very image that the pastor seems determined to banish from all churches. Most of the faces on the alter showing the Passion of Christ appear strange and wild to the boy: "in contrast to them the gentle face of Mary on the ground in front of the cross was consoling" (260). But later in his life, we find that he too has learned to appreciate the somber inscription that he hardly noticed in his youth (263). He has thus also undergone a transformation similar to Johannes's, and the persistent identification of his physical position with that of his seventeenth-century counterpart serves to reinforce their similarity in opinions as well.[26] In a certain sense we could even say that both narrators relate the same self-defeating story next to, or beneath, their tales of commemoration, sensuality, and admonition. By faithfully bringing the past to life, by mimicking Christ at Lazarus's grave, and by announcing realism as recollection, they both ultimately bear witness to the significance, as well as to the ultimate futility, of their own artistic gesture.

6

THE NARRATOR OF REALISM:
Orientalism in C. F. Meyer's *Der Heilige*

The oriental subject has the advantage of
independence. Nothing is certain. As
indefinite as the substance of the oriental is,
the character can be just as indefinite, free,
and independent. What for us is legality and
moral standards (*Sittlichkeit*) is there in the
state as well—in a substantial, natural way,
not in subjective freedom. Conscience does
not exist and neither does morality (*Moral*).
Georg Wilhelm Friedrich Hegel,
Lectures on the History of Philosophy

To this point we have witnessed two seminal fea-
tures about the poetics of realist texts. First, they call their own foundations into question by revealing aporias at the basis of realism itself.
We saw this self-destructive message delivered in both Lenz's "Kunstgespräch" and in the remarks about painting in *Aquis submersus*. Realism
discloses itself as an inconsistent artistic doctrine, and this very inconsistency—and the attempt to cover it up—led us to be suspicious of
what the text is concealing behind the realist façade. Second, we have
noticed that the implicit reflections on realism open onto ideological
spaces in which a moral code of both repression and renunciation is
evident. The task of remaining faithful to the external world, of adhering to the norms putatively imposed by reality, seems to entail the
simultaneous ideological rejection of actions and thoughts that would
threaten the restrictive ethics of the social order. Normed discourse

152

and normed ethics appear to go hand in hand, reinforcing each other. The lack of self-reflection or self-consciousness in the realist text corresponds to an apparently parallel unquestioning attitude toward the reality to be mirrored. In this and the next chapter, we shall see that the normed discourse that produces the effect of realism has other, perhaps more pernicious, implications. The social order can be threatened not only from within—by sexual desire, by repressed memories, or by the transgression of class boundaries—but also from without by groups or individuals that are perceived as destructive, parasitic, or foreign. The internal danger signaled by the sensual in each of society's members is complemented by an external threat that similarly endangers normal functioning. Otherness, that which announces its difference in either a poetic or an ideological fashion, must be warded off by the realist text.

In order to examine the xenophobic nature of realism, let us choose a slightly different starting point. We have seen in previous chapters that the works of bourgeois realism can generally be distinguished from the literature directly preceding and following by the absence of direct commentary on the relationship between text and reality. In contrast to romanticism the tendency during the last five or six decades of the nineteenth century is to separate the actual composing of literature from theorizing about it. Thus, although there is no dearth of commentary in journals, letters, and diaries concerning questions of aesthetics, these discussions are rarely incorporated into the texts themselves. Concomitant with this dichotomizing of theory and creative endeavor is a literature of closed forms, conventional narratives, and "objective" portrayal. Reflections on the writing process or on the nature of realism itself are usually marginal occurrences, such as the "Kunstgespräch," or else they must be adduced from indirect evidence, as I have done in the past three chapters.

But exceptions to this general rule do occur, and it behooves us to consider these texts as well. For the most part, reflections on realism seem to crop up at the borders of the movement, either in early works still influenced by late romanticism or in later prose anticipating the twentieth century. In Wilhelm Raabe's first novel, *Die Chronik der Sperlingsgasse* (*The Chronicle of Sparrow Alley*, 1856), for example, one easily detects the author's indebtedness to the playful reflexivity of Heine's early prose. Not only do we find the narrator occasionally adopting and then dropping personae, as the narrator of *Buch Le Grand* does, but we also get a glimpse of the process by which this putative non-novel is composed: "I have given it considerable thought as I folded this paper, and I also wrote it down: the contents will not have much coherence. I linger on a minute and then jump over a year; I paint images and supply no plot; I break off without letting the old tone fade out; I do not want to instruct, I want to forget. I am not writing a novel!"[1] We do not have to take this statement at face value, of course; just as in Heine's text, there may well be more coherence in the apparent confusion than the narrator cares to admit. The significance of this passage, however, lies in the reflection on how one might go about putting together a work of fiction so that it appears to be authentic. In implicitly preferring the subjective chronicle form to the more usual structure of a novel, Raabe's narrator gives us some insight into the complex relationship between composition and the reality it is supposed to capture.

The teacher in Theodor Storm's *Schimmelreiter* (*Rider of the White Horse*, 1889), the last novella he completed before his death, provides us with a similar, albeit more penetrating and skeptical, comment on this relationship. As the narrator of Hauke Haien's rise and fall, he assigns himself the task of separating fact from fiction, of relating to his eager auditor the reality rather than the myth. The ability of narrative to convey and contain truth is thus his central concern. But the teacher's version, we learn, is only one possible way to tell the story. Antje Vollmers, the elderly housekeeper of the current *Deichgraf* (official in charge of the dikes), would present the tale differently. Whether her account would be more accurate is impossible to adjudicate. Indeed, the suggestion is that accuracy and fidelity to reality have little relevance in the face of such obscure and awesome histories. The teacher, therefore, although he displays "a supercilious smile," does not claim privilege for his version of the events. With reference to Antje Vollmers, he states at the outset: "On this point we are not entirely of the same opinion";[2] and after he concludes his account, he again returns to this issue: "Of course the housekeeper of our Deichgraf would have told it [the story] to you differently."[3] Truth in narration is not unitary but perspectival; there are various valid opinions about what happened. Narrative does not provide access to the real events, but rather reflects a subjective impression, an "opinion," that may differ from that of another narrator. Confronted with this difficulty, the Storm persona listening to the tale understandably encourages the teacher not to try to eliminate the superstition from his account: "I have to ask you not to leave that out . . . . Just trust me to be able to separate the wheat from the chaff!"[4] In a world of varying perspectives, he is simply claiming his own right to a decision on the convoluted issue of fact and fiction.

As far as I can determine, similar reflections on realism, truth, and narrative can be found in the works of only one other author traditionally associated with nineteenth-century realism: Conrad Ferdinand Meyer. Once again we are not dealing with frequent occurrences; in the majority of his novellas, the relationship between the story being told and the manner in which it is told is taken for granted.[5] The two major exceptions, *Die Hochzeit des Mönchs* (*The Marriage of the Monk*, 1883) and *Der Heilige* (*The Saint*, 1879), are therefore all the more noteworthy. In the former novella Dante in exile at the court of Cangrande must tell a story as "payment" for sitting around the fire with his host and the other guests. The poet's decision to relate the characters in his tale of the renegade monk to the people in his presence enables him to play off the intrigues in Verona against the "fictional" events. While Dante thus uses the narrative to comment on the immediate reality around him, the reader is able to see how he is cleverly piecing together the story. The frequent interruptions in the narrative flow, sometimes by a listener but most often by Dante himself, also provide the reader with an insight into the process of telling. At one point Dante is corrected after he relates "false" information; at another point he is forced to correct a continuation of his tale that did not conform to his plan. Most frequently, however, he is called upon to justify or clarify a point in his story that has jarred the sensibility of his host. We are told at one such interruption: "His fable lay before him, spread out in all its fullness; but his disciplined mind selected and simplified."[6] Since we are exposed to this process of selection as well as to the ironic cat-and-mouse game that Dante plays with his listeners and that informs the course of the narration, the manner in which the story unfolds is also partially opened for our perusal. If this novella is less interesting for our purposes than *Der Heilige*, it is only because Dante's narrative is so consciously fictional. When asked at the beginning of the novella: "Are you going to tell us a true story, dear Dante, according to documents? Or a saga from the folk tradition, or an invention from your own crowned head?," he replies: "I will develop my story from an epitaph." Although he is not going to ignore reality—the characters in his tale are modeled, after all, on real persons, and Ezzelino, who plays a major role in the plot, is a historical figure—it is evident that he has opted for the third alternative. Truth in this tale is related to internal consistency and probability, and not to correspondence with external events. This novella thus comments throughout on the process of narrative, but only marginally on the ability of the narrative to capture that elusive quantity we call reality.

By contrast the self-reflexive structure of *Der Heilige* comments on this very issue. Again the frame is an important factor in the self-referentiality of the text. Indeed, the major reason for introducing Hans der Armbruster (maker of crossbows) as the narrator of Thomas Becket's biography and the Canon Burkhard as his auditor is to question conventional notions of narrative and truth, and thereby to comment on the problematic manner in which reality is reflected in texts (or oral reports). Burkhard lures Hans into his room because of his dissatisfaction with the accounts of Becket's life he has previously encountered. He expects to hear something different from what has been recorded on the parchment, the officially sanctioned vita of the new saint. It would be an exaggeration to state that he does not believe the official version promulgated by the church; at various points, as we shall see, he demonstrates his faith in the written word. But he seems to know that these facts do not represent the whole truth. What Burkhard wants, therefore, is more than the basic story; he wants the details, the behind-the-scenes account, authentic information. At first glance there seems to be no one better suited to supply him with this than Hans, for this aging and unassuming maker of crossbows was an eye witness to all of the most important events in Becket's career, both as statesman and archbishop. Standing behind his master's chair, delivering messages from Henry to Becket, or simply overhearing important conversations, Hans is in a unique position to relate the facts. Meyer has enhanced Hans's ability to function as an authority even further by making his life—somewhat artificially, most readers will feel —overlap in several places with Becket's.[7] Both have religious training, serve the king of England, and are acquainted with the class and racial differences of twelfth-century England at firsthand. Meyer even allows Hans to learn his trade in Moorish Spain so that he can understand Arabic, the language Becket seems to prefer for private matters, and acquire some familiarity with Moslem customs. Hans is thus established as the perfect narrator for this story precisely because he has unmediated access to the truth.[8] The authenticity of his account, apparently guaranteed by his personal experience and qualifications, is both the feature that attracts Burkhard to him and the source of his—at times—dogmatic insistence that his narrative is completely veracious.

Anyone reading this novella, however, can hardly fail to notice that Hans's authority as the guardian of the truth is constantly being undermined.[9] In the first place, it is fairly obvious that his interest in telling the story goes beyond relating Becket's activities. The very fact that he spends so much time at the beginning and at the close of his account with autobiographical details reveals something about his possible motives. His stated reason for including this information—"my poor career cannot be separated from that of the saint and of the king" (17)[10]—is hardly convincing. Parts of his life story are, of course, essential for establishing his credibility as narrator,[11] but too much time is spent with the particulars of Hans's life for this to be the only reason. Hans's admission of partial guilt in the deaths of Grace and Becket, the rather sharp rebuff he receives from the archbishop before he is murdered, and his feelings of relief after the conclusion of the story ("Telling the story relieved him like a kind of confession" [139]) indicate that his narrative is motivated by penance and self-justification as much as by love for the truth.[12] But even if we could not detect a cathartic undercurrent in his tale, we would still have to question the accuracy of the account. Since Hans is not only an observer and reporter but also an agent and accomplice, he sees events from a certain perspective. As Hilde's lover he could well harbor contempt for the Normans. As Henry's loyal servant he has sympathy for the king's point of view. And as an apparently repentant sinner when he tells the story, he may well have acquired a different understanding for Becket's actions and martyrdom. We can never be quite certain which of these biases is operating when he is speaking, but it is nonetheless not difficult to agree with his own comment when he is questioned for sympathizing with the Saxons: "Sir, passing judgment is like shooting arrows; it all depends on the point of view" (24).

This perspectival relativizing of Hans's story and its truth is persistently reflected in the novella. One of the chief ways this is accomplished is by the introduction of rival narratives that supplement and comment on the central account. The first and most important of these is the "fairy tale" of Prince Mondschein (Prince Moonlight), which Hans heard in Spain. It relates the story of a mysterious and anonymous foreigner who wins the favor of the caliph in Cordova and assists him, without bloodshed, to become the most powerful Moorish king. As a sign of his gratitude, the caliph gives Mondschein his sister in marriage, but she dies while giving birth to a daughter. Envied by the courtiers because of his favor, Mondschein discovers a cabal against him. He exposes the conspirators, but intercedes for their lives. When the caliph nonetheless delivers the heads of the plotters to Mondschein in sacks, the latter leaves the kingdom with his daughter; thereafter the caliph suffers losses in both power and happiness. This tale obviously functions, on one level, as part of Becket's biography, although neither the reader nor Burkhard realize this when it is first related. Later, however, we easily recognize several important elements in the archbishops life: most notably the existence of a daughter and the exposure to Arabic customs. It also serves, of course, as an introduction to Becket's character. The enchanting oratorical skills, the mastery of intellectual games, the political shrewdness, the paleness, the hatred of bloodshed and violence, the apparent mercy shown to enemies— all of these characteristics are shared by Mondschein and Becket. In a sense, then, this fairy tale both anticipates and begins the narrative proper by supplying information about Becket's pre-English activities and by outlining the major qualities associated with his enigmatic personality.

It also functions, however, as a comment on narrative and its tenuous relationship to truth.[13] One way that it does this is by prefiguring all of the major events in the conflict between Henry and Becket. In both instances a clever and loyal counselor helps his ruler to maneuver into a position of extreme power. In both cases the king showers favor upon his faithful servant. An exceptionally ruthless act, however, destroys the bond that had once existed, and the demise of the ruler is attributable in both Mondschein's and Becket's story to the disintegration of the relationship. Furthermore, one has no trouble recognizing the Fauconbridge episode in the tale of the conspirators. Envy as a motive for intrigue, an apparent absence of vengefulness on the part of Becket/Mondschein, and the certain destruction of the offenders are common to both occurrences. But if there is a parallel between the events in a fairy tale, the term Hans repeatedly uses to characterize this embedded narrative (*Märchen* or *Märe*), and the happening witnessed at firsthand, then not only does the status of the putative fiction become more real, but the purportedly real events appear more fictional. It is apparent in hindsight that Hans's oral report to Burkhard is a repetition of the very same fairy tale—with more detail, of course, with a different setting, and with slightly altered characters in the chief roles. Structurally, however, the similarity between the two narratives is too close to be coincidental, and the question that lingers in the reader's mind is whether Hans has been, or even could have been, more truthful than his Arab counterpart.

The similarity between the fairy tale and the "factual account" is further underscored by the similarity between the anonymous Moor and Hans. Just as Hans feels entitled to claim authenticity for his account because of his personal contact with Becket, so does the Arab narrator: "In the fervor of his narration the teller of the fairy tale swore that he had been personally acquainted with Prince Mondschein and had often greeted him in the square of Cordova, crossing his arms, humbly, over his chest" (23). Both thus relate from memory—we learn that Mondschein departed less than ten years prior to the telling of the fairy tale—events that they swear to have witnessed. But the similarity of the narrators is smuggled into the text by a linguistic trick as well. It is certainly not fortuitous that the humble greeting of the Arab is accompanied by the phrase *mit über der Brust gekreuzten Armen* (crossing his arms over his chest); the words *Armen* and *Brust* in this phrase echo the occupational title Hans has acquired (*Armbruster*). Indeed, since the setting of the main story is England, it is perhaps not too farfetched to consider the crossed arms as an allusion to Hans's favorite weapon, the crossbow.

Despite the obvious signs of identification, however, Hans goes out of his way to discredit his counterpart and, in doing this, tries to establish the privilege of his own narrative. Even before we hear the story of Prince Mondschein, Hans emphasizes that it is a fairy tale that is neither better nor worse than the other stories the Arab told. Thus from the very outset it is relegated to the realm of fiction and fantasy. After relating the story, he again underlines the fictitious nature of this account, informing Burkhard that despite assurances of truth, one has to doubt its veracity: "He was convinced that he was telling the truth, but I did not believe him completely; for the Moors, reverend sir, lie with more sincerity than we do because their vivid powers of imagination mislead them into confusing what didn't happen with what did" (23). Here Hans endeavors to distinguish sharply between his story and the Moor's. The inference is clear: he is able to recognize and exclude fantastic occurrences; the Arab is not. In the next paragraph, of course, Hans manages to cast doubt upon his own evaluation. Before his departure from Spain, it seems, he heard the Arab tell the same story "without any noticeable embellishment or alteration" (24). For Hans this is odd, since he apparently assumes that the ability to repeat a tale in the same manner signals a fidelity to reality. But on the whole, the distinction between a faithful account and an Oriental fiction is upheld throughout; the repetition is only surprising because Hans presumes that, in contrast to his own, the Arab's claims to truth are spurious.

One of the ironic twists in the novella later finds Hans on the receiving end of disbelief when Burkhard accuses him of fantastic insertions. Hans the listener is skeptical of the tale he hears, but when he is the teller, his auditor slips into the role he himself had assumed with regard to the Moor. This switching of roles among the Arab, Hans, and Burkhard thus becomes another moment in the relativizing of the truth of narrative. The reader may be able to see through Hans's transparent debunking of his counterpart, but precisely because we sense that Hans is not totally disingenuous, we are never quite able to separate out truth from fiction, to arrive at the reality that both narratives swear they have captured.

The two other rival narratives we encounter during the course of the novella are treated in a slightly different fashion by Hans. The first competitor comes in the form of a ballad sung by the golden-haired Hilde, the beautiful daughter of the Saxon bow-maker who is later abducted by the licentious Norman Gui Malherbe. Overcome by the recollection of Hilde and his love for her, Hans begins to sing the ballad for Burkhard: "In London was Young Beichen born / He longed strange countries for to see—" (26). But the latter, becoming impatient because of what he deems another digression, interrupts. Hans then reveals that this song is really to the point: it tells of the birth of a saint from the womb of a Saracen woman. It is, again, a duplicate of the story Hans himself is about to tell; and, if he had been permitted to continue his recitation, it would have anticipated his own narrative and perhaps made it superfluous. Here, too, we are dealing with legend, this time without author, source, and reassurances of veracity. Perhaps this is the reason that Hans does not discredit this account. Instead he substitutes his narrative for what the lyrics of Hilde's song would have related. In the process he covers the same ground that the fairy tale covered as well. To ensure Burkhard that his version is truthful—he is accused of fabricating as wildly as his Arab counterpart—he resorts to the familiar authority of the eyewitness. He himself, of course, was not yet in England when the heathen

Grace sought her beloved Gilbert Becket. But Hilde's father, who is "a precise and matter-of-fact man" (27), is able to vouch for what seems to be the stuff of legend. Accounting for Becket's early years is somewhat more difficult, and Hans is dependent on the rumors and stories that circulate in the bowman's shop. From these he pieces together the early career of Becket and manages, without Burkhard's notice, to recount in two sentences the Mondschein tale without the fantastic trappings. Thus the two legendary anticipatory narratives are furtively incorporated into the central account, while Hans, relying apparently solely on the solid testimony of firsthand observation, spins his tale in a fashion that is at once more linear, more familiar, and perhaps therefore more credible for his listener.

The final rival narrative is more troublesome for Hans since it too tells its story in a straightforward manner. But the parchment that Burkhard has in his possession is, as we have already noted, only an official version of sainthood; it is read for the edification of the local nuns at mealtime and contributed to the declaration of a holiday on the anniversary of Becket's death. In short, it is a piece of clerical propaganda. Still Hans has more respect for this account at first than Burkhard. He cites it as support for the Moorish origins of Becket found in the ballad, although he himself apparently never has seen the parchment. But as his tale progresses, it becomes clear that he strays from, or even contradicts, the official chronicle of events, while Burkhard, who at first sought something different from the parchment, clings to this simpler and less ambiguous version. His most significant departure from the parchment—and Meyer's from Thierry—is the story of Becket's daughter. Indeed, the special value of this episode is that it has been hitherto untold. "Now I come to tell you of a secret injustice that can be found in none of the chronicles. But it was the shovel that dug the graves of Sir Thomas and Sir Henry, one after the other" (43). In surpassing the chronicle in knowledge, Hans introduces motivation and, one presumes at this point, clarity into the sequence of otherwise incomprehensible events. We shall return to this point a bit later.

Although Burkhard does not object at this point—how can he since the story of Grace does not contradict the known facts?—he does protest later when he notices a discrepancy between the parchment and the oral account. Hans claims that the news of the excommunication of the bishop of York and the vassalage of Henry's son reached the king on the same day. According to the dates on the border of the chronicle, however, these events were separated by an entire year. Hans's reply endeavors to rescue his account by establishing two methods for measuring time:

> "Do not bother me with trivial numbers!" the Armbruster said with some resentment. Then immediately aware of the impoliteness of his words, he added to soften them: "It makes a difference whether a human being is still in the midst of time and everyday work, or whether death has closed his book of life. Once the last grain of sand has rolled down, man steps out of the sequence of days and hours and stands forth as a complete and distinct being at the bar of judgment, before God and man. Both are right and wrong—your chronicle and my memory, it with its letters on parchment, I with the signs engraved in my heart." (105–6)

Although his justification for the discrepancy is formulated in eschatological terms, it is not difficult to read it as a reflection on the preceding narrative and its relationship to truth. In the first place, it gives some insight into the construction of effective plots. The dramatic effect is greatest when the two events occur simultaneously; the "heartfelt" impact on auditors and readers is what concerns the storyteller most. But Hans's admission of "right and wrong" (*Recht und Unrecht*) also casts renewed doubt on the previous narrative. Indeed, it questions the ability of any account, whether a seemingly straightforward chronicle or an eyewitness report, to reflect faithfully a reality external to it. Reality consists of more than just numbers, dates, and facts; it also includes emotions, intentions, and motives—in short, items that are inaccessible to observers and often even to the person experiencing them.

This seems to be the point of the second conflict between the oral report and the chronicle toward the end of the novella. At issue is why Henry flayed himself at Becket's grave. Burkhard recounts the official version: "'According to the credible testimony of my chronicle,' the canon observed pensively, 'the king did indeed scourge himself at the grave of Saint Thomas of Canterbury, but not without shrewd and worldly purposes; for he wanted support in the conflict with his sons and was trying to win back the hearts of his Saxons, who had deserted him'" (137–38). The two key words here are "credible" (*glaubwürdig*) and "intentions" (*Absichten*). There is no dispute over Henry's actions, but rather over what lies behind them. The chronicle

162

sets up a narrative structure within which the intentions of its main characters are believable. But Hans is able to supply a different interpretation precisely because his narrative has had a different trajectory from the very outset. "By the thorn-crowned head of God, I tell you that no man has ever prayed more sincerely than King Henry during the hour when he covered the stone feet of the saint with kisses and tears!" (138). From the foregoing sequence of events and Hans's previous explanations, this too seems to be a valid statement; but from the internal commentary we have been examining, it would seem that there is no way to decide which interpretation is correct. Here too both may be "right and wrong." Although it may be possible to agree on what has occurred, on the "brute facts," as it were, why it has occurred and how its occurrence has an effect are impossible to ascertain.

The inclusion of rival narratives thus serves to undercut Hans's reliability as a narrator and, in general, to question the ability of narrative to tell what really happens. The very activity of telling seems to preclude reality, since telling establishes on its own logic a teleological movement whose relationship to reality is problematic. Hans winds up revealing the precarious relationship of his story to the truth. His repeated assurances concerning the fidelity and accuracy of his account ring hollow by the end of the novella. It is perhaps not coincidental, therefore, that at the very center of this work Hans is forced to confess that he may have strayed a bit in relating his tale. Burkhard interrupts after Hans has told of the conversation between Henry and Becket concerning the candidates for archbishop. The canon is obviously offended by the affronts to religious propriety; he cannot believe that a future saint, even if he is not particularly inclined to him, would have spoken so crudely about filling this vacant church office. His accusation is thus that Hans has made this up: "That part is an invention of your own!" (*Das kommt aus deinem Eigenem!*) (82). Thrown into the defensive, Hans is typically equivocal in his response. First he assures his auditor that he has faithfully rendered the spirit of the chancellor's conversation even if he no longer recalls the precise words he used. Then, however, he admits that he may have included his own opinions as well: "But it is not impossible that something of my own may have crept in." From now on, though, he will stick to the facts. "But even assuming that my story may have turned slightly inaccurate, from now on it will be genuine and incontestable as the gospel" (83). With these words he is able to placate the indignant canon temporarily.

Although this reassurance pacifies Burkhard, it can hardly satisfy the reader. In the first place, Hans is guilty of shifting ground once too often. While he first claims fidelity to the spirit of the words and then concedes the possibility of his own contribution, he finishes by casting doubt on his entire enterprise. His whole story may have crossed the boundary from fact to uncertainty (*ins Ungewisse geraten*).[14] Furthermore, his reassuring comparison—his story will now be as genuine as the gospel—is hardly persuasive to the modern reader, and it is almost certain that Meyer here, as so often throughout the novella, has employed a touch of irony.[15] There is also a lesson to be learned from this comparison, however. Hans selects the Bible precisely because the canon will consider it unshakeable truth. It would seem, then, that not only does the generation of narrative depend on perspective, as we have seen above, but also its reception. What seems likely to the canon in the twelfth century is not convincing for the more skeptical modern reader in the late nineteenth century.

The same point seems to be made in another fashion later in the novella when the bishop of York reports to Henry about Becket's arrival in England: "As one celebrating a triumph, with horse and chariot and a long procession of Saxons!" (124). The more sober account given by the cleric who accompanies him relates a more modest version of the same events. "That was the simple truth. It had been told to him as the truth [*getreulich*] by a member of the primate's staff who was under obligations to him." But the bishop also claims that his information stems from actual observation: "I have it from eyewitnesses!" (125). In this case, although Hans places more faith in the cleric's account, there is no way to decide who is correct. That Henry believes the bishop has to do with his predisposition, his horizon of expectations of what the truth is. In an analogous fashion the canon is more likely to believe an account that is as authentic as the Gospels or that is written on parchment by church officials. The point this implicit commentary seems to be making is that the perspective of the recipient, whether reader or auditor, is an essential factor in the linking of narrative and truth. If we distrust Hans's reassurances to Burkhard, therefore, it is not only because of his appeal to the Gospels, which we may recognize as "fiction," but also because from our reading perspective we have learned to be alert to the type of tergiversation so pervasive in Hans's account.

The problematic relationship between narrative, truth, and reality so often thematized by Hans would seem to relate to Meyer's own

creative activity as well, particularly to the manner in which he deals
with his historical sources.[16] It is generally accepted that the novella
is based on Augustin Thierry's *Histoire de la conquête de l'Angleterre*
(1825); indeed, some passages of *Der Heilige* are almost verbatim translations of the historian's work. It is also likely that Meyer drew from
some of the Latin chronicles available to him. In a letter to Alfred
Meißner on 27 May 1880, he agrees with the estimation "1/3 from
the chronicle, 1/3 Thierry, 1/3 belonging to me."[17] It would be unfair
and a bit peculiar to reproach Meyer for adding his own material,
for mixing fiction into the historical record, even if he did characterize
himself somewhat immodestly as "the outstanding representative of
the historical novella and the portrayer of world-historical powers."[18]
Obviously, Meyer, unlike his narrator Hans, nowhere promises fidelity
to reality. We have no reason to expect that this novella or any of
his works will correspond to historical facts—whatever that would
mean for a novella. Nonetheless, it seems to me that Meyer's adaptation
of history has something to do with the process of narration that Hans
is caught up in. In creating a conscious fiction, it is clear that Meyer
had to select his materials carefully to achieve the greatest effect. Sometimes this meant condensing events that occurred over a few years
into a much shorter span of time; sometimes it involved portraying
actions and intentions of characters without any basis in written historical accounts. But Meyer must have also realized that the historians
and chroniclers whom he had read had also included dubious, legendary, or apocryphal information, and that they too were involved in
a process of arranging and selecting that was informed by interests
and perspectives. It must have been clear to him, to cite only one
example, that the story of Becket's origins, which Thierry included
and he adopted, was not based on historical fact. It would be going
too far to assert that Meyer had recognized and fully appreciated the
nature of narrative as it limits and allows historical writing, as we have
been shown most recently in the work of Hayden White,[19]and it would
be wrong to think that he saw no essential difference between his activity as a creative writer and that of a historian. Nonetheless, the free
mixture of truth and fiction—indeed, at times the inability to separate
the two—is both the salient feature of Meyer's method and one of
the most important lessons in Hans's reflections.[20]

Up until now I have argued that Hans persistently undermines
his own repeated claims to tell the truth, and that his indifference
to fact and fiction is paralleled in Meyer's own process of composition.

Narrative is found to be incommensurate with the reality it pretends to reflect; an uncertainty or ambiguity necessarily accompanies the text. Now it is not difficult to see that the self-reflexive moments in the novella and the consequences we have drawn from them have something to do with the central issue in the secondary literature on *Der Heilige*, namely, Becket's ambiguity.[21] The connection between the self-reflexive narrative and characterization is, I think, twofold. On one level the two are related by analogy. Just as there are not unproblematic, straightforward narratives, so too there is no simple manner to comprehend character. The ambiguity of Becket's actions, motives, and statements parallels the epistemological ambiguity that riddles Hans's endeavor to relate his story. But the uncertainty of narrative in its relation to truth also shapes and is, in turn, shaped by the enigmatic nature of the central figure. Since the veracity of Hans's account is continually being challenged from within and without, an additional moment of doubt and uncertainty is injected into the already ambiguous personality. An illustration of this occurs in the passage cited above when the canon accuses Hans of putting his own thoughts into Becket's mouth. Since the Armbruster equivocates when he replies, we cannot be certain whether the future saint actually spoke so crassly about church matters or not. If he did, we might be inclined to see his conversion as a dramatic change in attitude—provided, of course, that we find his conversion sincere in the first place. If he did not speak in this manner, however, then we might give more credence to the signs of piety occasionally reported before his conversion. In this fashion the undermining of truth in narrative conditions the ambiguity of the character, and Becket's enigmatic nature, in turn, introduces further uncertainty into the narrative. Every time Hans or the reader has to guess what is really going on in Becket's mind, another element of obscurity is infused into the narrated chain of events.

This mutual conditioning of narrative and character is perhaps most evident in connection with motivation. If we read the novella as the story of Becket's revenge, then we will probably see him as a haughty, condescending person who secretly harbors contempt for the king and his court, perhaps from the outset. If we emphasize the conflict between the Normans and the Saxons, we may judge Becket to be a social reformer, motivated by a love of humanity and the desire to establish a better life in this world. And if we stress the change in Becket from ruthless minister willing to do anything to secure more power for Henry to a devout religious leader and martyr akin to Christ, then the sainthood in the title of the work would be partially stripped of its irony. Critics who choose only one of these alternatives[22]—or any other that could be construed from the textual clues dropped along the way[23]—are, I think, incorrect, and not just because Meyer himself, in a much-quoted letter, called his novella "intentionally ambiguous."[24] It seems to me that the significance and the realism of the novella are related to the multiple possibilities for motivation and hence for interpretation. It is significant because it presents a type of characterization more commonly found in the literature of the twentieth century. It is realistic because it may reflect more accurately the way the human mind actually works. Traditionally, of course, realism is associated with clarity and unequivocal motivation; if one cannot explain a character's actions on the basis of the preceding events and the given psychology of the character, then the work violates the unwritten code of realist depiction. But *Der Hei lige*—perhaps without Meyer's intention—suggests that someone may have an array of apparently contradictory reasons for actions. The complaint that Meyer's characters lack psychological realism may be thus misplaced;[25] their psychology may actually be more sophisticated and complex than those of the simpler, less problematic characters found in much of the realist prose of the nineteenth century. Indeed, that revenge and Christian piety can or even must be associated was shown at about the time of the novella's composition by the philosophical psychology of Friedrich Nietzsche.[26] A few years later, Freud claimed that a large part of our motives and desires is unavailable to our conscious mind. If we look at Becket from this perspective, he may remain enigmatic and contradictory, but he also appears more real—if not more realist—than we would have anticipated at first glance.[27] Paradoxically the question of the ability of narrative to do justice to reality may contribute, therefore, on the level of characterization, to a more accurate portrayal of reality. Here realism in motivation and psychology appears to be supported and enhanced by the very inability of the narrator to convey faithfully what has occurred.

Whether we view Becket's enigmatic personality as realistic or not, however, the question of ambiguity in the novella still presents us with a formidable problem. Surrounding Meyer's statements concerning the intentional ambiguity of the novella, we also find two noteworthy comments. The first occurs in a letter to his publisher, Hermann Haessel, in January 1877. Here Meyer writes of his plans for *Der Heilige* and states his intentions as follows: "I have two sketches. The first, a novella: 'der Heilige,' in agreeable garb tries to solve

167

[*enträthseln*] a medieval saint, Thomas Beket [*sic*], and in a greater scope tries to emphasize the difference between the legend, the conventional understanding of the life of a human being, and its cruel reality."[28] From these remarks, written while the novella was still in its incipient stages, it appears that Meyer was going to try to remove what is unclear in the historical account. It is very likely that he is thinking here of the inadequate motivation for Becket's conversion found in Thierry's work.[29] From his remarks to Haessel, at least, Meyer seems to be indicating that he will eliminate ambiguity by grounding the legend in "reality," that he will solve (*enträthseln*) what has remained a puzzle for the historian. Confirmation for this interpretation occurs in a conversation from 1890 reported by Fritz Koegel. Here Meyer again contrasts his conception of Becket with the historian's: "Dark figures such as these are very welcome for us; the motivation is not clearly established in history and the writer has the freedom to fill in the gaps."[30] Meyer clearly conceives of his work as a completion of the historical record, a filling in of the gaps in motivation. He must have realized, of course, that this finishing of history did not have to be based in fact. In motivating Becket more "realistically" than the historian, Meyer recognized, we must presume, that he would have to ignore "reality" and exercise poetic license. Nonetheless, it is not without significance that in a novella that Meyer and most critics label ambiguous, the author's intention was to explain what history leaves obscure and incomplete.

This apparent contradiction in Meyer's statements about *Der Heilige* can be resolved by looking more closely at what he was trying to clarify in the work. It seems clear that he was fascinated by the ambiguity of Becket's actions and that he therefore sought to retain, or even to enhance, this quality in the novella. What he endeavored to illuminate, on the other hand, was why and how this figure was ambiguous. He did not want to make Becket's motives more transparent—if he did, he was a dismal failure. Rather, it appears that he wanted to show the reader why Becket is an enigma. The chief way he accomplishes this is by drawing on the racial prejudices of the nineteenth century. On one level Meyer was simply staying close to his source when he introduced such issues. Thierry's account, after all, necessarily focuses on the conflict between the conquered Saxons and the Norman overlords.[31] That Thierry erroneously claims that Becket's father was a Saxon—both Becket's parents were Norman—serves Meyer well. Incorporating this legend into the text, Meyer makes his hero a furtive and then an open champion of the oppressed. In the very first episode in which he is involved, we can presume that Becket somehow rescues the Saxon girl Hilde from the clutches of her Norman abductor. Later we learn that while chancellor he was able to lighten the Saxon burden by persuading the king that this was in his best interest; and after he has become archbishop, we find him at the head of the Saxon hordes, defending their rights. Indeed, the highlight of his final meeting with Henry is the offer to grant the kiss of reconciliation if the king will liberate his Saxon subjects. It is thus easy to see that Meyer plays on this racial conflict to supply one important strain of motivation for his saint.

It is not Becket's fictitious origins as a Saxon, however, that lend him the mystery and ambiguity Meyer sensed in the historical figure, but rather his equally spurious Arab ancestry and affiliation. Becket's "Oriental" background crops up frequently in the course of the novella, serving as a convenient explanation for motives and actions. What the reader encounters with almost every allusion to Moslem culture is the nineteenth-century stereotype of the Arab. Becket is humbly submissive to his master, vengeful in an almost sadistic manner, and, above all, inscrutable for the outside observer. Hans continuously refers to his Arab nature, and this may be the reason that he emphasizes the motive of revenge in his account. Twice Hans speaks to Becket in Arabic, once quoting—incorrectly, as it turns out—from the Koran (65). He attributes Becket's unwillingness to mention Jesus by name to his "heathen blood" (82), and at another point suggests that his "Moorish constitution" (*das maurische Wesen*) may prevent him from considering Christ to be part of the Trinity (77). Indeed, Hans, whose career otherwise parallels Becket's in a remarkable and, as we noted above, somewhat artificial fashion, endeavors to distinguish himself from the saint with respect to Orientalism. While he repeatedly suggests Becket's furtive adherence to Arab customs and thought, he maintains that he himself remains "uncircumcised in body and unshaken in faith" (21). We should also recall that his remarks about twelfth-century Spain and Arab culture are highly stereotyped. His most prejudicial statement occurs when he describes the Arab storyteller. As we have seen previously, he discredits him by claiming that Moors have minds that cannot separate fact from fiction; lies are simply part of the Oriental personality. It is a further irony of the novella, as we have also witnessed before, that Hans's procedure—and Meyer's as well—hardly differs from that of the Moorish teller of fairy tales. Still, this obvious prejudice on

Hans's part adds another dimension to his perspectival inability to cope with truth. His story cannot be faithful to the facts not only because of the inherent discrepancy between narrative and reality but also because Orientalism everywhere intrudes to distort his account.

It is not surprising to find that most of the other characters in the novella reinforce this European prejudice against the East. The pious and narrow-minded Burkhard, for example, is amazed that someone with heathen blood could be raised to sainthood. Äscher is horrified at the Oriental upbringing Becket chooses for his daughter, and Henry wants Becket for his "Primus" because he is "an unbelieving philosopher and a disguised Saracen" (68)—although he later regrets selecting the "vengeful heathen" (121). Indeed, Becket himself contributes to this undercurrent of Orientalism. When Henry is trying to convince him to become archbishop, he stresses his Arab heritage by denying even his Saxon origins: "I am not a Norman; I am not even a Saxon! Foreign blood flows in my veins" (86). Later, at the meeting arranged by Richard, he again brings up his Moorish constitution: since he is a man of "heathen blood," he tells Henry, he is not as calm as he appears (118). Finally, in one of the most significant conversations between Henry and Becket before the latter is made archbishop, Becket attributes his servility to his race, speaking of "my nature, which inclines toward humility and being of service" (*mein zur Erniedrigung der Dienstbarkeit geschaffenes Wesen*) (75). The net result of this bombardment with biased references to the Orient is not that Becket's motives become more transparent but rather that his ambiguity becomes more comprehensible. If Becket is attuned to a foreign system of values, if he owes intellectual and spiritual allegiance to another culture and religion, in short, if he is so radically "other," then it is not astonishing that he remains forever an enigma. Such is the way that Orientalism in *Der Heilige* informs both the characterization and the narrative structure.

The most important and obvious function of Becket's Arab background—which remains significantly shrouded in the obscurity of fairy tales, folk ballads, and legend—is to supply him with a daughter and hence with a plausible motive for revenge. The episode with Grace is Meyer's chief contribution to Becket's biography; there is no basis for it in any of the historical sources he used. Even Hans, as we saw above, emphasizes that what he is about to relate is found in "no chronicle." Nonetheless, the tale of Fair Rosemund, either in the ballad collection of Thomas Percy[32] or in the tragedy by Theodor Körner,[33] evidently served as Meyer's inspiration for this incident. That this legend of seduction and murder is here placed against an Oriental backdrop, however, again demonstrates the enormous role played by the East in the ideological structure of the novella. During the course of the fifth chapter, we learn that Becket has secretly brought his daughter to England and has constructed a marvelous Arabian castle for her in a desolate forest. He speaks only Arabic with her, tells her "heathen fairy tales," and gives her no Christian religious instruction. In the middle of a narrative that is otherwise credible, this episode smacks of the fantastic. The only reason that it seems at all plausible is because it can be understood as part of Becket's mysterious Oriental quirk. Perhaps the most outlandish aspect of this chapter involves the motives for Grace's actions. That a fifteen-year-old girl in isolation in the woods would willingly give herself to the king and that she would then keep this a secret from her father is hard to believe. To make the unbelievable credible, however, the narrator need only call on the European bias about Arab subservience to rulers. Hans can thus explain to himself, to Burkhard, and to the reader why Grace acted as she did: "Grace was of heathen blood from both parents, and the submissive Arab women bow down to the dust before a scepter. For them a king represents God and the law, and more than father and mother. I could understand how Grace could keep silent to her father about the evil secret of the king" (54). Here again the "mysteries of the Orient" rescue the narrative from incredibility. Like Becket's ambiguity the seduction and silence of Grace only make sense if we are willing to buy into the racist system of values that underlies the narrative.[34]

Consideration of the Oriental dimension of *Der Heilige* is essential for an understanding of both motivation and ambiguity. This is clear from the text itself and would be true even if Meyer himself had never made reference to this issue. But as it happens, Meyer also stresses the importance of the East for an interpretation of the novella. He does not disclose that his source for a good deal of his knowledge about twelfth-century Spain was Schlosser's *Weltgeschichte für das deutsche Volk* (*World History for the German People*, 1846), especially the sections on medieval Spain,[35] but he does deal with the issue in two significant places. The first is evidently a blurb he composed for the novella and sent to Haessel in May of 1880. It reads, in part, as follows: "It [the novella] does not deal so much with the historical opposition between church and state personified in Thomas of Canterbury and Henry II of England; rather the writer has used the oriental origins of Thomas Becket as an occasion to give him a peculiar modern personality that necessarily had to come into conflict with the medieval, violent personality of the king."[36] Meyer's statement here coincides neatly with what we have found. This is not a novella about church and state—or, at least, not primarily—but rather an examination of an extraordinary personality. Becket can appear "modern"—and with this modifier Meyer no doubt understands ambiguous and multidimensional—because of his Oriental background.

Meyer's second statement about these matters, in a letter to Hermann Lingg of 2 May 1880, reveals even more clearly how prejudice informs the narrative. Ostensibly Meyer is simply explaining character motivation. At issue in particular is how Henry could have deceived himself so thoroughly about his apparently loyal chancellor. The major point that Mayer makes concerns the character of his central figure. Despite the length of the citation, it deserves to be quoted in full for what it discloses about the bias informing the novella:

> Personality of Th. Becket: 1. Oriental blood (utilization of the legend). 2. Highest education and fundamental contempt for his brutal era. 3. Superior calm, highest understanding, but (as Saxon and Oriental) an oppressed person, therefore a diplomat through and through. 4. Humane, morally pure, an aristocratic nature. 5. A touch of ambition, or rather a feeling of enormous intellectual superiority. 6. Orientally vindictive, I do not mean vengeful, but still (against vice and violent deeds) finely cruel [*fein-grausam*]. He plays with the king at the beginning and at the end as a cat plays with a mouse. All of these features, despite the conversion of Thomas, are to be maintained strictly from the beginning until the end.[37]

Three of the six points Meyer makes here concerning Becket's character have to do with his Oriental background. Although the final remark about his vengefulness is perhaps most offensive for its racism, the most significant is the first, "Oriental blood" (*Orientalisches Blut*). In all other cases an adjective or character trait is included, but Meyer evidently considered the mere mention of "Oriental blood" to be self-explanatory. For a European in the nineteenth century, it was clear from these two words alone what kind of character Becket would have.

By manifesting Orientalism, both Meyer and his novella partake in what Edward Said has termed "radical realism." According to Said, "anyone employing Orientalism, which is the habit for dealing with questions, objects, qualities, and regions deemed Oriental, will designate, name, point to, fix what he is talking or thinking about with a word or phrase, which then is considered either to have acquired, or more simply to be, reality."[38] In contrast to most forms of literary realism, "radical realism" is thus an active, creative variety; the word here is seen as constituting rather than mirroring reality. Located in the long heritage of European prejudice against the East, Meyer's novella thus maintains this tradition by creating anew the division between them and us, between native and foreign, between self and other. It should be noted in passing that in this respect *Der Heilige* has much in common with other celebrated works of its era, such as Freytag's *Soll und Haben* (*Debit and Credit*, 1855) or Raabe's *Der Hungerpastor* (*The Hunger Pastor*, 1864), both of which, as we shall see in the next chapter, set up pernicious oppositions of a slightly different racial composition. It also has affinities with Fontane's *Effi Briest* (1894/95), where the "Chinese" as outsider reinforces the distinction between what is apposite behavior for the Western world and what is to be repulsed as a threat to social stability. That Meyer, along with Raabe, Freytag, and Fontane, is most frequently labeled a *poetic* realist may be therefore slightly misleading. Indeed, even if we see him as a historical or symbolic realist,[39] as a writer who poeticizes historical accounts, often anticipating with his use of imagery the symbolist movement, we may still be missing the mark. If we take the explicit and implicit reflections on realism in *Der Heilige* as a basis, it seems that his case is much more complex. On the level of narrative, the repeated questioning of our ability to arrive at a true and accurate account of events undermines not only the narrator's own claims but also the conventional, simplistically conceived realist enterprise. On the level of characterization, we have noted that the tendency toward undecidability reflects a more sophisticated and ultimately more realistic presentation of how the human mind presumably functions. And on the level of ideology, the retention and propagation of what V. G. Kiernan calls "Europe's collective daydream of the Orient"[40] amounts to a different type of realism, one that shapes and divides reality along racial, if not racist, lines. All these aspects of realism have far-reaching ramifications for the twentieth century. It was unfortunately the final one, the active and prejudicial "radical realism," that has had the most telling and lasting effect on recent German reality. In the following chapter we shall be able to witness more directly the pernicious exclusory effects of the realist enterprise.

7

THE BUSINESS OF REALISM:
Ethical Preoccupations and Aesthetic Contradictions

> The villainy you teach me I will execute, and
> it shall go hard but I will better the instruction.
> Shylock in Shakespeare's
> *Merchant of Venice*

At the very beginning of this study, I noted that theorists of literary realism have traditionally found little agreement with respect to the phenomenon they are studying. Yet most, I think, would be compelled to concede that during the period to which we customarily attach the label "realism" there is a marked turn toward portraying a middle-class hero in a contemporary or nearly contemporary setting performing nonheroic and nonfantastic deeds. Exceptions may come to mind—particularly for the German branch of this European movement: Fontane's characters are frequently aristocrats, and C. F. Meyer writes almost exclusively historical novellas. But even if such examples would preclude the use of the aforementioned characteristics as part of a definition of realism, their occurrence and regularity in European literature of the nineteenth century can hardly be denied. Appeals to the "serious treatment of day-to-day reality"[1] or to the "objective representation of contemporary reality"[2] may be ultimately unsatisfactory for a description of realism, but it would be foolish not to admit that there are significant changes in the social status and activities of the characters most often encountered in European fiction during the postromantic era. Indeed, Hegel, whose remarks on the altered nature of aesthetic representation occur during the incipient

174

stages of the age of realism, is able to forecast and analyze rather precisely the course of literature for the coming decades. The "prosaic objectivity" that accompanies the decline of the romantic era allows the artwork the liberty to deal with previously "unaesthetic" realms. In this period "everything has a place, all spheres of life and phenomena, the greatest and the smallest, the highest and the lowest, the moral, the immoral, and the evil." Art becomes increasingly confined to "the finitudes of the world," its content is "normal, daily life."[3] The reason for this change has to do with changes in reality itself; in legal, moral, and political relations, there is little room for the development of "ideal formations." Even persons whose social positions formerly associated them with heroic deeds, e.g., monarchs, are now reduced to more mundane, administrative tasks.[4] These "present prosaic conditions," Hegel recognizes, are most adequately captured in prosaic form. The novel, "the bourgeois epopee," is well suited for grasping "a reality whose regime has already become prose."[5] In a world that itself produces nothing extraordinary, the novel has the task of portraying the nonheroic middle class going about its daily business.

Occupations therefore become a preoccupation for the realist writer. If the hero or heroine is no longer a monarch, a general, or an artist; if he or she is neither exceptional nor an outsider; if, in short, the work of art draws on the "prosaic" everyday world, then the writer will have to give some thought to what the characters do. The very selection of an occupation thus becomes a kind of reflection on realism, since, in the context of aesthetic theory, this choice is apt to break with established literary conventions. In Germany the social status of the hero is particularly important because of two historical circumstances. First is the fact that Germany, in contrast to England, experienced no appreciable industrialization during the eighteenth and early nineteenth century. Aside from isolated pockets of middle-class life, it remained essentially a feudally organized, rural nation until the middle of the last century. From 1850 to 1900, however, we find a rapid industrial growth accompanied by the concomitant urbanization of society. The age of realism in Germany, more than in France or England, overlaps with the rise of middle-class economic power, and the concurrent restructuring of society thrusts the theoretical question of apposite occupation into the center of literary debate. Of equal importance for the poetics of the latter half of the century, however, was the dismal failure of the revolution of 1848. The return of the *ancien régime* meant the end of hopes for a democratically based national unity and for the consolidation of bourgeois power. The bourgeoisie either retreated into a Schopenhauerian pessimism—the essentially romantic philosophy of *Die Welt als Wille und Vorstellung* (*The World as Will and Representation*) from 1817 was virtually ignored until the 1850s—or it restricted itself to economic and, within limits, cultural affairs, forfeiting political leadership in large measure to the aristocracy. Realism thus represents for the German bourgeoisie both a response to the revolution and a recognition of its altered role in society.[6] It is more than an artistic movement, a style, or an aesthetic doctrine. In Germany it coincides with, and is reinforced by, a "realism" in the economic and political spheres as well. This unique mixture of resignation and revitalization, of national, classist pride and political impotence, sets German realism apart from its European counterparts and makes the question of what characters do for a living an issue of both literary and political consequence.[7]

In this general poetic and historical context, one can more easily grasp the importance of the "programmatic realism" of the 1850s and the most celebrated novel to emerge from this doctrine, Gustav Freytag's *Soll und Haben* (*Debit and Credit*, 1855). The chief architect of this version of German realism, Julian Schmidt, was, along with Freytag, politically allied with the national liberal faction and initially supported the revolution of 1848. Of greater significance for literary developments, though, is that in the year of the revolution these two men assumed the editorship of *Die Grenzboten*, the most influential literary journal in Leipzig at the time, and in the next decade perhaps the most important platform for German criticism. Freytag's best-seller *Soll und Haben* follows closely the precepts he and Schmidt developed in *Die Grenzboten*.[8] The most important of these for our present purposes is the emphasis on the proper theme and setting for a realistic work. The frequently quoted epigraph to the novel captures in a nutshell this tenet of their literary theory: "The novel should look for the German people where they can be found to be most competent, namely, at work." It is not difficult to interpret this maxim as a response to the unsuccessful revolution. Having failed in its political aspirations, the middle class is now called upon to strengthen its position in the economic realm through industry and diligence, and literature is called upon to reflect and assist in this effort.

There are two other aspects of this epigraph, however, that deserve attention as well. The first concerns the novel as a form. Until the middle of the nineteenth century, the novel tradition in Germany was conspicuously weak. This was due in part to chance—there were few noteworthy practitioners of this form of narrative prose—and in part to historical circumstances—there was no literary center and no national unity. But it is also attributable to the low standing of prose in general in German poetic theory. As late as the 1840s, writers were still defending the use of prose in works of art; drama, lyric, and epic were ranked higher in the generic hierarchy well into the latter half of the nineteenth century. The novel was usually considered an inferior form, suitable perhaps for women; only in the most accomplished works did it escape the categorization of pulp literature. The theory and practice of Schmidt and Freytag aimed to change this evaluation and to reverse the hierarchy. The novel was now not only legitimate, but moreover the most appropriate genre for the age. The advent of the middle class was signaled by the valorization of the form suited to this class. The second significant dimension of this motto is that it amounts to a rejection of the scanty novel tradition that did exist at the time. By this I mean that Freytag and Schmidt were implicitly criticizing the heritage of the German *Bildungsroman*, represented most eminently by Goethe's *Wilhelm Meisters Lehrjahre* (*Wilhelm Meister's Apprenticeship*, 1795–96) and somewhat more derivatively by Karl Immermann's *Die Epigonen* (*The Epigones*, 1837). In the former work Wilhelm abandons the world of merchant capitalism in order to accomplish his maturation; in the latter work Hermann has to destroy his uncle's factory to make possible the utopian future. Freytag and Schmidt suggested that this tradition be reversed. Anton Wohlfahrt, the hero of *Soll und Haben*, can only realize his potential by entering the world of business. In a bourgeois perversion of Marx's most powerful vision, work here ceases to be the realm of necessity and becomes instead the path to self-fulfillment.

The theory and practice of realism as conceived by Freytag and Schmidt thrust the notion of work—understood as a bourgeois, not a proletarian, activity—into the center of poetic theory. That Wohlfahrt is a merchant is thus hardly coincidental; for in this occupation he is at the hub, as it were, of middle-class existence.[9] He is not involved in any particular trade or sphere, but has potential for contact with them all. More important, his activities as a clerk for the firm T. O. Schröter remove him from contact with the blatantly exploitative aspects of industrial society. There is no downtrodden proletariat in *Soll und Haben*. The only workers we encounter have the same fanatic loyalty to the patriarchal Schröter that Wohlfahrt displays throughout most of the novel. Neither are there any slum neighborhoods, subsistence wages, or other unpleasant trappings of industrialization. Merchant capitalism exports its exploitation at the same time that it imports its wares. In Anton's mind—and for the reader of the novel—capitalism presents itself as the exciting and exotic delight in foreign lands. Instead of the dull and monotonous sounds of the factory, Anton hears "the waves of the sea pounding against the shore in regular rhythm" when he saunters through the warehouse. Indeed, in the ethnocentric and classist perspective of the Central European bourgeoisie the world lies at the merchant's feet: "Barrels, crates, and bundles were also found here in total disarray, and only a narrow, winding path led through them. Almost every country on earth, every part of the human race, had worked and saved so that something useful and worthwhile would be piled up in front of our hero's eyes" (46).[10] Following these sentences is a lengthy passage in which the various countries and vehicles of commerce are evoked in Anton's fantasy. Such a pronounced imperialist vision recalls a discussion from English fiction from the previous century. In *The London Merchant* (1731), by George Lillo, we encounter a similar ideology in a discussion between the merchant Thorowgood and his clerk Trueman:

> I have observ'd those countries, where trade is promoted and encouraged, do not make discoveries to destroy, but to improve, mankind by love and friendship; to tame the fierce and polish the most savage; to teach them the advantages of honest trafick, by taking from them, with their own consent, their useless superfluities, and giving them, in return, what, from their ignorance in manual arts, their situation, or some other accident, they stand in need of.[11]

In both works the plot, the simplistically allegorical names (Wohlfahrt, Thorowgood, Trueman), and the words themselves tell us that trade is beneficial to all parties. It has no part in exploitation; it merely connects people previously unknown to one another for mutual benefit. Anton expresses this thought as follows:

> When I place a sack of coffee on the scale, I connect by an invisible thread the colonialist's daughter in Brazil who picked the coffee beans with the young farmer boy who will drink them at breakfast, and when I take a cinnamon stick in my hand, I see on the one side the squatting Malaysian who prepared and

packed it and on the other side the little old woman from our home city grating it over the rice pudding. (180–81)

Similarly, in the English play we read of the "mutual benefits diffusing mutual love from pole to pole."[12] The difference between these two merchant ideologies—besides the hundred and twenty years that separate them—is that Freytag's novel, unlike Lillo's drama, sought and received recognition for its realism. In German criticism of the nineteenth century, *Soll und Haben* is the first work to be acclaimed for its verisimilitude. Theodor Fontane, for example, called it "the first blossom of modern realism."[13] Even those who dispute this sort of accolade found it necessary to discuss the novel in similar terms; that is, at the time of its appearance there was for the first time a general awareness that realism was the poetic framework within which criticism of this work had to move.[14] For the postrevolutionary bourgeoisie, *Soll und Haben* becomes the "hymn to the bourgeois merchant class,"[15] the prototype of both the novel of business and the novel of realism.

Both of these claims can be easily disputed from a modern perspective. Since we now tend to attach the label "realism" solely to works of high literary quality, *Soll und Haben* would be considered by most current standards an illustration of kitsch rather than a paradigm of realism.[16] But it is also not difficult to show that it is not always—and perhaps not primarily—portraying business practices as they existed in the 1850s. The very comparison I introduced above indicates that it is promoting a somewhat obsolete ideology. Merchant capitalism belongs to an early phase of modern development; the German bourgeoisie of the mid-nineteenth century had its future in heavy industry, not in trade. Indeed, the narrator concedes as much while describing Schröter's business. His type of commerce is rapidly dying out:

> The business was a warehouse business, and nowadays there are fewer and fewer of these; nowadays, when railroads and telegraphs connect the seas with the inland areas, when every merchant from the coastal cities can have his goods sold deep in the interior of a country through his agent almost before they arrive in port; nowadays this type of business has become so infrequent that our descendants will find this kind of trade no less strange than we find the market bartering in Timbuktu or in a Kaffir kraal. (41)

It is significant for the ideological content that progress itself is responsible for the destruction of such mercantile business. But the antiquated nature of the business is also matched by its structure. It is a family enterprise—owned by Schröter and his sister Sabine—in which the clerks live and eat in the same house as their chief. Schröter himself is the prototypical patriarch, wise, honest, and good, yet, when it is appropriate, distant and stern. Referred to throughout the novel almost exclusively as *der Kaufmann* (the merchant) or *der Prinzipal* (the principal), Schröter assumes at times God-like proportions. That his first name is "Traugott" (lit. Godtrust) is certainly no coincidence, for he is less the magnate of trade and commerce than the lofty and omniscient lord and master of his limited universe. He rules with an austere authority and absoluteness, and his faithful clerks, like disciples, seem to worship and revere him. That the beneficent patriarchalism of Schröter's firm did not represent the path of the German bourgeoisie is obvious in hindsight, but probably perceptible even to contemporaries. However, the feature that perhaps tarnishes most the reputation of *Soll und Haben* as a novel of business is the very absence of actual business dealings—at least by the firm of T. O. Schröter. We do not see Anton very often behind his desk, nor do we find out what his colleagues are doing during business hours. After the brief description of the firm's activity cited in the passage above, we learn, in fact, almost nothing about future developments except as they relate to personnel. We even read in various places that the daily work routine was rather uniform and monotonous. Most of the events in the novel take place around or against the normalcy of Schröter's firm, but the reader is given very little in the way of detail about this normalcy.

What we encounter instead is the other side of the capitalist coin, the alternative to the ideal, honest, German world of T. O. Schröter. In *Soll und Haben* the shady dealings and disreputable business practices of the Jewish merchants occupy quantitatively more of the novel than anything Anton does for his principal. That Freytag here is drawing on and propagating anti-Semitism is obvious, although he amazingly still finds apologists in this regard.[17] No matter what he may have thought about Jews or written about them later, his novel documents and supports irrational anti-Jewish sentiments.[18] More important for our present purposes, however, is how the portrayal of Jewish speculators and usurers fits into the ideological framework described above; for almost all of the Jews presented in the novel are, like Anton and Schröter, involved in business. They are included, however, not so much to enhance the realism of the work through the presentation of an everyday, practical occupation, as to provide a contrast with the hero and his boss. Schmeie Tinkeles, a rather obsequious character who speaks broken German, seems to supply only comic relief until we learn that his greed almost causes Schröter's death. He appears to regret this transgression—although it remains unclear whether he is sincere in his penitence or only feigning so that he can resume his dealings with Schröter's firm—but to the very end we are supposed to get the impression that there is little he would not do for the right price. Hirsch Ehrenthal, who is partially responsible for the demise of the honorable but foolhardy Baron von Rothsattel, is somewhat more dignified in his business practices, but he too is marked from the beginning by servility and avarice. Although he is willing to renounce some of his aspirations to save his beloved son Bernhard, he is never quite able to make a definite choice between the life of his child and his desire for wealth and property. If he were not presented so shabbily from the outset, he could almost be a tragic figure in the novel. His endeavor to secure riches for his son and respectability for his wife and daughter is thwarted by a fatal course of events. Bernhard dies, his daughter winds up engaged to the man responsible for Bernhard's death, and he himself ends as a feeble-minded, babbling fool à la Lear. Here the attempt to improve one's lot by accumulating wealth is punished with disgrace and degeneracy.

The most offensive and villainous Jewish character in this novel, however, is Veitel Itzig.[19] This is significant because his career is made to parallel Anton's. They grow up in the same town, attend the same school, and even arrive in the big city (presumably Breslau, although it is never mentioned by name) on the same day to start their respective business careers. But whereas Anton finds employment as a clerk in the respectable firm headed by Traugott Schröter, Itzig learns his trade from the dubious dealer Ehrenthal and, later, from the alcoholic pettifogger Hippus. The instruction he receives from the latter character is particularly enlightening for the image of capitalism presented in the novel, for Hippus, who is the only non-Jew associated with fraud and deceitfulness, does not teach his eager pupil illegal practices but, rather, how to use the law as it already exists for one's own gain. Taking advantage of loopholes, knowing how to compose airtight contracts and mortgages, and a thorough acquaintance with legal codes are here depicted as the tools of unscrupulous businessmen. Itzig senses that by associating with Hippus he is selling himself to Satan (83), that he is about to do something evil (84), although it is difficult to say how his sort of training differs from Anton's in actual subject matter. Anton is also shown to be an exemplary learner: in Schröter's firm he receives a promotion in half the usual time. Both young men are obviously at the head of their respective classes: Itzig is the best Jewish businessman, Anton the exemplary German merchant, and we follow their rise in the trade through a series of parallel episodes.

A confrontation between the personification of good and the representative of evil is inevitable, however, since Itzig has schemed to ruin Baron von Rothsattel; and Anton, temporarily infatuated with aristocratic life and the baron's flighty daughter Lenore, has been called upon to save him from disgrace and financial insolvency, which in the ethos of the novel amount to approximately the same thing. Their meeting toward the close of the novel is described as a battle for which both men gird themselves with every weapon they possess. But before they enter into the fray, the narrator once again emphasizes the similarities between the two warriors:

> Many years of careful interchange with other people and the interests of commerce had given both men some similar characteristics. Both were accustomed to presenting the appearance of cold-blooded calm and to concealing the goal that they wanted to attain; both were accustomed to quick decisions, to bold initiatives; in language as well as gesture both showed something of the form that dealings with merchants lend to the businessman; today both were experiencing great inner excitement, and this reddened Anton's cheeks and covered Veitel's cheekbones with a bright glow. (590)

From this passage as well as from the previous experiences of Itzig and Anton, it seems that evil capitalism and good capitalism have a great deal in common. Although Freytag has obviously structured his novel to contrast Anton with Itzig, here, at a decisive moment, he stresses, perhaps inadvertently, their similarity.

This is not the only time that we find it difficult to differentiate between a Jewish and a German business morality. With respect to the fate of Rothsattel, Schröter seems to share an opinion with his less respectable colleagues. When Anton approaches him about helping the baron out of his financial quagmire, the principal makes it clear that he would not do anything even if he were personally asked to intervene. In a biting and pitiless harangue, Schröter implies that the baron has brought about his own demise and that sympathy for him is unprofessional and inappropriate. This sober, unfeeling appraisal of Rothsattel's financial situation corresponds precisely to the evaluation of the Jewish dealers who are, in part at least, responsible for his downfall. Itzig, for example, views the whole matter as another financial transaction, and Schmeie Tinkeles frankly concedes that he is indifferent to the fate of the Rothsattel family. Indeed, Ehrenthal is shown to be even more human than Schröter with respect to the Rothsattel affair. When his son demands that he not ruin the baron —and this seems to be within his power at one point—he is ready to make concessions. In a gesture of reconciliation toward Bernhard, he even agrees to help purchase a new estate for the Rothsattel family so that they will not be completely homeless. Schröter, by contrast, when asked by his future brother-in-law for his expert advice, flatly rejects any form of assistance. When Anton returns from his Polish adventures on the Rothsattel estate, Schröter has obviously not budged from this position in the least. Even though Anton had nothing whatsoever to do with the baron's initial, foolish financial transactions, even though Anton had devoted himself to extricating the fallen aristocrat from his difficulties and to making the new estate a viable enterprise, Schröter's only comment to him is that the association with such questionable affairs may have tarnished his business reputation. At no point does he display the least bit of concern for the plight of the Rothsattel family. This episode is included, of course, to demonstrate the decline of the nobility as nonproductive members of society. Nonetheless, it seems to show—undoubtedly against Freytag's intentions—that capitalism is a united front against the ancien régime. Here again Freytag's neat dichotomy between good and bad capitalism breaks down momentarily, revealing a fundamentally inhumane moral code.[20]

The obsolete nature of Schröter's firm, the introduction of disreputable Jewish speculators and usurers, and the impossibility of consistently distinguishing between honorable and base business moralities should indicate that *Soll und Haben* was not simply propagating nineteenth-century capitalism. Rather, it was advocating an ethical doctrine that speaks the ideology of business only at certain moments; at other times it implicitly protests against the logic of capitalism. That Freytag may have considered himself to have been supporting business values is of little consequence, since the ethos of the novel effectively drowns out any intention he may have harbored along these lines. If we examine the mores portrayed as exemplary in *Soll und Ha-*

ben, it soon becomes clear that they are often superficially pro-capitalist. The most obvious illustration of this occurs when we consider the attitude toward competition. The Jewish businessmen accept competition as a fact of capitalist life. They understand that they can gain an advantage only by putting someone else at a disadvantage, that their profit means somebody else's loss. For Anton and Schröter —and significantly for the naive scholar Bernhard and the inept Rothsattel—this is not at all clear. At various points in the novel, they express the view that the honest businessman should not make money at another party's expense. In keeping with their merchant mentality, which distances them from the inequities of the production process, they conceive of business as potentially nonexploitative. The raison d'être for their various activities in commerce is not profit or gain but the benefit of humankind. When Anton and Schröter journey to Poland to retrieve their goods, they are not acting out of selfish motives or for the sake of the firm's profit; something higher and more noble is at stake. Allowing disruptions in the flow of commodities is a sin against civilization itself: "When a businessman allows himself to be disturbed more than is necessary, he commits an injustice against civilization, an injustice for which he can never make amends" (267). This nonexploitative and noncompetitive version of capitalism also shuns risks and renounces expansion. Schröter persuades Anton that he is better off in his office than in America with his rambunctious friend Fink by telling him: "In my office you can never become a rich man, nor can you live the grand life; our business is limited, and the day will come when this limitation will be disconcerting for you. Everything that will secure for you independence in the future, namely, wealth and connections, you can attain over there more readily than here with me" (235). Ambition, riches, and autonomy are unimportant in Schröter's ethics. He is not the Mr. Moneybags whom Marx describes in *Capital*; he does not endeavor to revolutionize production, improve his efficiency, undercut his competitors, and maximize his profit at the expense of his employees. The business mentality in *Soll und Haben* is, rather, what one might call "ethical capitalism." That is, we find here the contradictory mixture of a probusiness stance combined with a morality derived from a more traditional humanism.[21] The irreconcilability of the two, kept in check throughout most of the novel, comes to the fore in those brief moments when the German and the Jewish opposition collapses.[22]

The business of German realism is thus neither purely pro-capitalist nor necessarily linked to any specific profession or occupation. Rather, it is a distinctly ethical entity.[23] The values it propagates are integrity, loyalty, perseverance, and subordination, not profit, production, and competition. The clarity with which this moral code is conveyed is due to the rigid dichotomies in Freytag's presentation. Anton and Itzig, Schröter and Ehrenthal, and German and Jew are the contrasts we encounter throughout the novel, and the entire narrative structure of the work is meant to demonstrate the moral superiority and ultimate invincibility of the first half of these pairs. In the universe of *Soll und Haben*, good inevitably conquers evil. Those who seek to enrich themselves or their families—and here one must include Baron von Rothsattel as well as the Jews—rather than to benefit society as a whole see their fortunes decline. Those who, like Anton, retain their honor and decency despite succumbing to occasional adventures and temptations receive the appropriate reward. At the close of the novel Anton is made a partner in the business and gains a partner in marriage, Schröter's sister Sabine. The reader may instinctively agree with Fink's evaluation of Anton earlier in the book—"He is a Philistine and will always be one"—but the inflexible logic of the novel, which allows one to be either a scoundrel or a saint, reaffirms Schröter's rejoinder: "In my view this public spirit [*Bürgersinn*] is a very respectable foundation for man's happiness" (235). If the sentiments Schröter here and elsewhere expresses were enunciated by an actual capitalist rather than a fictional merchant, the reader would correctly suspect deception or hypocrisy. But it is difficult to believe that in Freytag's novel the authorial intention matches the pernicious ideological effect. It is more likely that the ethos of the work is the result of a combination of naïveté, nostalgia, and misplaced utopianism. Recognizing the necessity of industrial development but disclaiming the consequences of a rigorously applied capitalist mentality, *Soll und Haben* endeavors to find a way to reconcile nineteenth-century business and humanist ethics under the aegis of programmatic realism.

The ethos of Freytag's novel, with its dual emphasis on work and integrity, found a great resonance in the German public.[24] It was one of the most widely read works of its time and went on to become one of the best-selling books in all of German literature. Among German realists it also had a distinct and powerful echo. Less than a decade after its publication, Wilhelm Raabe, a prose writer who is unfortunately largely unknown outside Germany, placed in his novel *Der Hungerpastor* (*The Hunger Pastor*, 1864) a similar narrative structure and ethical content. This coincidence is slightly unusual because Raabe does not otherwise share Freytag's views. In the first place, he has a much more cynical opinion of the bourgeoisie, and this is perhaps why he does not situate his novel in the world of commerce. His hero, Hans Unwirrsch, becomes a preacher, and his counterpart, Moses Freudenstein (a.k.a. Theophile Stein) achieves notoriety as a philosopher, theater critic, and journalist. In contrast to Freytag, Raabe satirizes the rising middle class as boorish parvenus. After completing his studies, Hans receives a position as a tutor for the children of a wealthy factory-owner who, we are told, "produces a foul-smelling substance that was very necessary in other factories for the production of other products" (169).[25] The instructions Hans receives for the education of his sons evidences Raabe's unmistakably ironic stance:

> "They should become good businessmen," he said, "but until they are old enough to go into apprenticeship, it will not hurt to teach them a little of what people call the humaniora. Time marches relentlessly onward, and we merchants and industrialists cannot complain about this at all; we are carried along with it if we are willing. Nowadays people have to learn how to deal with more things than in the age of our fathers. Therefore instruct as much as you want, my good fellow! I'll put a halt to it when I think that they have had enough and the more noble faculties are being flooded. Praxis is anyway my main concern." (173)

This speech could be almost a satirical comment on Anton Wohlfahrt's education values in *Soll und Haben*, but Raabe also disagrees with Freytag in regard to politics. An uncompromising liberal and democrat, he retained his ideals during the restoration of the 1850s. His portrayal of the revolution of 1848 is accordingly much more sympathetic to the lower classes. Whereas Anton and Schröter see only the disruption of trade and the perils of mob rule, Raabe has Hans dismissed from his position as tutor because of his alleged compassion with the rebelling masses.

Despite these differences Raabe's novel is obviously derivative of Freytag's in terms of structure and content.[26] Perhaps the most obvious aspect of borrowing involves the parallelism of a German and a Jewish life. In following Freytag's example, Raabe streamlines the contrast by excluding other elements (e.g., the aristocracy, the Polish adventure, the opposition Ehrenthal-Schröter) and expands upon the details. Where Freytag had only related the common origins and child-hoods in a sketchy retrospective, Raabe devotes several chapters to this phase of his heroes' development. Moses Freudenstein and Hans Unwirrsch are born in the provincial town of Neustadt on the very same day at about the same hour. They attend the same school and are first and second in their class respectively. A camaraderie of sorts even develops between the two boys, since Hans, like Anton, defends his Jewish schoolmate against the persecution of the neighborhood toughs. In both novels, therefore, the unscrupulousness of the Jew in later years is simultaneously a betrayal of an earlier trust. Upon graduation both young men leave their village and, like Anton and Itzig, make their pilgrimage on foot to the big city, in this case to study at the university rather than to become clerks. In these features the similarities between the two novels are unmistakable; it is difficult to escape the conclusion that Raabe, impressed by the success of Freytag's book, was here trying to capitalize on an already proven scheme.[27]

Unfortunately, however, despite his more enlightened politics, Raabe does not depart significantly from the anti-Semitism of his predecessor either.[28] He too draws upon the same clichés in his depiction of his Jewish characters. We do find a brief sociological explanation for anti-Semitism, and it does not appear that Raabe was particularly prone to racial prejudice, but this hardly excuses the presentation of Jewish characters in the novel.[29] From the very beginning Raabe's descriptions reinforce stereotypical attitudes. Moses' father, Samuel, who, like most of Freytag's Jewish figures speaks a broken, substandard German obviously affected by Yiddish, is a dealer in secondhand goods in Neustadt. In the past, we are told, he was involved in other business ventures of a speculative and risky nature. He is thus a small-time version of Itzig or Ehrenthal. Through various hints and innuendoes, we gain the impression that he, like the other Jews, is not particularly concerned with how he makes his money. More openly offensive is the depiction of his cellar store, which he set up "according to his taste" (44): "It was as dark as one could expect from a room that looked out onto such a dirty and dark courtyard. Moist walls sealed off every bit of fresh air from the low windows, and sunshine was really artificially shut out by the architect" (87). Dirt, darkness, moisture—an atmosphere of slimy evil is the impression we obtain of Freudenstein's environment. That the reader will then transfer these characteristics to his personality is inevitable. His only redeeming feature is that he, like Ehrenthal, possesses a fanatic paternal affection. But

Moses, the sickly boy with more logic than fantasy, responds to his father's devotion with indifference. After Samuel reveals to him the extent of his hard-earned savings, the narrator allows us to see his unfeeling reaction:

> His cold heart beat so heavily that it caused him physical pain. It was an evil moment when Samuel Freudenstein announced to his son that he was a rich man and that his son would be rich too one day. From this point in time a thousand threads ran into the future; whatever was dark in Moses' soul became even darker; nothing became brighter. His egotism raised itself up threateningly and reached out its hungry, polyp-like arms to grasp hold of the world. (109–10)

Like the Jewish businessmen in Freytag's novel, Moses is a coldhearted egotistical creature concerned only with self-aggrandizement.[30] Since in Hans we find only a slightly more dreamy and disgruntled (*unwirsch*) version of Anton, *Der Hungerpastor* repeats structurally the German-Jewish dichotomy that we found so pronounced in *Soll und Haben*.

The plot of Raabe's novel, then, also evidences similarities with that of Freytag's best-seller. At the center of both works stands a family threatened by the Jewish schemer and protected by the honest German. In *Der Hungerpastor* it is not an aristocratic family faced with financial disaster but, rather, an established bourgeois family named Götz on the verge of social disgrace. Moses Freudenstein had already managed to take indecent liberties with Franziska Götz while the two were living in Paris. (For many German writers in the nineteenth century, Paris was the epitome of sin and licentiousness.) Returning to a German metropolis, presumably Berlin, he takes advantage of the unsuspecting Hans, now a tutor in the house of Franziska's uncle, Privy Counsellor Götz, to make the acquaintance of her cousin, the beautiful, head-strong, and flighty Kleophea. Having ingratiated himself with both mother and daughter, he eventually persuades the latter to elope with him to Paris. Moses, it appears, collects women like Itzig collects promissory notes, and his sensual nature contrasts sharply with the chaste and prudish manners of his German counterpart. In Freytag's novel Rosalie, Ehrenthal's daughter, is his predecessor in this regard; for she too is shown to be more interested in the opposite sex than propriety would dictate. Since Hans feels called upon to defend the honor of the Götz family, a confrontation between the former friends is as inevitable as the showdown between Anton and Itzig. Nothing is accomplished at this meeting, however, except perhaps the confirmation that the opposition that existed between the two in their youth has become even more pronounced (270). Like Anton, Hans is unable to solve all of the family's difficulties, for in German realism, as we have seen, life only turns out happily for those able to resist the twin temptations of wealth and sex. At the end of the novel, Hans marries Franziska and ends up, like Anton, in a secure professional and domestic situation. Indeed, the parallels between the two novels even extend to the inexplicably rash actions of the Jewish villains. Itzig's resort to illegal activities to secure the Rothsattel estate is odd when we consider that his business acumen very likely would have procured it for him without this foolish and fatal risk. Likewise, it is difficult to explain Moses' elopement, since it appears that Kleophea's parents—particularly the domineering and gullible mother, Aurelia—would have either welcomed or at least not prevented a union of their daughter with the witty and charming Dr. Theophile Stein. There is something self-destructive and ultimately irrational about the calculating, logical Jewish figures in both novels, and although Moses does not receive quite the poetic justice Itzig does, from the description of his existence in Paris we cannot consider him to have been totally successful either.

In *Der Hungerpastor* the parallel structure of a German and a Jew that informs the plot is likewise ultimately a device for introducing an ethical message. Honest work is again of exemplary importance. Accordingly Hans is acquainted with "the greatest principle of work" (26) rather early in life; as a child he is recruited to help his aunt make dolls. Later in the novel Franziska's uncle, the kindly Lieutenant Götz, connects this concept with "hunger," the central leitmotif in the book. His ethical optimism, similar to Anton's and Schröter's, is revealed to the hero as they arrive together in Berlin: "A genuinely outstanding age," he assures his somewhat dejected companion, "like all ages in which a person has a great hunger for something that he knows he can achieve through work and effort" (194). By the end of the novel, Hans has adopted this view also. With his bride Franziska in the northern coastal village of Grunzenow, he finally has found contentment: "Labor and Love! this was the thought that thrilled both their [Hans's and Franziska's] hearts, and they knew that they had been granted both" (439). Hans's work, the activity so important for a wholesome bourgeois existence, is that of a pastor, and at first glance this profession might seem to conflict with the world of business extolled in Freytag's novel. But we should recall that the essence of capitalism as conceived by Anton is beneficent, almost charitable; thus it is no coincidence that Anton's best friend in Schröter's office is the clerk Baumann, a devoutly religious man who eventually leaves the firm to become a missionary. In the ethos of German realism, pastor and merchant are related occupations. The hunger that Hans experiences throughout the novel is thus perhaps not so far removed from the notion of *Kraft* (force or power) lauded by Anton and Schröter. Both serve as motivating impulses for useful, nonselfish activity in society; both forces lead their respective heroes to marital bliss and a productive existence. Although Anton will presumably be more socially involved and prosperous than Hans—he tells Franziska that he is bringing her into "deepest poverty and loneliness" (410)—their ideals are astonishingly alike. Both abstain from the adventures and possible gains offered by the ominous world around them; neither seeks to rise in society; and both affirm an active, honest, and benevolent existence against Jewish doubles who are characterized by discontent, unscrupulousness, and egotism. These novels thus preach an essentially conservative system of values at odds with the "revolutionary" spirit of capitalism:[31] the positive heroes are satisfied with their lot; their antagonists, who embody the ethos of business reality, seek to rise above their station in the social order.

Two decades after the appearance of *Der Hungerpastor* and *Soll und Haben*, Gottfried Keller repeated the structure and ethics we have been examining in his novel *Martin Salander* (1886). In this work we have once again returned to the world of commerce proper. Salander, after giving up his position as a secondary-school teacher in a small village, moves to the city of Münsterburg (the fictitious name given to Zurich) and becomes a businessman, "the model provider" (17),[32] thus duplicating the paths of Hans and Anton from town to urban center. At first he obtains a partnership in a small factory; then he turns to trade. Like Schröter and Anton, therefore, he selects the particular branch of business that conceals direct exploitation, although Salander's two voyages to South America, of which we learn only scanty details, potentially bring him into contact with the direct producers of the commodities he exchanges. But unlike Freytag, Keller appears to have a more sober view of the economics of trade. The relatively high standard of living that Europeans enjoy has a price that must be paid by someone. Thus when Martin, involved in his dreams of a perfect system of education, outlines an extensive pedagogical program that includes schooling until a child is twenty years old, his wife, Marie, who seems to have a much more practical bent than her husband, replies sarcastically that one important element in his plan is missing: "I mean the horrible expeditions to Asia and Africa that the Swiss will have to undertake in order to conquer an army of slave laborers or even better a country that will supply them. For without the introduction of slavery who is supposed to help the poor farmers take care of the work in the fields, who is supposed to provide for the youth?" (239). Marie seems to understand the dialectic of culture and barbarism that Walter Benjamin so clearly enunciated three-quarters of a century later.[33] Salander, by contrast, despite his business career, is obviously less attuned to economic realities. He shares with Anton and Hans a certain dreaminess, passivity, and gullibility. Indeed, in his notes for the novel, Keller consistently refers to him as an "idealist" (439). One of the important differences between *Martin Salander* and the literary predecessors I have discussed above is therefore that the "good" half of the ethical dichotomy receives something less than a wholehearted endorsement. Salander's naïveté is implicitly criticized and corrected, here by his wife and later, as we shall see, by his son Arnold.[34]

The evil contrast figure to Salander is supplied by Louis Wohlwend, whose very name announces his uncanny ability to turn seeming disaster into advantage (*Dinge zu seinem Wohl wenden*, to turn things to one's advantage).[35] That Keller intended the two characters to be ethical antagonists is evident from his notes, where he remarked: "Louis Wohlwend the bad type. Salander the good one" (447). In his almost innate disposition toward dishonesty and in his opposition to Salander, Wohlwend resembles Itzig and Moses in their respective relationships to Anton and Hans. But Keller also includes several details that bring Wohlwend into a more obvious proximity to these two literary precursors. He and Salander are old friends—in fact, best friends—who attended the same teacher's college. Here their relationship is not unlike that of Anton and Itzig. In *Soll und Haben* we are told that Anton assisted his Jewish friend with his homework; the same holds true for Salander and Wohlwend. As Martin reports: "We were already good friends in the same teachers' seminar. He was a slow learner and therefore stuck with me, since I found it easier. To the other students it seemed as if I were the one learning from him. God knows how that happened!" (14–15). From this example we can see that Wohlwend, like Moses, has the knack of appearing to know more than he actually does and to be more than he actually is. He is also

191

a skillful rhetorician, someone who knows how to manipulate situations to his own advantage.[36] Like Moses he changes his name, in his case presumably not to cover his racial origins but nonetheless likewise to enhance his social mystique; Wohlwend becomes Volvend-Glavicz (285). Like Itzig he is active in sectors of the business world that do not require "work," that is, speculative and financial enterprises. And like both his predecessors, he is meant to represent the dishonest parvenu whose position in society is attained by illicit means. The main difference in *Martin Salander* is that Wohlwend is not Jewish, although he duplicates a profile most often associated with anti-Semitic portrayals in nineteenth-century German prose. Besides being a dishonest financier who profits from others' misfortunes and gullibility, he also lacks any trace of nationalist feeling. It is significant that Salander hardly recognizes him when he returns from Hungary (266), that he changes his name so that he no longer appears Swiss, and that he, unlike Martin, feels no loyalty to Switzerland. What Moses Freudenstein tells Hans would seem to apply to both the Jewish figures we have examined and to Louis Wohlwend as well: "We Jews are really the true cosmopolitans, citizens of the world by the grace of God" (128). As Marx pointed out in the *Communist Manifesto* (1848), this "cosmopolitanism" is actually connected with the logic of capitalist expansion, a logic that each of the villains, whether Jewish or not, successfully internalizes. That Moses leaves Germany for Paris after his studies and that Keller, in sketching various alternatives for Wohlwend, jotted down "A parasite in Paris" (442), once again demonstrate the similarity between them in terms of morality and rootlessness. As in the Nazi ideology of the next century, realism finds the Jew/speculator/financier to be an eternal wanderer and parasite, sucking the wholesome red blood of devout patriots. But perhaps more astonishing in the consideration of Wohlwend's relationship to his Jewish predecessors is the narrator's description of him midway through the book. We read that he now looks "half-Asiatic," and that he has assumed a strange sort of German dialect (270); both of these features are characteristic of the Jewish stereotype in nineteenth-century Germany. Indeed, in one of the first notes Keller made for the novel, we find the following under the heading "Principle of Race" (*Princip der Race*): "Good and Evil, nobility and baseness is a question of the more refined or the cruder race" (*Die Güte u[nd] Schlechtigkeit, Noblesse u[nd] Gemeinheit der Personen ist Frage der feineren oder gröberen Race*)

(436). Now Keller, who was by no means completely free from anti-Semitic sentiments, probably did not mean *race* in any strict sense here. Nonetheless, his novel, like Freytag's and Raabe's, operates with a set of dubious and potentially dangerous dichotomies. Just as Raabe's character Moses Freudenstein is a "businessman" without being involved in industry or commerce, so too Louis Wohlwend is a "Jew" although he is never specifically identified with this faith.

By playing off Salander against Wohlwend, Keller is able to convey a familiar ethical message. Financial speculation and the business mentality of the initial years of the Second Empire—the so-called *Gründerzeit*—are criticized with the character Wohlwend. The alternative is the somewhat anachronistic "ethical capitalism" propagated by Salander. According to his ethical principles, one should engage in business deals not solely for personal gain but rather for the public weal. In fact, Salander becomes a businessman only because Marie's dowry carries with it, in his mind, a responsibility to the community: "I considered myself to owe everything because I possessed some wealth" (17). He lends money to the swindler Wohlwend not to make a profit but purely out of friendship; and after he has finally achieved success in the business world, he devotes his time and energy to local politics rather than to increasing his wealth. In this regard he is contrasted not only with Wohlwend but also with the Weidelich family, who sees in the Salander daughters only a means of climbing the social ladder: Netti and Setti are worth "a half million apiece" (119). Salander's ethics, on the other hand, are reinforced in the novel by the Kleinpeter episode. Ruined by the avarice and status-seeking of his wife and sons, Kleinpeter shares with Salander the sense that civic responsibilities, not self-aggrandizement, are of paramount importance: "As an affable and popular man, he placed more value on the demands of society and civic conduct than on the acquisition of riches" (222). Here we might note that the emphasis on political involvement distinguishes the ethos of *Martin Salander* from the novels previously discussed. This deviation is due largely to the different political situation in Switzerland at the time. Freytag's implicit plea for restricting one's activities to the economic sphere and Raabe's message of pursuing happiness through work and love in the provinces are more appropriate for the defeated, postrevolutionary middle class in Germany during the 1850s and 1860s. Nonetheless, all three works advocate an ideology that would retain capitalism but negate its unethical ramifications.

No one in *Martin Salander* expresses this ideology better than Arnold, Salander's son. When asked by his father if he thinks that they should risk expanding the business, he replies:

> "The gist of the question lies in the word 'risk' that you used; whether we can risk an expansion!" Arnold continued: "We are right at the point where we have to consider exactly that, namely, we are at the point where we would have to venture a part of our profit, perhaps everything, in order to acquire more. Speaking for myself I would have to confess that over there, on the other side of the ocean, I thought more than once in moments of calm about how far we really want to go with our business. Do we want to become little nabobs, who either change their lives or who have to bury anxiously the mammon that is in superfluity for their needs, and in either case make ourselves look ridiculous? You are a politician and a man of the people anyway; for my part I am an amateur historian and lawyer. It would be more appropriate for both of us therefore if we would remain within our middle-class relations and habits, as you have done in such exemplary fashion up till now." (391–92)

As in *Soll und Haben*, the emphasis is not on profit, business ventures, or expansion, but rather on being content with what one has, on security and self-realization. These latter qualities also connect it with Hans's provincial idyll in *Der Hungerpastor*. Once again, therefore, a novel of realism seeks to reconcile middle-class activity with a humanistic ethic of personal development and public benefit.

Let me summarize my arguments to this point. Although one might not want to use occupation as a defining characteristic for realism, both the theorists and the practitioners of German realism accord an important place to what the hero does for a living. Upon closer examination we found, however, that not just occupation in the sense of work, activity, or career, but also, and perhaps more decisively, the ethics accompanying the occupation are essential for the novels of realism. A relatively coherent and consistent message, potentially in conflict with the capitalist reality of the rising bourgeoisie, can be discerned in each of the novels we looked at. Integrity, public service, and domestic security, as well as a rejection of exploitation, profit, and expansion were the salient features of what I have termed the "ethical capitalism" in these works. This ethical content is conveyed by means of structural dichotomies. Jewishness is used primarily as a moral rather than a racial category. In each case a good-natured, somewhat idealistic, but thoroughly honest hero is juxtaposed with a ruthless, egotistical, and self-destructive villain. Through the use of parallel lives the reader should clearly differentiate between good and evil, although, as we have seen in *Soll und Haben*, the logic of capitalism often breaks down this neat opposition.[37] Indeed, the use of identical metaphors for Hans and Moses in *Der Hungerpastor*—both figures have a consuming "hunger," both use knowledge as a "weapon"—and the continued friendship of Martin and Louis despite the latter's double swindle suggest that the distinctions in these novels are not all that clear-cut either. Nonetheless, it is not difficult to distill from the structure and the plot the ethos that is the business of realism. With some modification other works could have been cited to demonstrate these ethics as well. Despite significant differences, Stifter's *Nachsommer* (*Indian Summer*, 1857), Otto Ludwig's *Zwischen Himmel und Erde* (*Between Heaven and Earth*, 1856), or Keller's *Der grüne Heinrich* (*Green Henry*, 1854/55), especially in the second version, are in their own way illustrations of this important dimension of German literary realism.

The choice of novels with strongly antinomic structuring principles was not completely fortuitous, however, for it seems to me that the very dichotomies I have been at pains to elaborate reflect on the realism of these works in a very special fashion. When theorizing about realism began in Germany in the 1850s, writers recognized that the alternative they were supporting must involve more than a mere copying of external reality. If the works of the new middle class were to stand on equal footing with those of previous generations, they would have to retain a creative, imaginative, and poetic element. In opposing the idealism of the Young Germans and the tendentious writings of the pre-March (*Vormärz*) period, these writers were not advocating a slice out of life, as the naturalists would later in the century, but rather a poeticizing of reality. This demand was captured most succinctly, perhaps, in Otto Ludwig's call for a "poetic realism."[38] In comparing the realist Shakespeare to the idealist Schiller, Ludwig clearly distances himself from any type of photographic imitation: "Art should not be impoverished reality, but rather enriched reality; it should not provide less fascination, but by means of thoughts that spring from the fantasy it should add new fascination, everything that arises out of the intertwined mixture in the two worlds of the serious and the comic. It should not be half of a world, but an entire world."[39] What Ludwig has in mind here is that writers should strive to create a separate and complete reality in their work. Other passages in his theory make it clear that he is concerned primarily with consistency of motivation, the illusion of a totality, and the typical in characterization. In the passage I have just cited and in the writings of other theorists of the era, however, it is also evident that imagination and inspiration are not to be excluded and that, therefore, realism entails a tension or a paradox at its very basis. On the one hand, we read of the necessity to remain true to reality, whether this is phrased in terms of an imitation of nature, character consistency, or the depiction of contemporary work. On the other hand, we encounter the demand to construct a work of art, to exercise one's fantasy and creativity, in short, to be "poetic." This tension between poiesis and mimesis is captured perfectly in the term "poetic realism."[40] With respect to the novels discussed above, however, we may also be reminded of the ethical polarity in the contrasting characters, for what is striking in the discourse surrounding poetic realism is the almost identical manner in which the positive hero of realism and the poetic are described and preferred. Both are imaginative, creative, and productive; both are shaped according to an ideal; and both are somehow more valuable and more worthy than their crude opposites, although not entirely separable from them. When Ludwig writes that "the thing represented should not be common [*gemein*] reality,"[41] is there not some hint of Itzig, Moses, and Wohlwend in this almost derogatory reference? Are not these characters also nonproductive (in the sense that they create no new value), parasitic (they live off the honest German/Swiss characters), and vulgar (they are consistently associated with shady, semicriminal elements in society)? Despite—or perhaps because of—their evil constitutions, however, are they not more in touch with the mechanisms of society, with the values of capitalism, and therefore with the reality of the nineteenth century? Indeed, could we not further speculate that there is an unconscious association of the Jewish speculators, who threaten the bourgeois social order, the masses in the revolution of 1848, whose radical demands alienated more moderate factions, and "crude" realism, all of which challenge cherished middle-class ideals? And if this is so, do we not then find in the term "poetic realism" an aesthetic program with a hidden political agenda cloaked in moral vestments? Do we not encounter in the literary doctrines of the age of realism the forced reconciliation of precisely those antagonisms which in the practice of realism, for ethical and political reasons, are necessarily rent asunder?

Soll und Haben, at least, seems to bear out this hypothesis. Anton

196

is continuously called upon to defend the poeticity of his existence, which is challenged from two distinct perspectives. The first of these is the realm of imagination and poetry itself. When Bernhard Ehrenthal, the multilingual scholar and student of poetry, judges the present to be "cold and monotonous," when he calls the life of a businessman "prosaic," reminding us of Hegel's evaluation of the nineteenth century in his *Aesthetics*, Anton voices an immediate protest. His profession, he counters, provides all the excitement, all the powerful feelings and deeds that have made up the "stuff of poetry" (181). "The merchant in our world experiences just as much grandeur in terms of feelings and deeds as any knight among the Arabs or the Indians" (181). The dull and uniform tasks of a real merchant are then stylized into an existence full of adventure, suspense, and magic. Anton likens the bankruptcy of a large business firm—the wailing of the wife, the desperation of the owner—to the classical tragic genre.[42] Indeed, Anton, who at one point is labeled the "Mignon of the office" (101), lives a life framed by the "poetry of business." As a child his aspiration to become a merchant is accompanied by the following narrative comment: "Let no one say that our life is poor in poetic mood; the good fairy of poetry still reigns everywhere over the doings of earthly creatures" (7). More than six hundred pages later, at the close of the novel, after he has been made a partner in the firm and has married the boss's sister, the identical dreams are recalled and identified with the ethical message of the book: "The poetic dreams that the young lad Anton had harbored in his father's house under the blessings of good parents have been honorable dreams. They were fulfilled" (640). As the personification of "realistic universal poetry"[43] in the business world, Anton has to distinguish himself not only from the "nonrealist" poetry of the bookish Bernhard[44] but also from the crass realism of business as represented by Itzig. In this regard their respective apprenticeships are particularly instructive. Itzig's initial opinion that success depends on learning a secret art (84) is mocked by Hippus, who proceeds to teach him dry legal technicalities. The more Anton, on the other hand, learns about his trade, the more mysterious and inspiring it seems:

> Mr. Jordan made a considerable effort to initiate his apprentice in the mystery of commodities, and the hour in which Anton first stepped into the storehouse of the business and became personally acquainted with hundreds of different materials and re-

markable formations in technical terms was for his receptive disposition the source of a peculiar poetry that was founded on a fairy tale-like fascination, which brings out strange and foreign qualities in the soul of human beings. (46)

Anton's worldview is that of the romantic idealist; Itzig's that of the crude realist. The former acts out of principles, the latter out of precise recognition of the actual circumstances. Perhaps part of the reason for the aesthetic failure of the novel, despite its commercial success, is attributable to the contrived manner in which poetry and realism are forced to coexist throughout. Anton cannot be truly realistic as a poetic merchant, and both the artistic and the ethical messages ultimately betray their precarious foundations, revealing themselves to be fantastic and propagandistic.

The reflection on poetic realism is handled differently and more skillfully in *Der Hungerpastor*. Again the German hero inclines toward the poetic and the Jew remains tied to a baser reality. Hans Unwirrsch is dreamy and soulful; like Anton, he acts on the basis of convictions, not "realistic" appraisal. Moses Freudenstein, as his antipode, is cold and ruthless, but therefore also objective and factual. This contrast between the two is presented most clearly during their school years. Hans has difficulties because he often allows his imagination to divert him from the task at hand. Moses has the "advantage" of possessing no imagination, and as he increases his knowledge, he strangles "the last remains of warm fantasy that were left in him" (88). It is thus fitting that in defending his dissertation—"The Material as an Instance of the Divine"—he is able to turn the tables and make the divine a moment of the material (133). The more serious and—from the perspective of literary theory—paradoxical reflection occurs later in the novel. After his varied experiences, Hans, we are told, wants to write an autobiography: "I have experienced so much, but I am all mixed up inside, and it is high time that I pull myself together and take stock of myself" (330). The title of his opus is "Book about Hunger" (*Buch vom Hunger*), and it requires little imagination on the part of the reader to recognize that the novel itself, with a slightly altered title, is something like the work he intends. Hans, who falls into a "completely romantic mood" (333) while thinking about his life, is unable to compose his "realistic" memoirs. His lively fantasy does not come to his aid; rather, it proves to be a barrier to writing: "the dancing, swirling thoughts did not want to restrain themselves and let themselves be fettered in my rough draft" (336). The problem is that our "poetic" hero cannot write in a realist vein: "The figures endowed with flesh and blood, the real, living relationships, in short, the things as they were had brought about a complete upheaval in his mind. A man like Hans Unwirrsch with such a completely subjective constitution could not deal with this as easily on paper as it appeared he could before he gave it a try" (337). For Hans reality itself becomes a hindrance to realism. By the end of the novel, when his own reality has become more idyllic, he has completely forgotten the book he intended earlier. The successful author in the novel, of course, is the loquacious dialectician Theophile Stein; but with his lack of fantasy and lack of sympathy, why would he be interested in a "Buch vom Hunger." From the perspective of "poetry" and "realism" delineated in *Der Hungerpastor*, the novel itself is impossible: if it is realistic (written by a type like Theophile Stein), then it will be without poeticity; if it is supposed to be poetic (authored by Hans Unwirrsch), it will remain unwritten. In a moment of ironic self-cancellation, this paradoxical reflection questions the fundamental precepts of any endeavor at poetic realism.

If *Soll und Haben* shows us the pretense of poetic realism and *Der Hungerpastor* exposes its aporetic demands, then we might conceive of *Martin Salander* as the proclamation of its demise. More than one critic has noted that this novel, in comparison with Keller's earlier work, signals a major change in his style.[45] Absent is the fairy-tale language of the Seldwyla novellas as well as the intrusive narrator commenting critically on the actions of the characters. Keller appears to have moved toward a naturalistic conception of literature; for although his language does not strive to be mechanically photographic or phonographic, it is noticeably drier, more monotonous, almost matter-of-fact. Thus when the earlier world of imagination does intrude, it has added significance. This occurs twice in the novel, as far as I can tell. In one of the opening scenes, the practical Marie, trying to divert the thoughts of her children from their hunger, resorts to pure fantasy. The fairy tale of the little people from the mountain that she relates, in contrast to the novel in which it is embedded, is meant to make its listeners forget reality (36–40). Wish fulfillment guides Marie's narrative, not probability, and at one point she experiences pangs of guilt because she believes that she is somehow deceiving her children. Fantasy is here opposed to reality and understood as manipulation. The inclusion of this episode, therefore, implicitly questions the compatibility of the poetic and the real world, casting doubt on the doctrine of "poetic realism" that sought to unite them.

Later in the novel we find a second and more crucial reflection on the conflict between poetry and reality, this time in the person of Myrrha Glawicz, Wohlwend's attractive sister-in-law. Because of her ideal features and seductive qualities, commentators justifiably have deciphered her as Keller's vehicle for criticizing poetic realism. At first Wohlwend intends to employ her to placate and distract Salander; later he evidently wants her to entrap Arnold. For a time his initial plan meets with success. The elder Salander is obviously infatuated with the mysterious but taciturn Myrrha, who thus tentatively and tenuously unites the "poetic" Martin with the "realist" Louis. The poetry that Myrrha personifies, however, turns out to be a mere façade for a less pleasant reality. In the penultimate chapter Arnold exposes the emptiness of beautiful appearances when he reveals to his father that this lovely woman is mentally deficient and that her mouth reeks of the sausage she ate for lunch (398–99). When the ideal is brought in touch with reality, it is no longer poetic; when it is thought to be poetic, it is no longer real. In disclosing the mindlessness and sterility of empty poetic realism, Keller thus reflects on the nonreflexiveness of poetic realism, on its inability or perhaps unwillingness to comprehend its constituent elements. Gerhard Kaiser has noted in this regard: "She [Myrrha] is the demented muse of a poetic realism that cannot thematize its poeticity, and that in this respect is without reflection and thus, in keeping with this, the real essence of reality remains absolutely given—and absolutely removed."[46] Or, in terms of literary history, she represents the silence and imbecility of a hollow poetic doctrine in the face of the harsh realities of the late nineteenth century.[47]

At the close of *Martin Salander*, Wohlwend, threatened with exposure by Arnold, loses his self-confidence and hurriedly leaves Münsterburg. His departure does not mark the disappearance of the type of speculative capitalism he represents but only of one of its most objectionable practitioners. Salander thus avoids being swindled a third time, but the future does not belong to his ilk of nonexpansionist, nonexploitative capitalist. Keller did not intend the saga of the Salander family to end here, however. In letters and conversations he repeatedly expressed his plan for a sequel to *Martin Salander* in which Arnold would have been the hero. There are probably many reasons why this continuation was never even started, and not the least of these may have been Keller's age and poor health. We might also be tempted to speculate that part of the problem Keller faced had something to do with the conflict between poetry and realism indirectly thematized in his last novel. A critical, realist work in the manner of the naturalists would be difficult to imagine with Arnold as the protagonist, since he, like his father, adheres to an obsolete business ethic. To have him champion merchant capitalism in the manner of Anton Wohlfahrt, opposing speculation and financial manipulation with naiveté and honesty, would signal either a return to the blatantly ideological message of a work like *Soll und Haben* or a conscious falsification of historical developments in nineteenth-century Europe. The only other possibility, a flight into totally subjective fantasy, would have been equally distasteful to Keller and not at all consonant with Arnold's sober and practical personality. When Keller, like his contemporaries, is confronted with the Hegelian alternatives of "prosaic objectivity," the capturing of the finitude of bourgeois existence, and a subjectivity that exerts its absolute authority over reality,[48] he elects silence. He had no other choice really; for Myrrha, the discredited and simpleminded muse of poetic realism, had already left on the train with her brother-in-law, and her departure signals a definitive turning point for the fragile and contradictory theory and practice of prose fiction that had dominated German literary circles for the greater part of the previous century.

8

AFTER REALISM:
The Nonreflecting Mirror and the Unchanging Portrait

The absurdity of the real insists on a form
that smashes the realist façade.
>   Theodor Adorno,
>   "Open Letter to Rolf Hochhuth"

Spiegel: noch nie hat man wissend beschrieben,
was ihr in euerem Wesen seid.
Ihr, wie mit lauter Löchern von Sieben
erfüllten Zwischenräume der Zeit.

(Mirrors: never yet has anyone described
knowing, what you are really like.
You, interstices of time
filled as it were with nothing but sieveholes.)
>   Rainer Maria Rilke,
>   *Sonnets to Orpheus*

The departure of the "muse" of poetic realism does not mean that the contradictions inherent in this label disappeared as well. The tension between the belief that literature must somehow reflect an external reality and yet retain a modicum of fantasy continues to be a central problem for authors at the end of the nineteenth century. What I have tried to show on the preceding pages is the extent to which issues relating to this crisis in representation were treated in the texts of the realists themselves. My contention throughout has been that the often inadvertent theoretical allusions in realist texts are quite

202

frequent and often more sophisticated than the consciously theoretical speculations of the same authors. The results are fairly uniform. When realism is thematized in the texts I have selected—all of which were composed between 1830 and 1890—it calls its own epistemological foundations into question. This is most evident in Büchner's *Lenz*, Storm's *Aquis submersus*, and Raabe's *Hungerpastor*, although this tendency to self-cancellation can be detected in several of the other prose works analyzed above. At this point of textual rupture, we have also witnessed that these texts are most vulnerable in terms of disclosing their ideological biases. Consistently, realist works carve out a space based on the exclusion of otherness. Sometimes the other is defined in terms of madness (*Lenz*), sometimes as illicit sexual desire (*Romeo und Julia auf dem Dorfe*, *Aquis submersus*, *Der grüne Heinrich*, *Der Nachsommer*); in other cases the exclusion is related to race (*Der Heilige*, *Soll und Haben*, *Der Hungerpastor*, *Martin Salander*). Common to all realist enterprises, however, is the creation of a normed discourse that protects itself from threats to bourgeois propriety by two central strategies. First, it implicitly asserts its own innocence. If realist prose merely mirrors what is "out there" in the society or the "real" world, then it can hardly be accused of creating a norm or of bias against otherness. Second, realist texts often have the overt pretension of themselves looking at social issues in a critical fashion. On the surface, Keller's novella, for example, chastises a narrow-minded, restrictive society; his autobiographically informed novel contains an obvious call for an active citizenry; and his final work lambasts the shady methods of capitalist speculation. Even Freytag's seemingly propagandistic best-seller criticizes more or less openly recent practices in the business world of his day.[1]

If we view realism in terms of the two strategies I have just defined, then naturalism would seem to be the culmination of the realist epoch.[2] This "super-realism" pushed the exact reproduction of the social world to its limits while taking up topics that even realist texts excluded. In naturalism the most extreme social questions are depicted in the most precise detail. Incest, sexual depravity, and alcoholism (*Vor Sonnenaufgang* [*Before Daybreak*, 1889]), the class struggle, religious hypocrisy, and proletarian misery (*Die Weber* [*The Weavers*, 1892]), women's emancipation (*Einsame Menschen* [*Lonely People*, 1891])—these issues, emarginated by most realist fiction, are at the very center of the naturalists' concerns. But though naturalism appears to shy away from none of the threats to realist propriety, it nonetheless closes off access to whole areas of human experience, in some cases exactly those areas that would illuminate the social phenomena it superficially treats. Paradoxically the reason for this is that it takes exact portrayal of reality as a serious proposition. Epistemologically the most consistent naturalists adhered to a naive empiricist notion of cognition based on dogmas of nineteenth-century natural science. A subject, wholly independent from an object, acts as mirror for the external world. From impartial description and induction, one can deduce the laws for natural phenomena. Artists, like their scientific counterpart, are called upon to be uninvolved and ideal observers, who then capture with words the events and persons of contemporary society. This dependence on distanced observation, however, coupled with a contentment with superficial depiction strips the subjectivity from both the observer and the human subject being observed. Social problems in naturalism are thus recorded merely as parts of reality; without a subjectivity reflecting upon them or a subjectivity of the human agents represented, these problems are abandoned in an objectivist sea of meaninglessness. Where naturalists do take up social causes, therefore, they are at odds with their demand for "objective depiction." With their restrictive epistemology and concomitant artistic practice, they can neither understand the psychological mechanisms of social problems nor derive a position on them from which they make sense.

The most representative theoretical pronouncements of this movement are therefore contained in Arno Holz's book *Die Kunst: Ihr Wesen und ihre Gesetze* (*Art: Its Essence and its Laws*, 1891), not only because it is typical in its reproductionist zeal but because it programmatically discloses the inherent contradiction in any (super-) realist dogma. Like most theorists of realism, the super-realist Holz proceeds from the visual and from the analogy with painting. Taking for granted that the goal of art is to create persons or scenes that the observer recognizes, he generalizes a materialist aesthetics for all artistic endeavor. The formulas "Artwork = Piece of Nature − x" and "Art = Nature − x" are the simplistic results of his reduction of the creative process to mathematical equations.[3] To assure the elimination of all subjectivity, he explains that the unknown quantity x should not be identified with *temperament*, as Emile Zola had suggested. Rather Holz claims that x relates only to artists' objective ability to represent reality with the tools at their disposal. Thus he can express his formula in terms of the following rule or law: "Art contains the tendency to become nature again. It will become this according to its conditions of reproduction [*Reproductionsbedingungen*] at any given time, and their accessibility."⁴ The tendency Holz discovers recalls the theory Büchner puts into the mouth of Lenz a half-century earlier. Lenz at several points conceives of art as a freezing, a halting of reality, indeed, in his allusion to the Medusa, as a petrifying in stone. We have seen above that such a theory winds up snarled in a series of aporias. The difference between Büchner and Holz is not simply that the latter has learned nothing during the intervening half century. Rather, the contrast between their theoretical statements is highlighted best by the fact that Büchner, by using a madman to advocate realism, uncovers its fundamental artistic contradictions, whereas Holz, in a perfectly serious and sane series of theoretical pronouncements, adheres madly to the obsolete doctrine itself. His claim to overthrow the entire history of aesthetic speculation on realism—he claims he makes a science (*Wissenschaft*) out of a pseudoscience⁵—ironically appears as the last gasp of a literary and artistic movement that had already run its course.

The naturalist insistence on the ability and necessity of art to reflect reality, this logical extension of realist poetics, is precisely what the twentieth-century novel calls into question. Although one could select almost any modernist piece of prose as evidence for this tendency, Rilke's *Aufzeichnungen des Malte Laurids Brigge* (*Notebooks of Malte Laurids Brigge*, 1910) is one of the most revealing.⁶ Critics have often noted that Rilke's novel departs radically from the usual narrative strategies found in realist fiction. Indeed, as in the works from the early nineteenth century that we examined in the initial chapter, the *Aufzeichnungen* foreground the difficulties of telling a story. Sometimes these difficulties are related to the impossibility of narration in the present age. In a remark that can be read as both a comment on his familial history as well as a reflection on the literary tradition, Malte notes: "The telling of stories, the real telling, must have been before my time" (244).⁷ This statement would appear to be a straightforward expression of the breakdown of traditional narrative structures if it was not followed by the contention that Malte's grandfather, Graf Brahe, supposedly possessed this rare ability. We have learned earlier in the *Aufzeichnungen* that Graf Brahe lives in an eternal present. "Chronological sequence played no role whatever for him, death was a trifling incident that he utterly ignored, persons whom he had once received into his memory continued to exist, and their dying off could not alter that in the least" (135). The ability to narrate appears to be associated with a feeling of timelessness. Narration, understood as the making present of something past (or future), as the re-presenting of events real or imagined, is only authentic when a correspondence exists between action and experience. It is not our lack of historical consciousness that inhibits narrative, according to this view, but rather a superfluity of this consciousness. Only those who, like Graf Brahe, live in unidimensional time are able to bring the past into the present with words.[8]

At other moments, however, the difficulties with narrative have to do with the simple incongruence between words and experience. After recalling the terrifying childhood encounter with his own hand (195), Malte relates, from the perspective of the child, his inability to communicate what had occurred.

> I swallowed a couple of times; for now I wanted to tell about it.
> But how? I made an indescribable effort to master myself, but it was not to be expressed so that anyone could understand. If there were words for this occurrence, I was too little to find them. (196)

The inability to narrate, however, is not the most frightening thought for Malte the child. He seems to fear even more the possibility that words can match his experience.

> And suddenly the fear seized me that nevertheless they might suddenly be there, beyond my years, these words, and it seemed to me more terrible than anything else that I should then have to say them. To live through once again the reality down there, differently, changed, from the beginning; to hear myself admitting it—for that I had no strength left. (196)

More horrifying than the insufficiency of language for representing experience is the quality language possesses to create new experiences by re-creating old ones. Here there is no question of an exact duplication of events; the reproduction in words is a new reality that is "different, changed" (*anders, abgewandelt*). Malte again emphasizes with this episode the close association between narration and presence. What is essential is not that language can capture or reflect reality but that words, whether spoken or written, have the ability to create a reality eternally present.

The nonreflexive quality of literary texts is emphasized most clearly in one of Malte's other childhood experiences, his confrontation with the mirror. As a true reflector of external reality, the mirror is quite obviously the central image of realist aesthetics. That it is connected solely with the visual does not diminish this association in the least. For we have seen repeatedly in the analyses above that this sense defines the realist enterprise, most often to the exclusion of all other senses. The occurrence of the mirror in the *Aufzeichnungen* would thus seem to reflect itself on this tradition. Indeed, the significance of this episode is apparent by the amount of space it occupies in the text. The typical occurrence is dispensed with in a few paragraphs, but Malte's recollections here extend over several pages. It begins with his memories of trying on different costumes from past centuries. When he passes in front of the mirror to examine himself, he receives anything but an accurate reflection of his appearance. "When out of the dimness something drew near, more slowly than oneself, for the mirror did not, so to speak, believe it, and did not want, sleepy as it was, to repeat promptly what had been said to it" (203). Although this unusual description can be attributed to Malte's assumption of the child's perspective, two features appear nonetheless important. First is the suggestion, reinforced by the personification of the mirror, that the traditional metaphor for reflection is misplaced. Mirrors in Rilke's *Aufzeichnungen* do not simply give back what reality presents; they assume a life of their own, creating impressions often only tangentially related to the object they are supposed to reflect. Second, the text here reinforces the suspicion that this passage is commenting on both images and the language that endeavors to capture these images. The metaphor Malte employs compares physical objects with words; the mirror refuses to repeat or echo (*nachsprechen*) what is said to it. Implicit in this metaphor is a poetological statement on realist texts. Not only does the supposedly passive mirror become active, it also refuses to regurgitate images in a language that is conceived as simply reflecting something external to it.

After a brief hesitation Malte's nonreflecting mirror ceases its resistance and apparently reflects Malte in his various costumes, but even in this reflection the text stresses the unusual and noncommensurate. What the child sees is "something very surprising, strange, altogether different from one's expectation, something sudden, independent" (203). Although the mirror supposedly reflects external reality, all of the words used to describe this activity point to the otherness of the reflection. And this nonidentical quality of the mirror and mirroring ultimately dominates in Rilke's work. After breaking two porcelain parrots, spilling a box of candy, and shattering a perfume bottle—

all because he had lost sight of the being in the mirror—Malte attempts to free himself from his disguise, but becomes ever more entangled as he struggles. He rushes forward to the mirror and peers into it through his awkward mask:

> But the mirror had just been waiting for this. Its moment of retaliation had come. While I strove in boundlessly increasing anguish to squeeze somehow out of my disguise, it forced me, by what means I do not know, to lift my eyes and imposed on me an image, no, a reality, a strange, unbelievable and monstrous reality, with which, against my will, I became permeated: for now the mirror was stronger, and I was the mirror. (208)

Once again we should not dismiss this description as merely the consequence of a child's imagination. The mirror, now active, controls representation. Whereas it formerly was compelled to reflect reality, it now creates reality. The medium has become agent. The lesson for literature and art is evident. As Malte himself states in an early passage, he was an imitator and a fool (125)—the two go together—as a would-be playwright at some undefined time prior to the composition of the *Aufzeichnungen*. Embarking on a new course as an author, Malte locates himself at a literary and historical moment in which reflection in the sense of the nineteenth century has become an impossibility.

As described by Malte, the mirror partakes of the phenomenon Freud had described in his essay "The Uncanny" ("Das Unheimliche"). In the *Aufzeichnungen* the mirror reflects something familiar, yet strange, identical, yet different. Just as the uncanny is "that kind of frightful thing that hearkens back to something that is well-known and familiar for a long time,"[9] so too Malte's experience with his own reflection is a horrifying memory caused by something both familiar and unfamiliar to him: his own ego. This is not the first time that Malte relates such an uncanny event. Indeed, the other terrifying recollection from his childhood, the experience with his hand,[10] is similarly a case of the reflection of a familiar and frightening object. Malte is not unduly disturbed by the sight of his own hand, or at least what he recognizes as his own hand. Searching for his crayon under the table, he becomes aware of his hand as something almost detached from his body, but this arouses curiosity, not fear. "I watched it, as I still remember, almost with curiosity; it seemed as if it knew things I had never taught it, groping down there so independently, with movements I had never noticed in it before" (195). Only when Malte observes another hand, does horror result. The description that he supplies, however, corresponds precisely to the mirror experience a few pages later. As the hand approaches the wall, searching for the crayon, its reflection, distorted by the darkness and Malte's fantasy, appears to come out of the wall, grow larger, and approach its mirror image:

> But how should I have been prepared to see suddenly come to meet it out of the wall another hand, a larger, extraordinarily thin hand, such as I had never seen before. It came groping in similar fashion from the other side, and the two outspread hands moved blindly toward one another. My curiosity was not yet used up but suddenly it came to an end, and there was only terror. (195)

The hand and the mirror experiences are thus in curious ways themselves reflections of one another.[11] In each case an image appears to gain power over the reality on which it supposedly depends, producing an uncanny reaction.[12]

If the mirror in postrealist literature does not reflect reality, what does it reflect? The *Aufzeichnungen* suggest two answers to this question. The first can be derived from two separate episodes in the novel in which mirrors also play a prominent role. Toward the end of the first book, Malte relates how he and his cousin Erik walked through the family portrait gallery. We have seen above that, in the literature of the nineteenth century, portraits frequently functioned as implicit commentary on realist poetics. It is not surprising to find that Rilke's text employs this association but subverts the usual valorization of reproduction. The two boys are searching for the portrait of Christine Brahe, the mysterious and purportedly dead relative who appears to her surviving family members occasionally as a ghost. When Malte hears that Christine herself is looking for her picture, he asks why. "She wants to see herself," is the answer he receives (216), and although he does not understand at this point, he pretends that he does. A moment later Erik tells him that he had brought her a mirror instead, but that she is not in it. Malte again does not comprehend, and he receives the following mysterious explanation: "One is either in it, . . . then one is not here; or one is here, and then one cannot be in it" (*Man ist entweder drin, . . . dann ist man nicht hier; oder wenn man hier ist, kann man nicht drin sein*) (217). Malte, fearful that he could be left alone in the dark gallery, hastily agrees; but he obviously has not appreciated Erik's words, or else he has taken them to be more mysterious than they actually are. The meaning of this passage hinges on the sense we attribute to the word *hier* (here). If it means "in the gallery," then Erik's statement is rather banal: when a person dies, his or her picture is hung in the gallery. The portrait is the substitute for the living mirror image. When persons are still alive and possess a reflection in the mirror, they will not appear in the gallery.[13] But if we read this statement in the context of the previous conversation— *sie ist nicht drin*—there is a second and more ghostly sense we can locate in his apothegmatic sentence. The word *hier* could also mean alive, on earth. In this interpretation Erik would be making a pronouncement in keeping with the nonreflecting poetics we have observed in other passages. If a person is alive, reflection is impossible. Only when persons no longer exist, only when they are a product of fantasy, do they appear in a mirror.

The lesson to be learned from this is that although mirrors produce the uncanny, they reflect only the unreal—understood as the product of subjective imagination. This contention appears to be confirmed by the lengthy entry at the close of the first book. Malte here describes tapestries representing the five senses.[14] In each a woman appears accompanied by a lion and a unicorn in various arrangements. His final description—which is also the final passage in the first part of the *Aufzeichnungen*—deals with the tapestry depicting the sense of sight. This may not have been completely fortuitous. As we have seen in previous chapters, the visual is always closely associated with realism, and that Malte chooses to end his account here may call into question the primary importance of this sense for his art. Indeed, in apparent defiance of the allegorical significance of these scenes, Malte endows them with a narrative structure.[15] Sight is the last sense treated; thus it is the culmination of a fiction, the product of an arbitrary narrative imagination. It occurs after "mon seul désir," the inscription on the sixth tapestry. At the close of his description, as if to emphasize the fictitious nature of reflection, Malte relates the central motif: "We have never yet seen her weary; is she weary? Or has she only seated herself because she is holding something heavy? A monstrance, one might think. But she curves her other arm toward the unicorn, and the creature bridles, flattered, and rears and leans upon her lap. It is a mirror, the thing she holds. See: she is showing the unicorn its image—" (229). The mirror, which is at the very center of the tapestry, is the last element on which Malte focuses. In this narrativized version the last element is the sense of sight, and it does not reflect a part of reality, but a myth. The unicorn, this "never-believed"[16] creature that never was (*das es nicht gibt*),[17] gazes at its own image. The fourth sonnet in the second part of the *Sonette an Orpheus* (*Sonnets to Orpheus*, 1923), which likewise depicts this scene, makes the fantastic nature of the unicorn clear.

> Zwar *war* es nicht. Doch weil sie's liebten, ward
> ein reines Tier.
> . . . .
> Zu einer Jungfrau kam es weiß herbei—
> und war im Silber-Spiegel und in ihr.

> (Indeed, it never *was*. Yet because they loved it,
> a pure creature happened.
> . . . .
> To a virgin it came hither white—
> and was in the silver-mirror and in her.)[18]

The unicorn, like the images Malte perceives in the mirror, is imagined; its reflection in and as fiction is contingent on subjective fantasy, not objective existence. Here again we find that the mirror operates in the *Aufzeichnungen* not as a metaphor for realism but as an affirmation of *poiesis*.

The cancellation of realist poetics in the *Aufzeichnungen* through internal allusions is the consequence and a reflection of the breakdown of nineteenth-century strategies on the level of narration and character. The subject-object dichotomy on which realism depends (despite its inadvertent questioning of this philosophical schema) is no longer valid for Malte.[19] Realism for him is unthinkable not because there is no external reality but because this reality is not shared, because it can only be perceived, experienced, described, and processed individually. Thus Malte can use the same visual vocabulary found in the texts and the poetics of the realists from the previous generation, but he means something radically different. Especially in the first half of the *Aufzeichnungen* Malte emphasizes seeing. This does not involve the perception of sense impressions from an external world, however, but rather the comprehension of his own psyche. "I am learning to see. I don't know why it is, but everything penetrates more deeply into me and does not stop at the place where until now it always used to finish. I have an inner self of which I was ignorant" (110–11). Reality is chiefly a catalyst for internal processes; it has no value in and of itself. For this reason reproducing reality in a text—assuming this is possible—cannot be the appropriate goal of literary endeavor. What is important is the impact of this reality on the perceiving subject. In a later passage Malte, commenting on a blind man he met on the street selling cauliflower, gives the reader a good indication of his artistic method: "He was blind and he shouted. I misrepresent when I say that, suppressing the barrow he was shoving, pretending I did not notice he was shouting 'cauliflower.' But is that essential? And even if it were essential, isn't the main thing what the whole business was for me? I saw an old man who was blind and shouted. That I saw. Saw" (148). In contrast to the visual imagery of realism, sight here refers to an interior, private world, one that is just as at home with the fantastic as the natural.[20] Likewise, the language that Malte employs is designed not to be referential but to relate to his personal impressions. Like the Prodigal Son, whose story closes the novel, Malte too searches for words to express experience (343–44). The poetics of the *Aufzeichnungen* thus redirect the outward glance associated with the realist enterprise to internal spaces. For Malte and the reader, the real, formerly associated with objects and events external to the self, does not extend beyond the boundaries of the individual mind.

How then does this reflection on (and rejection of) realism measure up against the preceding analyses? In the nineteenth-century texts discussed above, I have contended that at some point in the work a reflection on realism occurs. Most often we can discern a contradiction or paradox in this passage, particularly in the context of realist poetics. These passages serve simultaneously, however, as entries into an ideological reading of realism that demonstrates the limited and limiting nature of realist discourse. Texts that foreground such reflections, such as the two works included in the initial chapter, violate norms of realism. This does not mean that they do not establish a different norm —the *Nachtwachen* appears to validate a particularly extreme and bleak version of romanticism—nor does it mean that they are nonideological —the narrator of *Buch Le Grand* quite obviously "ironizes irony" for the sake of a political program that is fairly evident. It means, rather, that these messages are not situated in a textual rupture but are themselves the object of a reflexive activity. Rilke's *Aufzeichnungen* is a similar case. Here the chief symbol of realism is subverted in the process of positing an alternative model for producing texts. In contrast to a theory of appropriating reality, the *Aufzeichnungen* postulates describing experience as internal reality. This extreme subjectivity involves a reduction of all phenomenal events to private perceptions, and in this sense it represents one extreme path taken in the modernist critique of traditional modes of representation. Relinquishing all claims to a reproduction of reality, this direction in modernism contents itself with the exploration of an interior space devoid of overt ideological entanglements. This, of course, defines its very ideology. In closing down any common ground by which the reader could recognize world or self, it affirms an atomistic ideology of uniqueness at odds with the shared linguistic signs it employs, a longing for authenticity through private individualization, rather than political action or solidarity. In the *Aufzeichnungen des Malte Laurids Brigge*, the reflection on the impossibility of realism entails a reduction of reality to an unrealistic, solipsistic notion of self.

Modernism also took another direction in reflecting on its nineteenth-century predecessors, and this alternative path is perhaps most evident in a novel written less than a decade after Rilke's *Aufzeichnungen*: Franz Kafka's *Der Prozeß* (*The Trial*, 1925).[21] In this work, as we shall see, it is not the subject but the object that reigns supreme. The allusion to realism that helps to show this hegemony of the objective occurs in the seventh chapter, when K. meets the painter Titorelli. Heinz Politzer has noted that this name is "a resounding blend of illustr[i]ous prototypes such as Titian, Tintoretto, Signorelli."[22] As a composite of various Italian artists, however, it also may refer obliquely to the opening chapter of Freud's *Zur Psychopathologie des Alltagslebens* (*Toward a Psychopathology of Everyday Life*, 1904). Here Freud analyzes his own forgetting of the proper name Signorelli. In contrast to the psychoanalytic process, however, Titorelli is neither repressed nor forgotten. Instead he appears to K. as the most open and useful of his various helpers. In one of the fragmentary chapters, Kafka even refers to the assistance of Titorelli as the most favorable chance for K.: "Here, if anywhere, he realized, it would be possible to break through" (210).[23] Indeed, Titorelli's apparent candor and extensive knowledge of the inner workings of the court have led some critics to think that he is the key figure among K.'s contacts.[24] This interpretation, like almost all attempts to arrive at determinate meaning in the novel, is open to a great deal of doubt. Neither the painter's atelier nor his living situation give the reader (or K. at first) confidence that he is an influential and authoritative individual. The manufacturer claims that he is "almost a beggar" and adds that he certainly lies (117). Indeed, even if we assume that he is in a position to give an accurate representation of the procedures of the court—an assumption that is undercut by his artistic practice—his conversation leaves K. in the same predicament he was in before he encountered him.

Because he has been seen as a key figure in the novel, and because he is the only person associated with the arts, it is somewhat strange that critics have not paid more attention to his actual occupation.[25] In the aesthetics he implicitly advocates is a clue, I believe, to any evaluation of his potential usefulness to K.[26] In light of our previous considerations, it is also not unimportant that his profession played such a prominent role in realist prose of the past century. Painting, as we have seen, is the art form around which the concept of realism developed, and the vocabulary of theories about realism, from Plato to Lukács, relies heavily on vision and the visual arts. But in our first introduction to Titorelli, as in the discussions around Johannes in *Aquis submersus*, business appears to be more important than creativity. The manufacturer considers the purchase of his work to be a kind of charity; although he is not displeased by the landscapes he buys, he evidences no interest in art or artistic theory. These sporadic sales, however, are not the chief source of income for Titorelli, and the manufacturer is astounded to learn that he is chiefly a portraitist for the court. Josef K. shares this lack of concern for Titorelli's artistic work. He goes to see him only because he feels that he can obtain information pertaining to his case, and he, like the manufacturer, purchases landscapes without interest in the aesthetic principles that inform them. Titorelli, on the other hand, introduces himself as "*Kunst*maler Titorelli" (my emphasis), obviously conscious of his art; and when K. questions him about the judges he paints, hoping to receive insight into the proceedings of the court, Titorelli frequently steers the conversation in the direction of his odd and antirealist aesthetics. In paying no attention to art, K. duplicates the manufacturer's philistine attitudes, and as a consequence he remains ignorant about the very matters he comes to discuss.

In order to avoid K.'s mistake, let us take a closer look at the artistic principles underlying Titorelli's work. The reader's first acquaintance with his aesthetics occurs before we encounter the artist himself. Sitting with Leni in the darkened office of the lawyer, K.'s eyes gradually make out objects in the room. Most conspicuous to him is a large portrait of a judge hanging to the right of the door. The judge is depicted in official robes seated on an impressive, throne-

214

like chair. What strikes K. as unusual about the picture is that the judge is not seated calmly and in a dignified posture; rather, he is shown rising from his seat, as if he were about "to say something decisive or to pronounce a judgment" (94). Unfamiliar with Titorelli's unusual artistic prescriptions, K. treats the picture as a realistic portrayal of a person. His initial comment to Leni is that this is perhaps his judge. But Leni, who has gained some insight into a nonrealist aesthetics through simple exposure to reality and its nonidentical image, clarifies the situation. Since she knows the judge personally, she can verify that he looks nothing like his portrait; even in his youth he could not have resembled the image on the canvas, since there he appears much taller than he is in reality. Although Leni then tries to distract K. with flirtation, he perseveres in his queries about the portrait, inquiring about the status of this judge. He is surprised to learn that he is only an examining magistrate since he is seated on such an imposing chair. But Leni explains that this aspect of the painting also has nothing to do with reality: "That's all invention . . ., actually he is sitting on a kitchen chair, with an old horse-rug doubled under him" (94). K. is here guilty of committing the mimetic fallacy; he believes that the function of art is to reproduce elements of the external world. He has not yet learned that there is no necessary match between reality and artistic representation in a postrealist world.

His opportunity to gain an understanding of modernist representation occurs in his conversation with Titorelli. But K. is too preoccupied with the court and his case to comprehend the lesson Titorelli's strange aesthetics teaches. K. comes to the painter with a letter from the manufacturer that presumably recommends Titorelli for his unofficial expertise in matters of the court, but the painter ignores this and begins to speak about his art. After reading the letter, he asks K. whether he wants to purchase paintings or sit himself for a portrait. K. is confused by this response since he presumed the manufacturer had mentioned his case. As it turns out, he has, but Titorelli is evidently more intent on art than on supplying information at this point. Or perhaps he detects an opportunity to make a quick sale. In an attempt to distract Titorelli, K. directs his attention to the portrait on which he is currently working. It is similar to the picture K. had seen in the lawyer's office. Portrayed is a completely different judge in precisely the same posture. This unusual representation of a seated figure about to rise and pronounce judgment has been traced by Malcolm Pasley to Michelangelo's statue of Moses,[27] and it is not unlikely that Kafka was influenced here by descriptions of the artwork found in Freud's essay "Der Moses des Michelangelo" ("The Moses of Michelangelo"), published in *Imago* in February 1914. From careful attention to details, Freud overturns most contemporary interpretations, which saw Moses as rising from his throne in anger. The statue, Freud maintains, depicts Moses a moment after he has decided not to rise. This is the reason he gives the impression of movement and stasis at the same time. K. emulates Freud in examining his judge closely, but instead of focusing on the details of the judge himself,[28] he notices a vaguely defined figure on the back of the chair. The painter identifies it as an allegory of justice, but claims at the same time that it is the goddess of victory. This figure, like Freud's Moses and perhaps like the judges, partakes of an undecidability quality, an ambiguity that goes to the heart of a nonrealist aesthetics. Neither seated nor rising, neither justice nor victory, art in the hands of Titorelli/Freud is emancipated from both a definitive referent in the world and from a single meaning. K., who yearns for certainty in this and other issues, finds the two contradictory allegorical associations an "unfortunate combination" (126). He cannot comprehend the simultaneity of opposites. But for a postrealist art, such tensions, as well as the frustration of an audience accustomed to determinate reference and meaning are normal.

To this point in their conversation, K. has shown more of a propensity for discerning inconsistencies in the symbolism—and the underlying ideals—of the court than for understanding Titorelli's artistic raison d'être. Just how much he misunderstands the function and goal of his art is shown by their subsequent exchange. Titorelli, rather than trying to interpret the contradictory allegory, rather than searching for a meaning concealed in the figure, explains that he is merely following the orders of his client. K.'s false assumption is that both Titorelli and the judges of the court subscribe to his representational values: "You have painted the figure as it actually stands above the high seat [*Thronsessel*]" (126). But the painter denies this emphatically. In fact, he claims to have seen neither the figure nor the judge's chair, and although he therefore maintains everything is "invention" (just as Leni had claimed in the episode described above), the clarification he supplies indicates that this is not a totally accurate designation. For there is no sense here that Titorelli is painting according to his subjective fantasy. He is not inventing in the sense that he has the liberty to select whatever suits him at the moment or to exercise his fantasy. On the contrary, everything he paints is prescribed exactly. His invention here turns into a kind of repetition, recalling perhaps Keller's ambivalence toward these two words in the opening paragraph of *Romeo und Julia auf dem Dorfe*. The difference is that the repetition of the painter Titorelli has nothing whatsoever to do with reality. Rather, it is convention that absolutely determines every stroke of Titorelli's brush. Even though this portrait is painted for private enjoyment—"it is intended for a lady" (126)—it must still conform to the rules. What K. fails to recognize in Titorelli's aesthetics—and in his own predicament—is the inescapability of the law. In contrast to Rilke's subjective iconoclasm in the *Aufzeichnungen*, here the individual, whether artist or accused, cannot escape the invisible web of structures that determines art and action.

When Titorelli returns to the topic of his painting later in the conversation, he confirms this initial impression that the rules by which he works are both secret and binding. Endeavoring to secure the confidence of the painter, K. inquires about his initial employment as court portraitist. We learn that his position has nothing to do with artistic talent; he inherited it from his father. His qualifications are simply that he has a familiarity with the requisite rules. "There are so many complicated rules laid down for the painting of the different grades of functionaries that a knowledge of them is confined to certain families" (130). In addition, Titorelli has sketches from his father, which he shows to no one. Even without these his knowledge of the rules —not his ability, style, or originality—would still enable him to retain his post. He alone knows how to paint the judges in the style of the old, great judges of yesteryear, the manner in which these conceited men of the court all want to be portrayed. The world we have entered in accompanying K. into Titorelli's atelier is therefore a hermetic, not a reflexive, system of artistic representation. We customarily think of portraiture as a form of painting in which the artist closely copies an original, emphasizing the individuality of the subject, but Titorelli adheres to aesthetic principles that abandon any notion of verisimilitude, promulgating instead an anonymity of types. Reproduction is a central concern, but it is not the reproduction of world but of another portrait for which the original does not exist. This, at least, is the sense one gets from the bequest of the position from one generation to the next. Art has entered an age of mechanical reproducibility in which genius and creativity, on the one hand, and fidelity to nature, on the other, are subordinated to the blind production of art objects according to prescribed formulas.

Indeed, when he is not acting as court painter, Titorelli evidently obeys a set of even more rigid prescriptions. His heathscapes, the non-commissioned paintings he creates when he is outside the restricted purview of the court, are not only unimaginative and bleak, they are exactly identical, consisting of two trees, grass, and a sunset. One could ascribe this monotony to an overexposure to the court, and at one point Titorelli himself explains that his position there has robbed him of artistic élan (130). But we should not overlook that here too the paintings of Titorelli the "Kunstmaler" serve as both a comment on the superannuated notions of realism from the past century and an allusion to some of the central motifs of a modernist aesthetics. If K. had seen only one heathscape, he (and the reader) could have assumed that Titorelli had remained faithful to some real landscape. Although the scene depicted does remind one of the North and there-fore contradicts somewhat the artist's Italian *nom de palette*, nothing in the description the narrator provides would indicate any deviation from nature. The reader and K. may suspect at this point that when Titorelli is freed from the constraints of the court, he subscribes to the familiar nineteenth-century heritage of realism, but this view is negated by the second picture Titorelli offers for sale. He calls it a *Gegenstück*, a companion piece, but there is no noticeable difference between the two heathscapes. When K., who is more intent on leaving the premises than examining the identity of the two landscapes, pur-chases it as well, the painter reaches under the bed for a third painting, which he describes as similar. But it is not similar at all, we are told; it is the exact same picture. Here the narrator, obviously speaking from K.'s limited perspective interprets as follows: "The painter was exploit-ing to the full this opportunity to sell off his old pictures" (140); but this is not necessarily a correct inference. After all, the painter had already stated earlier that it was not necessary to talk with him about his art first in order to obtain information about the court later (127). Titorelli is willing to tell K. what he knows whether or not K. buys his work. Although K. may conceive of his purchases as pay-ments for service rendered, there is no indication that the painter shares this view. Thus the motives K. (through the narrative voice) imputes to the painter probably tell us more about his own intentions and the way he operates with people. As a result he totally ignores what has been most important: the nonrealist aesthetics implied by the series of heathscapes. On the one hand, this aesthetic theory denies a corre-spondence between reality and representation; on the other, it suggests a complete codification of existence, in which difference and subjectivity disappear.

In this regard Titorelli's antirealism, in fact, underscores the very problems Josef K. confronts in his own struggles with the court, an institution that he similarly misconstrues. What K. does not seem to understand is that the tenets that made realism possible are no longer valid; the previously assumed correspondence between inner and outer, reality and appearance, signified and signifier no longer holds. As a consequence truth is not determined by the match between word, symbol, or picture and the external world; and justice is not the product of a sifting and weighing of evidence to arrive at a determinate and indubitable judgment. Rather, such universal concepts disappear in a codified structure of norms, analogous to the aesthetics employed by Titorelli. The final exchange with the prison chaplain concerning the parable "Before the Law" ("Vor dem Gesetz") serves as a confirmation of this antirealist message. K., insisting that the chaplain's last interpretation of the doorkeeper's message would compel us to accept everything he says as true, is quickly contradicted: "'No,' said the priest, 'it is not necessary to accept everything as true, one must only accept it as necessary.' 'A melancholy conclusion,' said K., 'It turns lying into a universal principle'" (188). These two statements clearly show that K. and the chaplain approach the same problem from two different systems of value. The chaplain is simply affirming necessity; truth is irrelevant in this discussion, just as the match between reality and picture is insignificant for Titorelli's art. But K. is unable to situate his thought in a matrix that does not validate a transcendental notion of truth (or the derivative realist notion of art). His reply is inappropriate because it switches back to the inoperative dichotomy of truth and falsehood. The passage Kafka deleted bears witness to this as well. Almost directly after K.'s last rejoinder, the narrator remarks: "He had been pulled into a train of thought that was completely unfamiliar" (221). Unable to accept a world in which expression is a function of rigid structuring, he falls back on an obsolete system of signification unequipped for coping with the altered social reality of twentieth-century existence.

The importance of the Titorelli episode thus does not reside in the painter's conversations about the possibility for acquittal or in other information he supplies about the workings of the court, but rather in the insight he provides through his aesthetic theory.[29] Indeed, if we take his aesthetics seriously, then we would have to conclude that his description of the court is of very little value. The message that he has tried to convey, and to which K. has remained impervious, is that there is an irreducible difference between reality and its representation in pictures or words. Even if he were not someone who is "certainly a liar," (117) in fact, someone, whose very name is a misrepresentation, he would be unable to depict the court and its procedures accurately. The court, like his art, depends on rules and conventions that have hardened almost into ritual. It is particularly conspicuous that throughout the novel most of the persons K. encounters have no notion of any ultimate value for their actions. They perform their tasks as part of an unchanging and unchangeable routine. This is evident in the opening scene of the novel, when Willem and Franz arrest him, and later in the book when they are beaten for transgressions. It is also one of the chief features of the parable "Vor dem Gesetz," where the doorkeeper, himself a paradigm for rigidity and convention, responds according to prescribed formulae. For the most part, this quality of actions and words as repetitions of codified structures escapes K. Only once, as far as I can tell, in his final visit to his attorney, Huld, does he become aware of this reified side of existence. Allowed to listen in on the conversation between Block and Huld, he recognizes that what he is witnessing has occurred many times before: "K. had the feeling that he was listening to a well-rehearsed dialogue that had been often repeated and would be often repeated and only for Block would never lose its novelty" (166). The reason K. can discern the ritualistic character of the proceedings is that he is not involved and thus attentive to a level of meaning beyond what the words denote directly. In his usual intercourse with the official and semiofficial employees of the court, he is too occupied with himself to hear how he and they interact within convention. Even in his interpretation of the parable with the chaplain, he is unable to gain this perspective because he immediately and continuously identifies with the man from the country. This identification is correct, no doubt, but it precludes his comprehension of the simple fact that the chaplain conveys: although the commentaries vary, the law itself is always the same, an unalterable text that defies determinate interpretation.

In *Der Prozeß*, therefore, structure, text, tradition, and prescription always rule over the subject, entrapping it in a web that it can neither comprehend nor avoid. In contrast to Rilke's *Aufzeichnungen*, where the world was reduced to the subjectivity of the narrator, in Kafka's novel the world overwhelms the subjectivity of both the main character and the narrator, who generally speaks from his perspective. Whereas the space defined by the reflection on realism in the *Aufzeich-nungen* opens onto an almost solipsistic perspective on reality, the analysis of the role of painting in *Der Prozeß* discloses a world at the other extreme, in which individuality is effaced and engulfed by an anonymous and ominous structuring of action and belief. In both cases, however, the illusory harmony that produced the realist text is undermined. The poetics of modernism thus link up with the romantic tradition of irony discussed in the initial chapter: both involve self-reflections upon the very principles of creative endeavor that produced the text. The difference here is that realism with its nonreflexive surface has intervened, changing both the direction and the significance of textual reference to external reality. The romantics exhibited the playfulness of irony or the farce of comedy, but modernism seems more troubled with its reflections on realism. Kreuzgang and Heine (the narrator) were able to laugh at themselves and their world, even if this meant affirming nihilism and personal tragedy. The figures that populate the *Aufzeich-nungen* and *Der Prozeß* suffer in a world they do not understand or control. Perhaps for this reason both of these twentieth-century works evidence a slight touch of nostalgia for the realist past. Both Josef K. and Malte recall a time when the world was different, when narrative was possible or when truth entailed a match between signifier and signified. The problems they encounter in their altered situations, whether they are seen as neurosis, guilt, or alienation, are at least in part the consequence of their inability to fit into a nonrealist scheme.

That even this hint of nostalgia is a misapprehension, a ruse propagated by the writers and theoreticians in the mid-nineteenth century, has been the theme of this book. The texts of realism, despite their veneer of serenity and naturalness, despite their façade of normalcy and propriety, contain an implicit poetics that, like the works of the preceding and subsequent generations, discloses both the impossibility and the exclusory ideology of the realist enterprise. It is uncertain how clearly this was understood by Kafka and Rilke personally, but in passages in their novels where they bear witness to the distance between the modern predicament and the poetics of an earlier age, they indirectly comment on the futility of a renewal of realism. In the *Aufzeich-nungen*, as we have seen, this is expressed by the simple inability to fathom a time in which narration could occur in a straightforward fashion. "The telling of stories . . . must have been before my time" (244) is Malte's comment; and by the very vagueness and tentativeness of this remark, he casts doubt upon its possibility. In *Der Prozeß* the same effect is achieved by pushing the origin of the rules and regulations for art into the distant past and by making the post of court painter a matter of inheritance. At some point in the past, one might assume, the original conventions by which Titorelli now carries out his commissions were established. At that time some ancestor of his may have actually painted what he saw; he may have faithfully copied the reality before his eyes. As in the case of the *Aufzeichnungen*, however, this age of realism seems to have receded so far into the past that its very occurrence seems questionable. The texts discussed in this chapter, these creations of the postrealist age, thus not only affirm their own adherence to a modernist poetics, they also call into question the very existence of the literary movement that preceded them. My contention has been that if we read the realists themselves attentively enough, their own more furtive, more ideologically laden reflections on the nature of their art perform precisely the same function.

NOTES

INTRODUCTION

1. Richard Brinkmann, *Wirklichkeit und Illusion: Studien über Gehalt und Grenzen des Begriffs Realismus für die erzählende Dichtung des neunzehnten Jahrhunderts,* 2d ed. (Tübingen: Niemeyer, 1966), pp. 1–82.

2. Gerhard Kaiser, "Um eine Neubegründung des Realismusbegriffs," *Zeitschrift für deutsche Philologie* 77 (1958): 161–76.

3. Peter Demetz, "Zur Definition des Realismus," *Literatur und Kritik* 2 (1967): 333–45.

4. Marshall Brown, "The Logic of Realism: A Hegelian Approach," *PMLA* 96 (1981): 224–41; here p. 233.

5. René Wellek, "The Concept of Realism in Literary Scholarship," *Neophilologus* 45 (1961): 1–20.

6. Ibid., p. 10.

7. Roland Barthes's essay "L'Effet de Réel," *Communications* 1 (1968): 84–89, is only partially relevant here. In the first place, he only considers superfluous detail or description as contributing to "the effect of the real," whereas I believe that many different textual aspects can contribute to this effect. Second, he opposes description to narrative, an opposition that is of no concern to me. Finally, his discussion of the relationship of the real to the probable (*vraisemblable*) makes an interesting historical point: "il y a une rupture entre le vraisemblable ancien et le réalisme moderne; mais par là-même aussi, un nouveau vraisemblable naît, qui est précisément le réalisme" (88). Barthes is obviously thinking here of the distinction Aristotle draws in the poetics. My focus, however, is on the nineteenth century, when this merger of the real and the probable has already taken place. More relevant for German realism is the study

by Nancy A. Kaiser, *Social Integration and Narrative Structure: Patterns of Realism in Auerbach, Freytag, Fontane, and Raabe* (New York: Lang, 1986). Kaiser's concern, unlike my own, is to examine patterns of communication prevalent in German prose in the second half of the nineteenth century.

8. This is the view propagated by Roman Jakobson in "On Realism in Art," *Readings in Russian Poetics: Formalist and Structuralist Views*, ed. Ladislav Matejka and Krystyna Pomorska (Cambridge, Mass.: MIT Press, 1971), pp. 38–46.

9. In *Partial Magic: The Novel as a Self-Conscious Genre* (Berkeley: University of California Press, 1975), Robert Alter argues that the realists did not abandon reflecting on the fictive status of their texts because they adhered to a doctrine of realism but, rather, because they were such great "*imaginists*—writers caught up in the autonomous power of their own fantasy world even as they strive to make it a true image of the world of contemporary society" (p. 97). He too, of course, sees the realist movement as a temporary hiatus in self-reflexivity. (Alter uses the term *self-consciousness*.) Indeed, Alter shows how Balzac in *Lost Illusions*, in contrast to, say, *Tristram Shandy*, shuns the opportunity to reflect on the writing and publishing process (pp. 104–15). I am in substantial agreement with Alter's general outline, although, as will become obvious, I think that there is a good deal more of furtive "self-consciousness" in prose fiction in the nineteenth century in Germany than most critics have previously uncovered.

10. Emile Benveniste's distinction between *discours* and *histoire* might seem to be applicable here, but I think it is clear from my previous discussion of realism as effect that it will not completely overlap with the distinction between realist and nonrealist texts. Benveniste considers texts where no one speaks, where "the events seem to narrate themselves," to belong to historical texts, and those in which a speaker and a hearer are implied are discursive. Realist texts, however, may be either historical or discursive; similarly one could find nonrealist texts of both these types. The distinction I am drawing does not relate so much to the perceived presence or absence of a narrator as it does to the type of reflection and the degree of foregrounding that occur. See Emile Benveniste, "The Correlations of Tense in the French Verb," *Problems in General Linguistics*, trans. Mary Elizabeth Meek (Coral Gables, Fla.: University of Miami Press, 1977), pp. 205–15.

11. In *The Political Unconscious*, Fredric Jameson suggests that some sort of overt reflexivity lies at the core of realism. He claims that "any number of 'definitions' of realism assert . . . that processing operation called narrative mimesis or realistic representation has as its historic function the systematic undermining and demystification . . . of those preexisting inherited traditional or sacred narrative paradigms which are its initial givens" (p. 152). It is difficult to know precisely what Jameson has in mind with this comment. He cites Jakobson's essay "On Realism" as support for his view, but it is well known that the Russian formalists considered that the function of *all* art was the undermining of inherited paradigms, and that this function is in no way peculiar to realism. One of Jameson's problems is that he appears to identify the tradition of the novel, starting with *Don Quixote*, with the tradition of realism. As far as I can tell, in the vast literature on realism, there are no definitions that come close to what Jameson maintains "any number of 'definitions' assert." Indeed, in most cases scholars have ignored any type of reflexivity in realist texts. See Fredric Jameson, *The Political Unconscious: Narrative as a Socially Symbolic Act* (Ithaca, N.Y.: Cornell University Press, 1981).

12. In a recent essay Valerie D. Greenberg argues that *Effi Briest*, one of the classic texts of German realism, is "a text about narrative, reminding the reader of storytelling and its inevitably fragmentary characters" (771). She also shows how eroticism is "driven underground" (772). Her study of Fontane's novel thus fits well into the scheme I am trying to establish for other works of realism. Therefore, I would have to disagree slightly with her closing remarks, which situate Fontane's oeuvre at the beginning of modernism because of the self-referentiality in *Effi Briest*. Indeed, the point of the following chapters is to demonstrate that this self-reflexivity exists below the surface throughout German realism. Fontane is neither an early modernist nor a renegade realist, but rather typical for nineteenth-century writers of prose. See Valerie D. Greenberg, "The Resistance of *Effi Briest*: An (Un)told Tale," *PMLA* 103 (1988): 770–82.

CHAPTER ONE

1. The most complete book on the topic is still Ingrid Strohschneider-Kohrs, *Die romantische Ironie in Theorie und Gestaltung* (Tübingen: Niemeyer, 1960). A convenient summary of Strohschneider-Kohr's thesis can be found in her essay "Zur Poetik der deutschen Romantik II: Die romantische Ironie," *Die deutsche Romantik: Poetik, Formen und Motive*, ed. Hans Steffen (Göttingen: Vandenhoeck & Ruprecht, 1967), pp. 75–97. Also helpful is Ernst Behler, *Klassische Ironie, romantische Ironie, tragische Ironie: Zum Ursprung dieser Begriffe* (Darmstadt: Wissenschaftliche Buchgesellschaft, 1972).

2. Friedrich Schlegel, *Kritische Friedrich-Schlegel-Ausgabe*, Erster Abteilung, vol. 2, *Charakteristiken und Kritiken I (1796–1801)*, ed. Hans Eichner (München: Schöningh, 1967), p. 160. (Lyceum Fragment 108).

3. Schlegel, vol. 18, *Philosphische Lehrjahre 1796–1806, Erster Teil*, ed. Ernst Behler (1963), p. 85.

4. Ibid., p. 128.

5. Among the most popular candidates for authorship who have been mentioned besides Jean Paul and the philosopher Schelling (who used the pseudonym Bonaventura in other works) are Friedrich Gottlob Wetzel and Clemens Brentano. A few years ago Rosemarie Hunter-Lougheed revived the proposal that E. T. A. Hoffman authored the *Nachtwachen*. See Rosemarie Hunter-Lougheed, *Die Nachtwachen von Bonaventura: Ein Frühwerk E. T. A. Hoffmanns?* (Heidelberg: Winter, 1985). However, Jost Schillemeit's hypothesis that August Klingemann is the author of the *Nachtwachen* has recently been supported by a finding in the library of the University of Amsterdam. It now seems certain that Klingemann, director of the court theater in Braunschweig and author of many prose works, is the person behind the pseudonym Bonaventura. See Jost Schillemeit, *Bonaventura, der Verfasser der Nachtwachen* (München: Beck, 1973); and Ruth Haag, "Noch einmal: Der Verfasser der *Nachtwachen von Bonaventura*," *Euphorion* 81 (1987): 286–97. For an excellent review of the literature on the *Nachtwachen* from 1965 to 1985, which concentrates on the now apparently solved question of authorship, see Jeffrey L. Sammons, "In Search of Bonaventura: The *Nachtwachen* Riddle, 1965–1985," *Germanic Review* 61 (1985): 50–56. For a quick overview of the secondary literature and the major issues in this research, see Gerhart Hoffmeister, "Bonaventura: *Nachtwachen* (1804/05)," *Romane und Erzählungen der deutschen Romantik: Neue Interpretationen*, ed. Paul Michael Lützeler (Stuttgart: Reclam, 1981), pp. 194–212.

6. Blackall emphasizes the circularity of form since at the end of the fifteenth night watch (Blackall considers the sixteenth a "Hogarthian tailpiece") we arrive at the point where the narration began. See Eric A. Blackall, *The Novels of the German Romantics* (Ithaca, N.Y.: Cornell University Press, 1983), pp. 209–20.

7. Parenthetical citations are taken from Bonaventura, *Nachtwachen*, ed. Wolfgang Paulsen (Stuttgart: Reclam, 1964). Translations are my own.

8. See Dieter Arndt, *Der poetische Nihilismus in der Romantik*, vol. 2 (Tübingen: Niemeyer, 1972), pp. 482–536. "The ironic distancing, which in any case has to be conceded to the writer, is sufficient evidence for the fact that in the middle of romanticism there exists a critical consciousness going beyond romanticism" (p. 533).

9. Fichte's philosophy was often misunderstood to imply the positing of a solipsistic ego that then creates the world. At times Bonaventura appears to share this misconception. What is certain, however, is that the *Nachtwachen* is filled with allusions to the philosophical terminology popularized by Fichte. The most thorough study of the relationship of the *Nachtwachen* to Fichtean philosophy is Walter Pfannkuche's *Idealismus und Nihilismus in den "Nachtwachen" von Bonaventura* (Frankfurt: Lang, 1983).

10. Kathy Brzovic's "Nachtwachen von Bonaventura: A Critique of Order," *Monatshefte* 76 (1984): 380–95, is one of the few efforts I have come across that tries to refute the nihilistic nature of this text. Unfortunately, although much that she writes about Kreuzgang's critique of the social order is accurate, she does not manage to overturn the prevailing wisdom about his nihilism.

11. Georg Wilhelm Friedrich Hegel, *Werke*, vol. 11 (Frankfurt: Suhrkamp, 1970), p. 233.

12. Hegel, 11: 80.

13. Jean Paul Friedrich Richter, *Sämtliche Werke*, Erste Abteilung, vol. 11, *Vorschule der Ästhetik* (Weimar: Hermann Böhlaus Nachfolger, 1935), p. 22.

14. See Richard Brinkmann, "Nachwachen von Bonaventura: Kehrseite der Frühromantik?", *Die deutsche Romantik: Poetik, Formen und Motive*, ed. Hans Steffen (Göttingen: Vandenhoeck & Ruprecht), pp. 134–58. "This book is the most decisive application of irony; in a consequential fashion it even tries to include itself in the ironic sublation. Annihilation as the only utterable possibility" (p. 153).

15. Although the topic of Heine and romantic irony has been quite popular, most critics of *Buch Le Grand*, though they do not fail to note the obvious self-conscious text, have chosen to deal with other issues. See, for example, Jeffrey L. Sammons, *Heinrich Heine, the Elusive Poet* (New Haven, Conn.: Yale University Press, 1969), pp. 116–49; Jost Hermand, *Der frühe Heine: Ein Kommentar zu den Reisebildern* (München: Winkler, 1976), pp. 102–18; and Jocelyne Kolb, "The Sublime, The Ridiculous, and the Apple Tarts in Heine's *Ideen. Das Buch Le Grand*," *German Quarterly* 56 (1983): 28–38.

16. Page numbers for citations from *Ideen. Das Buch Le Grand* are taken from Heinrich Heine, *Sämtliche Schriften*, ed. Klaus Briegleb, vol. 2 (München: Hanser, 1976). I have consulted the English version in the volume *Heinrich Heine: Poetry and Prose*, ed. Jost Hermand and Robert C. Holub (New York: Continuum, 1982) for the translations.

17. A recent essay by Richard T. Gray, "Free-Lancing: Heine's 'Ideen. Das Buch Le Grand,'" (*Heine-Jahrbuch* 27 [1988]: 33–66), does an excellent job of analyzing the intricate connection between Heine's predicament as writer in the restoration and his political critique. Although Gray does not concentrate on the self-reflexive moments in the text, I believe he is essentially correct when he characterizes Heine's technique

as "hypermimetic," since his text "does not simply reflect the exoteric surface of the real, but penetrates to its esoteric core" (p. 53).

18. It is also quite possible that Heine is here alluding to Goethe's *Werther* in his reference to death and unrequited love. In *Der frühe Heine* (pp. 59–80), Jost Hermand has argued that *Die Harzreise (The Harz Journey)* contains several hidden references to that work, but the connection between *Buch Le Grand* and *Werther* appears to me to be more direct.

19. See Hanna Spencer, *Heinrich Heine* (Boston: Twayne, 1982). "Unlike the ironic flights of the Romantics which allow them to escape reality, Heine's irony has precisely the opposite effect; it bursts the idealistic bubble by confrontation with reality" (p. 23).

20. See Viktor Shklovsky, "Die Kunst als Verfahren"; and Jurij Tynjanov, "Das literarische Faktum"; both in *Texte der russischen Formalisten*, ed. Jurij Striedter (München: Fink, 1969), pp. 2–35, 392–431.

21. Hegel, 13: 97.

22. Ibid.

23. Heine, 3: 429.

CHAPTER TWO

1. The most recent overview of the literature on the novella can be found in Karlheinz Hasselbach, *Lenz* (München: Oldenbourg, 1986).

2. Parenthetical citations in this chapter refer to Georg Büchner, *Sämtliche Werke und Briefe*, ed. Werner R. Lehmann (Hamburg: Christian Wegner, 1967–). For the English I have consulted Henry J. Schmidt's translation in *Georg Büchner: Complete Works and Letters* (New York: Continuum, 1986).

3. Heine first used this term in 1828 in a review of Wolfgang Menzel's *Die deutsche Literatur (German Literature* [1827]). The term became more widely known when it appeared in the first paragraph of Heine's *Die romantische Schule (The Romantic School,* 1835).

4. The stylistic differences between the *Kunstgespräch* and the rest of the novella have been somewhat overemphasized in previous research. It is not quite true, for example, as Maurice Benn asserts, that this speech "is not disfigured by the broken sentences and mental blockages which characterize his more distracted utterances" (206). See Maurice Benn, *The Drama of Revolt: A Critical Study of Georg Büchner* (Cambridge: Cambridge University Press, 1976). There are at least two instances of incomplete sentences. In describing the girls on the hillside, Lenz makes the following remark: "and a serious, pale face, and yet so young, and the black dress, and the other one working with such care" (1. 87). And in his description of the painting of Christ and the Apostles, we read: "It's a gloomy, dusky evening, a straight red streak on the horizon, the street half dark" (1. 88). There are also other common features, for example, the use of "so" plus an adjective or the paratactic constructions. The conversation on art is indeed more coherent syntactically, but the obvious differences should not prevent us from seeing similarities that are just as apparent.

5. J. M. Ritchie, "Realism in Germany, from the Death of Goethe," *The Age of Realism*, ed. F. W. J. Hemmings (Middlesex, Eng.: Penguin, 1974), pp. 218–64; here p. 222.

6. Stephan Kohl, *Realismus: Theorie und Geschichte* (München: Fink, 1977), p. 110.

7. Benno von Wiese, "Lenz," *Die deutsche Novelle von Goethe bis Kafka*, vol. 2 (Düsseldorf: August Bagel, 1965), pp. 104–26; here p. 109.

8. Martin Swales, *The German Novella* (Princeton: Princeton University Press, 1977), p. 113.

9. John J. Parker, "Some Reflections of Georg Büchner's *Lenz* and Its Principle Source, the Oberlin Record," *German Life and Letters* 21 (1967/68): 103–11.

10. Peter K. Jansen, "The Structural Function of the *Kunstgespräch* in Büchner's *Lenz*," *Monatshefte* 67 (1975): 145–56.

11. I am assuming that the *Kunstgespräch* does not represent the views of the historical Lenz. The similarities between the views here and in Lenz's theoretical works are, in my view, few. Erwin Kobel has found a few points of agreement (pp. 188–99). But Peter Jansen's "hope" to write an extensive study on this subject has, to my knowledge, never been fulfilled (p. 153), and lacking more convincing evidence, I am compelled to agree with Hans Mayer's evaluation: "The more one confronts Lenz, above all his *Anmerkungen übers Theater* [*Remarks about Theater*], with the thoughts that Büchner has him utter, the more perceptible is the opposition between them" (425). See Erwin Kobel, *Georg Büchner: Das dichterische Werk* (Berlin: Walter de Gruyter, 1974); and Hans Mayer, *Georg Büchner und seine Zeit* (Frankfurt: Suhrkamp, 1972).

12. Thomas Michael Meyer, "'Wegen mir könnt ihr ganz ruhig sein . . .': Die Argumentationslist in Georg Büchners Briefen an die Eltern," *Georg Büchner Jahrbuch* 2 (1982): 249–80.

13. See Wolfgang Proß, "Spinoza, Herder, Büchner: Über 'Gesetz' und 'Erscheinung,'" *Georg Büchner Jahrbuch* 2 (1982): 62–98; and Joachim Kahl, "'Der Fels des Atheismus': Epikurs und Georg Büchners Kritik an der Theodizee," *Georg Büchner Jahrbuch* 2 (1982): 99–125.

14. The assumed connection between the *Kunstgespräch* and Büchner's aesthetic views involves other questions rarely posed by commentators. Why, for example, should Büchner choose to have his theory explicated (in such a strange form) by a man who is obviously not of sound mind? Lenz's very instability would seem to disqualify him as a persuasive advocate for an alternative to idealism. Furthermore, it does not appear that Lenz expressed Büchner's opinions on other matters—on religion or society, for example. Why then should he be singled out in this area as a vehicle? But perhaps the most important question is why Büchner should want to have his views stated in this form at all. From the fragments of correspondence we have, it is clear that he had ample opportunity to publish an essay of any length he chose on literary theory. Gutzkow seemed willing to print just about anything he could get from him (2. 480). That Büchner would opt for smuggling his views into the middle of this novella seems, therefore, odd, even if the evidence cited above were more convincing.

15. Albrecht Meier, "Georg Büchners Ästhetik," *Georg Büchner Jahrbuch* 2 (1982): 196–208.

16. For a finely differentiated view of Büchner, see Reinhold Grimm, *Love, Lust, and Rebellion: New Approaches to Georg Büchner,* (Madison, Wisc.: University of Wisconsin Press, 1985).

17. Herbert Fellmann, "Georg Büchners Lenz," *Jahrbuch der Wittheit zu Bremen* 7 (1963): 7–124; here p. 86.

18. One of the few exceptions is Albrecht Schöne, who sees signs of insanity in the *Kunstgespräch*, especially in the almost eerie description of the paintings (pp. 46–

49). Nonetheless, he considers the views here to be Büchner's own. See Albrecht Schöne, "Interpretationen zur dichterischen Gestaltung des Wahnsinns in der deutschen Literatur," Ph.D. diss., Münster, 1951.

19. Letter of 5 May 1835.

20. See René Wellek, "The Concept of Realism in Literary Scholarship," *Neophilologus* 45 (1961): 1–20; and Kohl for a discussion of the origins of the term.

21. Roman Jakobson makes a strong case for distinguishing between realism in the visual arts and in literature: "While in painting and in the other visual arts the illusion of an objective and absolute faithfulness to reality is conceivable, 'natural' (in Plato's terminology), verisimilitude in a verbal expression or in a literary description makes no sense whatever" (p. 39). Roman Jakobson, "On Realism in Art," *Readings in Russian Poetics: Formalist and Structuralist Views*, ed. Ladislav Matejka and Krystyna Pomorska (Cambridge, Mass.: MIT Press, 1971), pp. 38–46. As far as I can tell, Jakobson is unique in this dissociation of realism from literature.

22. For a brief introductory account of this relationship, see Walter J. Ong, *Orality and Literacy: The Technologizing of the Word* (London: Methuen, 1982).

23. I am thinking here in particular of Wolfgang Iser, who from his phenomenologically informed perspective affirms without question that the reader forms images when reading. See especially his most important theoretical work, *The Act of Reading: A Theory of Aesthetic Response* (Baltimore: Johns Hopkins University Press, 1978).

24. J. P. Stern, *On Realism* (London: Routledge & Kegan Paul, 1973), esp. pp. 46 ff.

25. The reference is to Friederike Brion, a woman with whom both Lenz and Goethe were acquainted. He associates the death of the girl with Friederike, and this has led some editors of the text to assume that the girl's name was also Friederike.

26. Both Richard Brinkmann and Marshall Brown consider realism to be related to the stability of the subject-object relationship. In contrast to my view, however, they feel that the breakdown of this relationship and the subsequent search for reality is constitutive for realist prose. This seems to be the case for Büchner, but I would have misgivings about extending this thesis to other writers in the nineteenth century. See Richard Brinkmann, *Wirklichkeit und Illusion: Studien über Gehalt und Grenzen des Begriffs Realismus für die erzählende Dichtung des neunzehnten Jahrhunderts*, 2d ed. (Tübingen: Niemeyer, 1966); and Marshall Brown, "The Logic of Realism: A Hegelian Approach," *PMLA* 96 (1981): 224–41.

27. It is not essential to my argument that Büchner had already made his notes on these two philosophers before composing *Lenz*, since his other works exhibit a general familiarity with these theological and epistemological issues as well. Customarily the composition of the novella is dated toward the end of 1835 or the beginning of 1836, thus presumably before he began the more extensive excerpting from Descartes and Spinoza. To my knowledge only Wolfgang Wittkowski has dated the composition of *Lenz* to be as late as 1837. Wolfgang Wittkowski, *Georg Büchner: Persönlichkeit Weltbild Werk* (Heidelberg: Carl Winter, 1978).

28. For example, by Fellmann, pp. 100–102; or Kobel, pp. 183–86.

29. In a recent essay Mark W. Roche contends that the Medusa runs counter to Lenz's notion of realism. I remain only partially persuaded by his argument. The parallels between the Medusa and the realist artist are too obvious: both are observers of a scene; both endeavor to capture the reality they witness. In any case, we both seem to agree that Lenz is arguing against the ability of art and literature to capture external

reality. See Mark W. Roche, "Die Selbstaufhebung des Antiidealismus in Büchners *Lenz*," *Zeitschrift für deutsche Philologie* 107, Sonderheft (1988): 136–47.

30. See Herbert Lindenberger, *Georg Büchner*, (Carbondale: Southern Illinois University Press, 1964), p. 81.

31. See Helmut Kreuzer, "Zur Theorie des deutschen Realismus zwischen Märzrevolution und Naturalismus," *Realismustheorien in Literatur, Malerei, Musik und Politik*, ed. Reinhold Grimm and Jost Hermand (Stuttgart: Kohlhammer, 1975), pp. 48–67.

32. Fellmann is one of the few critics who has noted this reversal (p. 98), but his overall view of the *Kunstgespräch* is disappointing. Büchner is credited with the ideas Lenz articulates as long as they are noncontradictory and coherent. When contradictions arise, Fellmann simply claims that the literary figure is no longer speaking for his creator. Richards also speaks of the "literary perspective" of the descriptions, but he draws no significant conclusions from this astute observation (David G. Richards, *Georg Büchner and the Birth of Modern Drama* [Albany: State University of New York Press, 1977]).

33. In *Laokoon* Lessing had tried to establish the essential differences between the pictorial arts and literature. For a review of this controversy in the century before Büchner's novella, see Niklaus R. Schweizer, *The Ut pictura poesis Controversy in Eighteenth-Century England and Germany* (Bern: Lang, 1972).

CHAPTER THREE

1. Page numbers for quotations from Stifter and Keller are from the following editions: Adalbert Stifter, *Sämmtliche Werke*, ed. August Sauer et. al., 24 vols. (Prague: Calve; Reichenberg: Kraus, 1904–72); and Gottfried Keller, *Sämtliche Werke*, 22 vols. (Erlenbach and Zürich: Eugen Rentsch, 1926–31; Leipzig: Benteli, 1931–49). For my translations I have consulted Wendell Frye's translation of Stifter's *Indian Summer* (New York: Lang, 1985), and A. M. Holt's *Green Henry* (New York: Grove Press, 1960).

2. See Klaus Amann, *Adalbert Stifters "Nachsommer": Studie zur didaktischen Struktur des Romans* (Wien: Wilhelm Braumüller, 1977), pp. 70–83; and Hans Dietrich Irmscher, *Adalbert Stifter: Wirklichkeitserfahrung und gegenständliche Darstellung* (München: Fink, 1971), pp. 326–41.

3. The term *Bildung* is notoriously difficult to translate. "Education" suggests something too formal. "Self-cultivation," the translation evidently preferred by W. H. Bruford in his *The German Tradition of Self-Cultivation: 'Bildung' from Humboldt to Thomas Mann* (Cambridge: Cambridge University Press, 1975), may be more accurate, but it is a bit awkward. In the following pages I use a variety of terms, depending on the context, for *Bildung* and its derivatives.

4. The standard German book on this topic is Jürgen Jacobs, *Wilhelm Meister und seine Brüder: Untersuchungen zum deutschen Bildungsroman* (München: Fink, 1972); the latest English monograph is Martin Swales, *The German Bildungsroman from Wieland to Hesse* (Princeton,N.J.: Princeton University Press, 1978). A useful work for information about the *Bildungsroman*, particularly in the eighteenth and nineteenth centuries, is Rolf Selbmann's *Der deutsche Bildungsroman* (Stuttgart: Metzler, 1984).

5. See E. M. Butler, *The Tyranny of Greece over Germany: A Study of the Influence Exercised by Greek Art and Poetry over the Great German Writers of the Eighteenth, Nineteenth, and Twentieth Centuries* (Cambridge, 1935; rpt. Boston: Beacon Hill, 1958);

and my study, *Heinrich Heine's Reception of German Grecophilia: The Function and Application of the Hellenic Tradition in the First Half of the Nineteenth Century* (Heidelberg: Carl Winter, 1981).

6. See Marianne Schuller, "Das Gewitter findet nicht statt, oder Die Abdankung der Kunst: Zu Adalbert Stifters Roman *Der Nachsommer*," *Poetica* 10 (1978): 25–52; here p. 38.

7. I am here following the tripartite scheme outlined by Ludwig Arnold in *Stifters "Nachsommer" als Bildungsroman (Vergleich mit Goethes "Wilhelm Meister" und Kellers "Grüner Heinrich"* (Gießen: Otto Kindt, 1938), p. 38.

8. See Christine Oertel Sjörgen, *The Marble Statue as Idea: Collected Essays on Adalbert Stifter's* Der Nachsommer, (Chapel Hill: University of North Carolina Press, 1972): "The *Marmorgestalt* is like a nucleus that holds all the elements of the novel together in its gravitational field" (p. 95); and G. Joyce Hallamore, "The Symbolism of the Marble Muse in Stifter's *Nachsommer*," *PMLA* 74 (1959): 398–405.

9. Although he may not have had this aspect of Plato's philosophy in mind, Walther Rehm's suggestion that one should call this work a "Platonic utopia" rather than a realistic novel fits in nicely here. See Walther Rehm, *Nachsommer: Zur Deutung von Stifters Dichtung* (Bern: Francke, 1951), p. 81.

10. This statement would appear to contradict the contention in an essay by Lauren Small that "painting succeeds where language fails" (p. 13). Small fails to recognize that Stifter promulgates a hierarchy of art forms. Painting is indeed more accurate and preferable for descriptions of nature, but it is not superior to literature. See Lauren Small, "White Frost Configurations on the Window Pain," *Colloquia Germanica* 18 (1985): 1–17.

11. See Heinrich Landesmann, Rev. of *Nachsommer*, by Adalbert Stifter, *Wiener Zeitung* (23 December 1857). Rpt. in *Adalbert Stifter im Urteil seiner Zeit*, ed. Moriz Enzinger (Wien: Böhlau, 1968), pp. 205–9; here p. 206.

12. See the amusing and critical piece by Arno Schmidt, "Der sanfte Unmensch: Einhundert Jahre Nachsommer (*Adalbert Stifter*), *Nachrichten von Büchern und Menschen*, vol. 2, Zur Literatur des 19. Jahrhunderts (Frankfurt: Fischer, 1971), pp. 114–36; here p. 132.

13. Hannelore Schlaffer and Heinz Schlaffer discuss this equation under the category of the "restoration of art" in their *Studien zum ästhetischen Historismus* (Frankfurt: Suhrkamp, 1975), pp. 112–20.

14. Emil Staiger makes a similar point with respect to the artist: "The creative artist does not *invent* these laws [the objective laws of nature], he only discovers them" (p. 195). Emil Staiger, "Adalbert Stifter: 'Der Nachsommer,'" *Meisterwerke deutscher Sprache aus dem neunzehnten Jahrhundert* (Zürich: Atlantis, 1945), pp. 188–203.

15. E. H. Gombrich, *Art and Illusion* (Princeton, N.J.: Princeton University Press, 1960).

16. See Christine Oertel Sjörgen, "The Monstrous Painting in Stifter's *Der Nachsommer*," *JEGP* 68 (1969): 92–99.

17. Dieter Borchmeyer confuses the issue when he makes Roland's painting a prototype of future art. He is correct, of course, from the perspective of the history of art, but he is incorrect when he implies that Risach (or Stifter) welcomes this direction. The point of the episode is the very opposite of what Borchmeyer uses it for. Dieter Borchmeyer, "Stifters Nachsommer—Eine restaurative Utopie?" *Poetica* 12 (1980): 59–82; esp. pp. 78–79.

18. See Gerald Gillespie, "Ritualism and Motivic Development in Adalbert Stifter's *Nachsommer*," *Neophilologus* 18 (1964): 312–22.

19. See Gerhard Kaiser, *Gottfried Keller: Das gedichtete Leben* (Frankfurt: Insel, 1981), p. 210.

20. As Hans Meier points out in his book *Gottfried Kellers Grüner Heinrich: Betrachtungen zum Roman des poetischen Realismus* (Zürich: Artemis, 1972), both Heinrich Lee and Heinrich Drendorf learn to recognize the essence of things (p. 72).

21. In a discussion of Keller's novel, Winfried Menninghaus writes the following: "Painting appears only in the medium of language, indeed, *as* language, and conversely language, even when it is not even dealing with painting, literally presents images; it brings figures behind glas and frame" (p. 39). Although he is referring only to *Der grüne Heinrich*, his depiction is equally applicable to Stifter's *Nachsommer*. Winfried Menninghaus, *Artistische Schrift: Studien zur Kompositionskunst Gottfried Kellers* (Frankfurt: Suhrkamp, 1982).

22. For a discussion of Feuerbach's influence on the novel, see Ernst Otto, "Die Philosophie Feuerbachs in Gottfried Kellers Roman Der Grüne Heinrich," *Weimarer Beiträge* 6 (1960): 76–111; and Christine Träger, "Gottfried Kellers 'Der grüne Heinrich': Das Modell des Bildungsroman in der geschichtlichen Entscheidung," *Weimarer Beiträge* 31 (1985): 2008–24.

23. Keller was probably influenced here by the wall paintings in Goethe's *Wilhelm Meisters Lehrjahre*.

24. See Wolfgang Preisendanz, "Keller: Der Grüne Heinrich," *Der deutsche Roman vom Barock bis zur Gegenwart: Struktur und Geschichte*, ed. Benno von Wiese, vol. 2. (Düsseldorf: August Bagel, 1963), pp. 76–125; esp. pp. 95–101.

25. See Gail K. Hart, "Keller's Fictional Readers: Heinrich, Pankraz, and Jacques," *Seminar* 23 (1987): 115–36. "Excesses of the imagination are the main focus of interest in Keller, and he is continually exploring the problem of reconciling imagination . . . with life in the world, a problem he never succeeds in solving" (119). The relationship between literature and life in Keller's works is the topic of Hart's recent study *Readers and Their Fictions in the Novels and Novellas of Gottfried Keller* (Chapel Hill: University of North Carolina Press, 1989).

26. The best recent study to approach Keller from a psychoanalytic perspective is by Adolf Muschg. Muschg emphasizes throughout his monograph Keller's peculiar relationship to his mother. Adolf Muschg, *Gottfried Keller* (Frankfurt: Suhrkamp, 1980).

27. In "Gottfried Keller: *Der grüne Heinrich* (1854/55; 2. Fassung 1879/80): Gesellschaftsroman, Seelendrama, Romankunst," *Romane und Erzählungen des bürgerlichen Realismus*, ed. Horst Denkler (Stuttgart: Reclam, 1980), pp. 81–123, Gert Sautermeister has pointed to the importance of the father as a model in the novel. Part of the hero's problem is due to his father's untimely death and to the demise of the ideals he represented.

28. It is interesting to note in this connection that Keller himself wrote in a letter to Hermann Hettner on 4 March 1851 that in this novel he wanted "to make myself objective for myself" (*mich selbst mir objektiv machen*). Gottfried Keller, *Gesammelte Briefe*, ed. Carl Helbling, vol. 1 (Bern: Benteli, 1950), p. 357.

29. Goethe may have received an impulse for this tragic ending from Winckelmann, who wrote: "An ornamented column from an old Roman hand will have the same relationship to its Greek original as Virgil's Dido has, in her entourage with Diana among the oreads, to Homer's Nausikaa, which the former endeavored to imitate."

See Johann Joachim Winckelmann, *Kleine Schriften und Briefe* (Weimar: Hermann Böhlaus Nachfolger, 1960), p. 30. One might note in passing that Winckelmann, like the nineteenth-century realists we have been examining, also moves freely between the visual and the literary in his example.

30. Johann Wolfgang Goethe, *Werke*, vol 5, ed. Josef Kunz (Hamburg: Christian Wegner, 1952), pp. 68–72, 431–40.

31. The "Nausikaa" fragment first appeared in print in 1827; both Stifter and Keller were well aquainted with Goethe's writings.

32. See Moriz Enzinger, "Adalbert Stifters Nausikaa-Plan," *Gesammelte Aufsätze zu Adalbert Stifter* (Vienna: Österreichische Verlagsanstalt, 1967), pp. 180–91. The only book on this topic, Hermann Augustin's *Goethes und Stifters Nausikaa-Tragödie* (Basel: Benno Schwabe & Co., 1941), is unfortunately worthless as scholarship.

33. J. P. Stern is simply wrong when he asserts that "Mathilde *is* right" (290–91)—at least from the logic of the novel. See J. P. Stern, *Re-interpretations: Seven Studies in Nineteenth-Century German Literature* (London: Thames and Hudson, 1964). Margret Walter-Schneider's attempt to lay the blame at the feet of Mathilde's parents is similarly inattentive to the crusade against passions throughout the work, and ignores the fact that parents are almost invariably prudent in the world sketched in Stifter's works. See Margret Walter-Schneider, "Das Licht in der Finsternis: Zu Stifters *Nachsommer*," *Jahrbuch der deutschen Schiller-Gesellschaft* 29 (1985): 381–404.

34. Barton W. Browning, in "Stifter's *Nachsommer* and the Fourth Commandment," *Colloquia Germanica* 7 (1973): 301–16, argues that the relationship fails because Mathilde misconstrues the parental bond established between her own parents and Risach.

35. See Schuller, p. 33

36. For a more extensive discussion of Stifter's unusual views on passions (*Leidenschaften*), see Irmscher, esp. pp. 47–52.

37. One can therefore agree with Victor Lange's conclusion that the novel, in presenting the process of sublimation, is perhaps not so much concerned with Heinrich's development as with the transformation of a passionate relationship into a "reasonable" and "exemplary" one. See Victor Lange, "Stifter: Der Nachsommer." *Der deutsche Roman vom Barock bis zur Gegenwart: Struktur und Geschichte*, vol. 2, ed. Benno von Wiese (Düsseldorf: August Bagel, 1963), pp. 34–75; here p. 49. In contrast to Lange, however, we should ask how "reasonable" this "exemplary" relationship actually is.

38. We should note, however, that Stifter's polemic against passion and subjectivity predates the actual revolution and may be found in incipient forms in novellas from the forties, for example, in *Brigitta* (1844), whose plot is a prototype of the plot in *Der Nachsommer*.

39. Uwe-K. Ketelsen, "Adalbert Stifter: *Der Nachsommer* (1857): Die Vernichtung der historischen Realität in der Ästhetisierung des bürgerlichen Alltags," *Romane und Erzählungen des bürgerlichen Realismus*, ed. Horst Denkler (Stuttgart: Reclam, 1980), pp. 188–202.

40. Friedrich Schiller, *Werke: Nationalausgabe*, ed. Lieselotte Blumentahl and Benno von Wiese, vol. 20 (Weimar: Hermann Böhlaus Nachfolger, 1962), p. 412.

41. Schiller, vol. 20, p. 319.

42. See Marcus Tullius Cicero, *Cato maior de senectute* (München: Heimeran, 1963). It is not uninteresting to note that Cicero too associates political excesses with passions: "hinc patriae proditiones, hinc rerum publicarum eversiones, hinc cum hostibus

clandestina colloquia nasci, nullum denique scelus, nullum malum facinus esse, ad quod suscipiendum non libido voluptatis impelleret" (p. 52).

43. Here I differ from the evaluation of W. H. Bruford, who considers Stifter's novel "a swan-song of liberal individualism of the eighteenth-century type" (p. 146). It actually signals a new phase of liberal bourgeois ideology.

44. Horst Albert Glaser, "Stifters 'Nachsommer': Eine Studie zum Verhältnis von ästhetischer Utopie und Gesellschaft," Ph.D. diss., Johann Wolfgang Goethe-Universität Frankfurt, 1965.

45. Even the early review by Landesmann, cited above, notes this quality (p. 207).

46. One of the most interesting books on Stifter in recent years, Thomas Keller's *Die Schrift in Stifters "Nachsommer"* (Köln: Böhlau, 1982), reads the novel as a "postmodernist text" (p. 330). Although I disagree with this conclusion, Keller's work contains many important insights into the novel. I agree to a large extent with Russell Berman's interpretation of Stifter's "version of the end of man." Berman regards the explicit renunciation of anthropocentrism in the novel as a call for subsuming individuality under an overarching order. In this order the individual passively "mirrors the external order in his own universal education" (p. 112). See Russell Berman, *The Rise of the Modern German Novel: Crisis and Charisma* (Cambridge, Mass.: Harvard University Press, 1986), pp. 105–33.

47. Klaus-Detlef Müller, in "Utopie und Bildungsroman: Strukturuntersuchungen zu Stifters 'Nachsommer,'" *Zeitschrift für deutsche Philologie*, 90 (1971): 199–228, repeatedly refers to the reification (*Verdinglichung*) that informs the novel.

48. In a slightly different context, Adorno twists the argument one more time. For him it is the very ideological exaggeration of the novel that lends the work an unideological dimension of "truth" and makes it superior to other, more consoling literature of the era. Theodor W. Adorno, *Ästhetische Theorie*, ed. Gretel Adorno and Rolf Tiedemann (Frankfurt: Suhrkamp, 1970), pp. 346–47.

49. On this point see Michael Böhler, "Die Individualität in Stifters Spätwerk: Ein ästhetisches Problem," *DVjs* 43 (1969): 652–84; and Ketelsen, pp. 196–99.

50. See Sautermeister, p. 115.

51. Kaiser also points to this parallel (p. 188) and connects the names Anna and Agnes with D*iana* as well.

52. Friedrich A. Kittler, "Fleur de Lys," *Fugen* 1 (1980): 99–113.

53. See, for example, Bernhard Spies, *Behauptete Synthesis: Gottfried Kellers Roman "Der grüne Heinrich"* (Bonn: Bouvier, 1978), p. 155.

54. The pun stems from the fact that *dort* in German means "there." Thus the phrase means "Dortchen is not here" or "There is not here."

55. In a slightly different interpretation of Heinrich's possibilities, Joachim Hörisch connects the loss of Dortchen (for him the last erotic adventure) with the rise of Heinrich's economic prosperity. Eroticism and economic wealth are thus inversely related in the novel. See Joachim Hörisch, *Gott, Geld und Glück: Zur Logik der Liebe in den Bildungsromanen Goethes, Kellers und Thomas Manns* (Frankfurt: Suhrkamp, 1983), pp. 116–79.

56. Gail K. Hart, in an astute analysis of Heinrich's activity of reading in the two versions of the novel, evaluates the episode with Judith as a turning point in the hero's development. See her "The Functions of Fictions: Imagination and Socialization in Both Versions of Keller's *Der grüne Heinrich*," *German Quarterly* 59 (1986): 595–610.

57. This is the tendency in the seminal essay on Keller by Georg Lukács in *Deutsche Realisten des 19, Jahrhunderts* (Berlin: Aufbau, 1956), pp. 146–228. The essay was originally published in 1939.

58. Rilla comments appropriately: "But even the new ending plays in the subdued colors of a mood of resignation" (p. 89). Rilla attributes this atmosphere, however, solely to Heinrich's failure as an artist. See Paul Rilla, *Essays* (Berlin: Henschelverlag, 1955), pp. 51–108.

59. Considering Keller's dislike for Stifter's writings, it is unlikely that he consciously adopted the ending from *Der Nachsommer*. One of the few critics who suggests a connection between Keller's revision and both *Der Nachsommer* and the novella "Brigitta" is Walther Rehm (p. 70).

60. It is interesting to note that the association of painting, mimesis, and renunciation is already present in the "original" Bildungsroman, *Wilhelm Meister*. As Christoph Schweitzer has noted in "Wilhelm Meister und das Bild vom kranken Königssohn," *PMLA* 72 (1957): 419–32, a painting foreshadows not only the hero's success in love in the *Lehrjahre*, but also his renunciation in the *Wanderjahre*. The latter novel, of course, announces renunciation as a major theme in the subtitle: "Die Entsagenden."

CHAPTER FOUR

1. Page numbers for the parenthetical citations from Keller's work are taken from Gottfried Keller, *Sämtliche Werke*, 22 vols., ed. Jonas Fränkel and (since 1942) Carl Helbling (Erlenbach/Zürich: Eugen Rentsch, 1926–31; and Leipzig: Benteli, 1931–49). Unless otherwise indicated, parenthetical citations refer to volume 7. I have consulted the translation of Paul Bernard Thomas as adapted by Frank G. Ryder in *Gottfried Keller: Stories*, ed. Frank G. Ryder (New York: Continuum, 1982), pp. 52–118.

2. Gottfried Keller, *Gesammelte Briefe*, ed. Carl Helbling (Bern: Benteli, 1950–54), 1: 400. For a discussion of this notion see Klaus Jeziorkowski, *Literarität und Historismus: Beobachtungen zu ihrer Erscheinungsform im 19. Jahrhundert am Beispiel Gottfried Kellers* (Heidelberg: Carl Winter, 1979), esp. pp. 185–203.

3. Quoted from Jürgen Hein, ed., *Gottfried Keller: Romeo und Julia auf dem Dorfe*, Erläuterungen und Dokumente (Stuttgart: Reclam, 1971), p. 40. The review originally appeared in the Beilage to Nr. 108 of the *Augsburg Allgemeine Zeitung* (17 April 1856), pp. 1721–23.

4. Keller, *Briefe*, 3/2: 186.

5. See Wolfgang Preisendanz, "Voraussetzungen des poetischen Realismus in der deutschen Erzählkunst des 19. Jahrhunderts," *Wege des Realismus: Zur Poetik und Erzählkunst im 19. Jahrhundert* (München: Fink, 1977), pp. 68–91.

6. The notice is cited in full in volume 7 and in Hein on p. 31.

7. See Arthur Henkel, "Beim Wiederlesen von Gottfried Kellers 'Romeo und Julia auf dem Dorfe,'" *Text und Kontext* 6 (1978): 187–99; esp. 189–90.

8. Keller apparently eliminated just the initial word "Auch" for the second edition of *Die Leute von Seldwyla I* in 1873. For a discussion of the changes in the various editions, see Fränkel's afterword to vol. 7.

9. Keller, *Briefe*, 3/2: 262.

10. Quoted in Alfred Zäch, *Gottfried Keller im Spiegel seiner Zeit: Urteile und*

Berichte von Zeitgenossen über Menschen und Dichter (Zürich: Scientia, 1952), pp. 43–48; here p. 46.

11. This is the error Marshall Brown and others have committed when they oppose, with good reason, the rigid opposition between romanticism and realism; they overcompensate and force more of a continuity than actually exists. See Marshall Brown, "The Logic of Realism: A Hegelian Approach," *PMLA* 96 (1981): 224–41.

12. Hans Richter's interpretation of this passage has reality forcing the writer to retell the *Urfabel*: "it is therefore reality that compels the modern writer and at the same time allows him to tell anew the old story of the tragic pair of lovers from feuding families" (p. 112). This interpretation takes too many liberties with the text, for grammatically it is the fables that force the writer to grasp them. As strange and confused as this thought may be, the text should be respected. Hans Richter, *Gottfried Kellers frühe Novellen* (Berlin: Rütten & Loening, 1960).

13. Quoted in Heim, p. 38.

14. Quoted in Zäch, p. 47.

15. Keller, *Briefe*, 3/2: 186.

16. Ibid., p. 262.

17. See Ernst Feise, *Xenion: Themes, Forms, and Ideas in German Literature* (Baltimore: Johns Hopkins University Press, 1950), p. 156.

18. Robin Clouser, "*Romeo und Julia auf dem Dorfe*: Keller's Variations upon Shakespeare," *JEGP* 77 (1978): 161–82. For another comparison of Shakespeare and Keller, see Heinrich Richartz, *Literaturkritik als Gesellschaftskritik: Darstellungsweise und politisch-didaktische Intention in Gottfried Kellers Erzählkunst* (Bonn: Bouvier, 1975), pp. 57–69.

19. See Walter Schmiele's discussion of the Romeo and Juliet theme in his edition of the play. The authoritative study of this literary theme was written by Olin H. Moore and published in 1950. According to Moore the motif of awakening from apparent death goes back to Boccaccio. The introduction of a friar and a sleeping potion is credited to Masuccio in the thirty-third of his *Novellino* (1476). By the time we reach Luigi da Porto's *Giulietta e Romeo* (1524), the basic plot is fairly well established. Walter Schmiele, "Nachwort," *Romeo und Julia*, by William Shakespeare (Frankfurt and Berlin: Ullstein, 1963), pp. 89–117. Olin H. Moore, *The Legend of Romeo and Juliet* (Columbus: Ohio State University Press, 1950).

20. Walter Silz, "Motivation in Keller's *Romeo und Julia*," *German Quarterly* 8 (1935): 1–11.

21. Georg Wilhelm Friedrich Hegel, *Werke*, ed. Eva Moldenhauer and Karl Markus Michel (Frankfurt: Suhrkamp, 1970), 15: 567.

22. Ibid., p. 566.

23. One of the worst offenders in this regard is Heinrich Karl Roeder, "Gottfried Keller: Romeo und Julia auf dem Dorfe," *Deutsche Novellen des 19. Jahrhunderts: Interpretationen zu Storm und Keller* (Frankfurt: Diesterweg, 1964), pp. 93–119. See also Reginald H. Phelps, "Keller's Technique of Composition in *Romeo und Julia auf dem Dorfe*," *Germanic Review* 24 (1949): 34–51.

24. As far as I can determine, Emil Ermatinger was the first critic to consider this sort of motivation in connection with Feuerbach's ethics: see Emil Ermatinger, *Gottfried Kellers Leben*. Mit Benutzung von Jakob Baechtolds Biographie, 4th and 5th ed. (Stuttgart and Berlin: Cotta, 1920), pp. 357–58. Among those who have followed him on this point are Edith A. Runge, "Ein kleiner Blick in die künstlerische Verwandlung: Zu Kellers 'Romeo und Julia auf dem Dorfe,'" *Monatshefte* 52 (1960): 249–52;

and Robert Clair Warner, "The Death Problem in the Life and Works of Gottfried Keller," Ph.D. diss., University of Connecticut, 1973.

25. See Richter, pp. 138–39.

26. Hanspeter Gsell in *Einsamkeit, Idyll und Utopie: Studien zum Problem von Einsamkeit und Bindung in Gottfried Kellers Romanen und Novellen* (Bern: Lang, 1976), feels that this is the most important obstacle to a happy solution to the conflict (p. 43).

27. Bernd Neumann, *Gottfried Keller: Eine Einführung in sein Werk* (Königstein/ Ts.: Athenäum, 1982), p. 137.

28. Gerhard Kaiser, "Sündenfall, Paradies und himmlisches Jerusalem in Kellers *Romeo und Julia auf dem Dorfe*," *Euphorion* 65 (1971): 21–48; here p. 30.

29. In this connection Henkel writes: "Her dreams too betray the inhibition in her subconscious" (p. 195). One could argue that the dreams reinforce the actions I have described at the river.

30. Fritz Martini in *Deutsche Literatur im bürgerlichen Realismus* (Stuttgart: Metzler, 1964), also recognizes this lack of clarity: "Keller weaves them [the motivations] in such a manner that they make themselves unclear" (*daß sie sich gegenseitig verunklären*) (p. 83). Kaiser, by contrast, makes a virtue out of necessity when he tries to show that the various arguments support each other: "in reality the arguments do not weaken each other, but rather belong together like the two sides of a coin" (p. 41).

31. For a review of the psychoanalytic literature on Keller, see Uwe Lemm, *Die literarische Verarbeitung der Träume Gottfried Kellers in seinem Werk* (Bern: Lang, 1982), pp. 6–42.

32. Adolf Muschg, *Gottfried Keller* (Frankfurt: Suhrkamp, 1980).

33. Sigmund Freud, *Studienausgabe*, ed. Alexander Mitscherlich et. al. (Frankfurt: Fischer, 1969–79), 2: 252, 397.

34. For a nonpsychological but basically accurate account of Keller's life and works written in English, see J. M. Lindsay, *Gottfried Keller: Life and Works* (London: Oswald Wolff, 1968)

35. Freud, 10: 169–79.

36. Freud, 1: 329.

37. See Eduard Hitschmann, *Gottfried Keller: Psychoanalyse des Dichters, seiner Gestalten und Motive* (Leipzig: Internationaler Psychoanalytischer Verlag, 1919). "The feelings of incest toward the mother are regularly transferred through displacement to the sister" (p. 34). Hitschmann's study, which exhibits the characteristic strengths and weaknesses of trying to psychoanalyze a writer, is based on two earlier essays: "Über Träume Gottfried Kellers," *Internationale Zeitschrift für ärztliche Psychoanalyse* 2 (1914): 41 ff.; and "Gottfried Keller: Psychoanalytische Behauptungen und Vermutungen über sein Wesen und sein Werk," *Imago* 4 (1916): 223–47, 274–316.

38. See Muschg, pp. 64–66.

39. Keller, *Briefe*, 1: 46.

40. We could also observe that the age difference between Keller and his sister— about two years and three months—is the same as that between Sali and Vrenchen.

41. Keller, *Briefe*, 1: 119.

42. Ibid., p. 121.

43. Muschg, p. 53.

44. Hitschmann, p. 73.

45. Keller, *Briefe*, 1: 121.

46. Ibid., p. 23.

47. Ermatinger, p. 352.

48. See W. Daniel Wilson, "Science, Natural Law, and Unwitting Sibling Incest in Eighteenth-Century Literature," *Studies in Eighteenth-Century Culture* 13 (1984): 249–70; Inge Vielhauer, *Bruder und Schwester: Untersuchungen und Betrachtungen zu einem Urmotiv zwischenmenschlicher Beziehung* (Bonn: Bouvier, 1979); and William Henry Hagen, "The Metaphysical Implications of Incest in Romantic Literature," Ph.D. diss., University of South Carolina, 1974.

49. Muschg, p. 20.

50. In this context it is not uninteresting to note Keller's response to Theodor Storm's poem "Geschwisterblut" ("Sibling Blood"), whose first stanza appears as an epigraph to this chapter: "On the other hand I place *your* poem 'Geschwisterliebe' [*sic*] ("Sibling Love") not among epic poetry, but among lyric poetry in the highest sense of the word; the last two lines are everything, and this everything is the most moving lyric there can be; it makes every heart that has no intimation of incest tender and sad, and at the same time it consoles" (Keller, *Briefe*, 3/1: 498). The last strophe reads as follows:

> Die Schwester von dem Nacken sein
> Löste die zarten Hände:
> "Wir wollen zu Vater und Mutter gehn,
> Da hat das Leid ein Ende."

(The sister loosened her gentle hands from his neck: "Let us go to father and mother; then our suffering will cease.")

In Theodor Storm, *Sämtliche Werke* (Leipzig: Insel, 1919), 1: 159.

51. With the expression "structure of incest," I am endeavoring to distinguish the unconscious and repressed incestuous feelings underlying *Romeo und Julia* from actual brother and sister relationships (e.g., *Moll Flanders*, *Nathan der Weise*, or *Wilhelm Meister*). In Keller's novella we encounter certain patterns of thought or action that suggest incest, as well as textual clues that support this thesis.

52. Both Richartz, pp. 62–63, and more recently Winfried Menninghaus *in Artistische Schrift: Studien zur Kompositionskunst Gottfried Kellers* (Frankfurt: Suhrkamp, 1982), p. 123, note this cancellation of difference between the two fathers.

53. That only one mother appears in the novella, Vrenchen's mother having died without any introduction to the reader, is also suggestive for my thesis.

54. I have found only two comments to this effect in the secondary literature. Warner, in his dissertation on the death problem, states: "It violates an ancient moral code of life which states that the child does not raise his hand against the parent" (90). And Helmut Rehder in "Romeo und Julia auf dem Dorfe: An Analysis," *Monatshefte* 35 (1943): 416–434, claims in the same connection: "It is the gravest revolt against the order of life with children raising their hand against their progenitor" (422). Neither explores this matter any further though.

55. Lemm, p. 108.

56. For example, Clouser, pp. 166, 169–70; or Roeder, p. 96.

57. See Henkel, p. 191.

58. Kaiser, p. 26. "The stony field of the paternal fall from grace [*des väterlichen Sündenfalles*] is for them a paradise of childhood."

59. Although Menninghaus does not associate the guilt with incest, he nevertheless recognizes a connection between the children's actions here and their later guilt: "The cruelty in the game with the doll is an expression of childlike innocence *and* a premonition of future guilt" (p. 126).

60. Hitschmann interprets this scene as a direct reflection of Keller's own experience: "One cannot escape the assumption that Keller's fantasy would not have been so attracted by the theme of the novella *Romeo und Julia*, and he would not have added his own poetic representation of the children's love, if he had not experienced a tender, comradely relationship himself as a child and spun it further in his thoughts, and this relationship was probably with Regula" (p. 74).

61. This is Otto Rank's claim in *Das Inzest-Motiv in Dichtung und Sage: Grundzüge einer Psychologie des dichterischen Schaffens* (Leipzig: Franz Deuticke, 1926). Fortunately the studies in the book are more differentiated than the claim.

62. See A. T. Cooke, "Gottfried Keller's 'Romeo und Julia auf dem Dorfe,'" *German Life and Letters* 24 (1971): 235–43; here p. 240.

63. See Kaiser, p. 28.

64. See Hildegarde Wichert Fife, "Keller's Dark Fiddler in Nineteenth-Century Symbolism of Evil," *German Life and Letters* 16 (1963): 117–27; and Lee B. Jennings, "Gottfried Keller and the Grotesque," *Monatshefte* 50 (1958): 9–20; here pp. 11–12.

65. See Mary E. Gilbert, "Zur Bildlichkeit in Kellers 'Romeo und Julia auf dem Dorfe,'" *Wirkendes Wort* 4 (1953–54): 354–58; here p. 358.

66. Dancing in the moonlight is, of course, an ancient symbol for death. See August Obermayer, "Gottfried Kellers 'Romeo und Julia auf dem Dorfe': Ein realistisches Märchen?" *Jahrbuch der Grillparzer-Gesellschaft*, dritte Folge, 12 (1976): 235–55; here p. 246.

67. Inge Graichen, *Der frühe Gottfried Keller: Menschenbild und poetische Konzeption*, (Frankfurt: Lang, 1979).

68. See Muschg, p. 257.

69. See Kaiser, pp. 30–31; Menninghaus, p. 127.

70. The recurrence of this phrase later in the novella is suggestive for the thesis presented here. The description of the lovers' first night together includes the following sentence: "With that thought they fell asleep on the uncomfortable hearth, without pillow or bolster, and slept as peacefully and quietly as two children in a cradle" (7: 144).

71. E. Allen McCormick, in "The Idylls in Keller's Romeo und Julia: A Study in Ambivalence," *German Quarterly* 35 (1962): 265–79, notes in this connection the resemblance between Vrenchen and the doll (p. 270).

72. Quoted in Zäch, p. 109.

73. Ibid., p. 110. "Brüderchen und Schwesterchen," of course, refers to one of Grimms' fairy tales.

CHAPTER FIVE

1. The parenthetical notation refers to the page number in the fourth volume of Theodor Storm, *Sämtliche Werke*, ed. Albert Köster, 8 vols. (Leipzig: Insel, 1919). Translations are my own.

2. This is analogous to the point Roland Barthes makes about Gustave Flaubert's *Un Coeur Simple* in his essay "L'Effet de Réel," *Communications* 11 (1968): 84–89.

3. Rudolf Buck in "Theodor Storm: 'Aquis submersus,'" *Deutschunterricht* 5(1) (1953): 92–107, points out that this opening also anticipates the theme of recalling the past.

4. The question of guilt in *Aquis submersus* has been controversial since the novella's appearance. It is well known that Storm denied that the lovers bear personal guilt for the tragedy. See Gertrude Storm, *Theodor Storm: Ein Bild seines Lebens*, vol. 2 (Berlin: Karl Curtius, 1913), pp. 175–76. From the recent literature on this topic, the three most interesting contributions are David A. Jackson, "Die Überwindung der Schuld in der Novelle 'Aquis submersus,'" *Schriften der Theodor-Storm-Gesellschaft* 21 (1972): 45–56; W. A. Coupe, "Zur Frage der Schuld in 'Aquis submersus,'" *Schriften der Theodor-Storm-Gesellschaft* 24 (1975): 57–72; and Gerhard Kaiser, "Aquis submersus— versunkene Kindheit: Ein literaturpsychologischer Versuch über Theodor Storm," *Euphorion* 73 (1979): 410–34.

5. It is well known that Storm utilized the chronicle of Johann Melchior Krafft for many details in *Aquis submersus*. For a discussion of the local color Storm borrowed from Krafft, see Therese Rockenbach, "Theodor Storms Chroniknovellen: Eine Untersuchung ber Quellen und Technik," Ph.D. diss., University of Müster, 1916.

6. A schematic and, unfortunately, vastly oversimplified view of the interplay between romanticism and realism in Storm's works may be found in Paul G. Bez, "The Relation of Romanticism and Realism in the Novellen of Theodor Storm," Ph.D. diss., University of Michigan, 1943.

7. Hans Bracher, *Rahmenerzählung und Verwandtes bei G. Keller, C. F. Meyer und Th. Storm: Ein Beitrag zur Technik der Novelle* (Leipzig: H. Haessel, 1909). For a discussion of the frame-story relationship in *Aquis submersus*, see Franz Stuckert, *Theodor Storm: Sein Leben und seine Welt* (Bremen: Carl Schünemann, 1955), p. 335; E. Allen McCormick, *Theodor Storm's Novellen: Essays on Literary Technique* (Chapel Hill: University of North Carolina Press, 1964), pp. 91–107; Josef Kunz, *Die deutsche Novelle im 19. Jahrhundert* (Berlin: Erich Schmidt, 1970), pp. 143–44; Leonard L. Duroche, "Like and Look Alike: Symmetry and Irony in Theodor Storm's *Aquis submersus*," *Seminar* 7 (1971): 1–13; and Reinhard Struve, "Funktionen des Rahmens in Theodor Storms Novelle 'Aquis submersus,'" *Schriften der Theodor-Storm-Gesellschaft* 23 (1974): 28–32.

8. W. F. Mainland, "Theodor Storm," *German Men of Letters*, ed. Alex Nathan, vol. 1 (London: Wolff, 1961), p. 162. See Struve: "This function of the frame—mediation between the present of the reader and the past of the material—simultaneously serves to make the representations credible. The objectivity is increased by the coincidence of finding the chronicle and by the removal of the author from the narrative; at the same time this enhances the receptive posture of the reader" (p. 30).

9. Storm's dependence on recollection has long been a topic of scholarship. For two early examples see Richard M. Meyer, *Die deutsche Literatur des Neunzehnten Jahrhunderts* (Berlin: Georg Bondi, 1910), pp. 466–69; and Ottokar Fischer, "Das Problem der Erinnerung," *Das literarische Echo* 15.24 (1911): 1717–24.

10. See Georg Lukács, *Die Seele und die Formen: Essays* (Neuwied: Luchüterhand, 1971), p. 111.

11. Karl Laage, "Das Erinnerungsmotiv in Theodor Storms Novellistik," *Schriften der Theodor-Storm-Gesellschaft* 7 (1958): 17–39.

12. Bracher, p. 110. In this regard I agree with Preisendanz's assessment: "Al-

though Storm distanced himself from the conventional norms of completely transparent plot developments, of air-tight motivation, and of the clearly developed portrayal of conflict, he did not want to focus attention on the problems of poetic and linguistic consistency building, but rather he wanted to bring to light something about the reality of human existence." Wolfgang Preisendanz, "Gedichtete Perspektiven in Storms Erzähl-kunst," *Wege des Realismus: Zur Poetik und Erzählkunst im 19. Jahrhundert* (München: Fink, 1977), p. 214. See also Dieter Lohmeier, "Erzählprobleme des Poetischen Realis-mus: Am Beispiel von Storm's Novelle 'Auf dem Staatshof,'" *Schriften der Theodor-Storm-Gesellschaft* 28 (1979): 109–22; here p. 114.

13. Terence John Rogers, *Techniques of Solipsism: A Study of Theodor Storm's Narra-tive Fiction* (Cambridge, Eng.: Modern Humanities Research Association, 1970), pp. 117–26.

14. Fritz Martini hit upon a felicitous phrase when he called Storm's brand of realism "psychological realism of experience" (*psychologischer Erfahrungsrealismus*) (p. 650). Fritz Martini, *Deutsche Literatur im bürgerlichen Realismus: 1848–1898*, 3d ed. (Stuttgart: Metzler, 1974).

15. For an overview of the various time segments, see Ernst Feise, "Theodor Storms 'Aquis submersus': Eine Formanalyse," *Xenion: Themes, Forms, and Ideas in Ger-man Literature* (Baltimore: Johns Hopkins University Press, 1950), pp. 226–40; esp. pp. 230–31. Feise errs, however, in placing the time of composition of the first notebook before the events of 1666.

16. See Thea Müller, *Theodor Storms Erzählung "Aquis submersus"* (Marburg: N. G. Elwert'sche Verlagsbuchhandlung, 1925), pp. 32–33; and Peter Goldhammer, *Theo-dor Storm: Eine Einführung in Leben und Werk* (Leipzig: Reclam, 1966), pp. 181–82.

17. Concerning the lack of reflection in Storm's work, Preisendanz writes: "This literature does not yet reflect on itself, it does not yet enter into a debate with itself, it does not make its own problematic, its own failure, its own potential, a theme" (p. 214). I could only agree with this statement if one adds that Storm did not *consciously* or *intentionally* reflect on these matters in his work in the way in which twentieth-century (and romantic) writers often do. As the following discussion will show, there is a great deal of reflection on the basis of realistic portrayal—perhaps in spite of Storm—in the text of *Aquis submersus*.

18. I am ignoring in this essay the relationship between the paintings in the novella and the portraits in Drelsdorf, which evidently served as an inspiration for the work. For an account of the scholarly confusions surrounding this real-life influence, see Karl Friedrich Boll, "Das Bonnixsche Epitaph in Drelsdorf und die Kirchenbilder in Theodor Storm's Erzählung 'Aquis submersus,'" *Schriften der Theodor-Storm-Gesellschaft* 14 (1965): 24–39.

19. The best discussion of the dual nature of commemoration and the paintings in *Aquis submersus* is found in the first section of Clifford A. Bernd's *Theodor Storm's Craft of Fiction: The Torment of a Narrator* (Chapel Hill: University of North Carolina Press, 1963). By a slightly different route, Bernd arrives at similar conclusions concerning the contradictions in the novella.

20. Recollection is thus also related to Storm's conception of history. As Walter Brecht has shown in "Storm und die Geschichte," *Deutsche Vierteljahrsschrift* 3 (1925): 444–62, Storm conceived of history primarily as family history, such as those recollected by his narrators.

21. See McCormick, p. 127.

22. Storm, *Werke*, 4: 215.
23. Ibid., pp. 124–25, 147.
24. Ibid., 3: 118–19, 143–44.
25. Coupe also points to this paradox in his essay.
26. See Coupe, p. 65.

CHAPTER SIX

1. Wilhelm Raabe, *Sämtliche Werke*, Braunschwieger Ausgabe (Göttingen: Vandenhoeck & Ruprecht, 1965), 1: 74–75.
2. Theodor Storm, *Sämtliche Werke*, ed. Albert Köster (Leipzig: Insel, 1923), 7: 256.
3. Ibid., p. 375.
4. Ibid., p. 257.
5. See Klaus Jeziorkowski, "Die Kunst der Perspektiven." *Germanisch-romanische Monatsschrift*, Vol. 48, NF 17 (1967): 398–416; here p. 399.
6. Conrad Ferdinand Meyer, *Sämtliche Werke*, Historisch-kritische Ausgabe, ed. Hans Zeller and Alfred Zäch (Bern: Benteli, 1961), 12: 56.
7. See W. D. Williams, *The Stories of C. F. Meyer* (Oxford: Oxford University Press, 1962), p. 49.
8. See Marianne Burkhard, *Conrad Ferdinand Meyer* (Boston: Twayne, 1978), pp. 77–78.
9. See Kathleen L. Komar, "Fact, Fiction, and Focus: Their Structural Embodiment in C. F. Meyer's 'Der Heilige,'" *Colloquia Germanica* 14 (1981): 332–41.
10. The numbers in parentheses refer to volume 13 of Meyer's *Sämtliche Werke*. I have consulted the translation entitled *The Saint* by W. F. Twaddell (Providence, R.I.: Brown University Press, 1977).
11. See Sjaak Onderdelinden, *Die Rahmenerzählungen Conrad Ferdinand Meyers* (Leiden: Universitaire Pers Leiden, 1974), p. 109.
12. Hans's interests, motives, and contradictions have rarely received sufficient attention in secondary literature. An exception is the essay by Michael Shaw, "C. F. Meyer's Resolute Heroes: A Study of Becket, Astorre and Pescara," *Deutsche Vierteljahrsschrift* 40 (1966): 360–90.
13. See Gunter H. Hertling, *Conrad Ferdinand Meyers Epik: Traumbeseelung, Traumbesinnung und Traumbesitz* (Bern: Francke, 1973), p. 100.
14. See Uwe Böker, "C. F. Meyers 'Der Heilige': Die Bedeutung der Erzählhaltung für die Interpretation der Novelle," *Studia Neophilologica* 39 (1967): 60–79. "The story can never be told objectively since in bringing the events into the present time a part of the consciousness of the narrator is always mixed in" (p. 72).
15. For a study of irony in *Der Heilige* see Tamara S. Evans, *Formen der Ironie in Conrad Ferdinand Meyers Novellen* (Bern: Francke, 1980), pp. 59–76.
16. The most detailed study of Meyer's sources is by R. Travis Hardaway, "C. F. Meyer's *Der Heilige* in Relation to Its Sources," *PMLA* 58 (1943): 245–63. Volume 13 also supplies useful information on pp. 301–5.
17. Conrad Ferdinand Meyer, *Briefe*, ed. Adolf Frey (Leipzig: H. Haessel, 1908), 2: 279.

18. Ibid., p. 140.

19. See especially his *Metahistory: The Historical Imagination in Nineteenth Century Europe* (Baltimore: Johns Hopkins University Press, 1973).

20. Walter Silz, *Realism and Reality: Studies in the German Novelle of Poetic Realism* (Chapel Hill: University of North Carolina Press, 1954), speaking of Meyer's work, states the following: "Here a supreme master in the poetic recreation of the past seems to call into question the very possibility of history as a true record of 'reality' in the higher sense" (p. 96).

21. Almost every critic deals with this issue to some degree. Two studies of particular importance for this matter are those by Walter Hof, "Beobachtungen zur Funktion der Vieldeutigkeit in Conrad Ferdinand Meyers Novelle 'Der Heilige,'" *Acta Germanica* 3 (1968): 207–23; and Manfred R. Jacobson, "The Narrator's Allusions to Art and Ambiguity: A Note on C. F. Meyer's *Der Heilige*," *Seminar* 10 (1974): 265–73.

22. For an illustration of a one-dimensional reading of this novella, see Colin Walker, "Unbelief and Martyrdom in C. F. Meyer's *Der Heilige*," *German Life and Letters* 21 (1967–68): 111–22.

23. Lewis W. Tusken, for example, in "C. F. Meyer's *Der Heilige*: The Problem of Becket's Conversion," *Seminar* 7 (1971): 201–15, suggests that Becket discovers that his will and God's are identical with respect to Henry.

24. Meyer, *Briefe*, 2: 300.

25. See Leo Löwenthal, "Conrad Ferdinand Meyers heroische Geschichtsauffassung," *Zeitschrift für Sozialforschung* 2(1) (1933): 34–62.

26. Most strikingly in his *Zur Genealogie der Moral* (1887).

27. Meyer himself seems to have just this in mind when he comments as follows in a letter to Klinkel on 16 March 1879: "It is a composition that is without a doubt magnificent, but unpleasant on account of its realism and ambiguous as life itself." Quoted from *Sämtliche Werke*, 13: 287.

28. Meyer, *Briefe*, 2: 66.

29. See W. A. Coupe, "Thierry, Meyer and 'Der Heilige,'" *German Life and Letters* 16 (1962–63): 105–16; here p. 108.

30. Quoted in *Sämtliche Werke*, 13: 130.

31. Many of the related works Meyer probably read, for example, Walter Scott's *Ivanhoe*, stress this racial factor as well.

32. Thomas Percy, ed., *Reliques of Ancient English Poetry*, vol. 2 (London: J. M. Dent, 1906), pp. 19–26.

33. See *Rosamunde* (1812) in Körner's *Sämtliche Werke*, vol. 3 (Stuttgart: Cotta, n.d.), pp. 159–248.

34. For a more traditional interpretation of this episode, see Mary Crichton, "Zur Funktion der Gnade-Episode in C. F. Meyers *Der Heilige*," *Lebendige Form: Interpretationen zur deutschen Literatur*, Festschrift for Heinrich E. K. Henel, ed. Jeffrey Sammons and Ernst Schürer (München: Fink, 1976), pp. 245–58.

35. See Friedrich Christian Schlosser, *Weltgeschichte für das deutsche Volk*, Unter Mitwirkung des Verfassers bearbeitet von G. L. Kriegk, vol. 5 (Frankfurt: Franz Varrentrapp, 1846), particularly section 13 of the initial chapter.

36. Meyer, *Briefe*, 2: 99.

37. Ibid., p. 205

38. Edward W. Said, *Orientalism* (New York: Pantheon, 1978), p. 72.

39. This is Silz's suggestion on p. 109 of his study.

40. V. G. Kiernan, *The Lord of Humankind: Black Man, Yellow Man, and White Man in an Age of Empire* (Boston: Little, Brown & Co., 1969), p. 131.

CHAPTER SEVEN

1. Erich Auerbach, *Mimesis: Dargestellte Wirklichkeit in der abendländlischen Literatur*, 2d expanded ed. (Bern: Francke, 1959), p. 458.

2. René Wellek, "The Concept of Realism in Literary Scholarship," *Neophilologus* 45 (1961): 1–20; here p. 10.

3. Georg Friedrich Wilhelm Hegel, *Werke in zwanzig Bänden* (Frankfurt: Suhrkamp, 1970), 14: 221.

4. Ibid., 13: 253–54.

5. Ibid., 15: 392.

6. The notion of programmatic realism as a "compensatory ideology" is developed in an essay by Ludwig Stockinger in "Realpolitik, Realismus und das Ende des bürgerlichen Wahrheitsanspruchs: Überlegungen zur Funktion des programmatischen Realismus am Beispiel von Gustav Freytags *Soll und Haben*," *Bürgerlicher Realismus: Grundlagen und Interpretationen*, ed. Klaus-Detlef Müller (Königstein/Ts.: Athenäum, 1981), pp. 174–202.

7. The best study of the social and historical environment in which German realism originated and thrived is Peter Uwe Hohendahl's *Literarische Kultur im Zeitalter des Liberalismus 1830–1870* (München: Beck, 1985). Hohendahl concentrates in particular on the notion of the public sphere and the institution of literature.

8. See Claus Richter, *Leiden an der Gesellschaft: Vom literarischen Liberalismus zum poetischen Realismus* (Königstein/Ts.: Athenäum, 1978), pp. 140–48; and Hermann Kinder, *Poesie als Synthese: Ausbreitung eines deutschen Realismus-Verständnisses in der Mitte des 19. Jahrhunderts* (Frankfurt: Athenäum, 1973), pp. 139–99.

9. To understand where Freytag and Schmidt fit into the tradition of novels about the merchant class see Wolfgang Kockjoy, *Der deutsche Kaufmannsroman: Versuch einer kultur- und geistesgeschichtlichen genetischen Darstellung* (Strassburg: Universitätsbuchdruckerei Heitz & Co., 1932); and Harald Obendiek, *Konturen des Kaufmanns: Die Entstehung eines beruflichen Leitbildes in der belletristischen Literatur des 19. Jahrhunderts* (Gelsenkirchen: Müller, 1984). A stimulating study of the depiction of merchants in German literature of the eighteenth century can be found in John W. Van Cleve, *The Merchant in German Literature of the Enlightenment* (Chapel Hill: University of North Carolina Press, 1986). Of particular relevance for my concerns in this chapter are his remarks on Jewish merchants.

10. Parenthetical citations to the novel are taken from Gustav Freytag, *Soll und Haben* (München: Droemer, n.d.). Translations are my own.

11. George Lillo, *The London Merchant or The History of George Barnwell* (Boston: Heath, 1906), p. 53.

12. Ibid., p. 52.

13. Theodor Fontane, *Schriften und Glossen zur europäischen Literatur*, vol. 2, ed. Werner Weber (Zürich: Artemis, 1967), p. 375.

14. See Hartmut Steinecke, "Gustav Freytags *Soll und Haben* (1855): Weltbild und Wirkung eines deutschen Bestsellers," *Romane und Erzählungen des Bürgerlichen*

Realismus: Neue Interpretationen, ed. Horst Denkler (Stuttgart: Reclam, 1980), pp. 138–52; and "Gustav Freytags Soll und Haben—ein realistischer Roman?" *Formen realistischer Erzählkunst: Festschrift für Charlotte Jolles*, ed. Jörg Thunecke (Nottingham: Sherwood Press, 1979), pp. 108–19.

15. Leo Löwenthal, *Schriften*, vol. 2, ed. Helmut Dubiel (Frankfurt: Suhrkamp, 1981), p. 360.

16. In *The Rise of the German Novel: Crisis and Charisma* (Cambridge, Mass.: Harvard University Press, 1986) Russell Berman attaches the label "realism" to the novel and contends that it is the key work in the transformation of the German bourgeoisie from liberalism to imperialism. His interpretation, in contrast to mine, emphasizes that Freytag's realism propagates an "aesthetics of capitalist commodities" (p. 92) in form, content, and modes of reader interaction (pp. 79–104).

17. The most recent, as far as I can tell, is Helmut Schwitzgebel, who defends Freytag's portrayal of Jewish characters with an appeal to realism: "These are not monstrous outgrowths of hatred for Jews; nor are they characters that originate in an anti-Semitically colored literary tradition, but figures from an environment which he had experienced himself and for which there were numerous prototypes and models in Breslau." Helmut Schwitzgebel, "Gustav Freytags 'Soll und Haben' in der Tradition des deutschen Kaufmannromans," *Gustav-Freytag-Blätter* 24 (1980): 3–12; 25 (1981): 3–11; and 26 (1982): 3–13; here 24: 8. On the claim that these characters are not part of a literary tradition of anti-Semitism, Schwitzgebel is simply wrong. Just how stereotypical Freytag's figures are can be easily seen from a brief look at anti-Semitic writings from the first half of the nineteenth century, for example, the works of Friedrich Freiherr von Holzschuher (whose pen name for his anti-Semitic works was Itzig Feitel Stern) or Hartwig Hundt-Rudowsky. In their works one finds all the clichés that reappear in Freytag's novels. Freytag, in short, perceived the reality of Breslau as he was conditioned to see this reality by prejudices rampant in German society. If we are charitable, then Schwitzgebel's remarks can be seen as merely hopelessly naive; but I fear that they are more likely themselves a continuation of the pernicious tradition from which he would like to extricate Freytag.

18. For a review of Freytag's relationships with three prominent Jewish intellectuals of his era—Berthold Auerbach, Karl Emil Franzos, and Jakob Kaufmann—see Margarita Pazi, "Wie gleicht man auch ethisch Soll und Haben aus?" *Zeitschrift für deutsche Philologie* 106 (1987): 198–218.

19. For the possible origins of this name, see Mark H. Gelber, "Die literarische Umwelt zu Gustav Freytags *Soll und Haben* und die Realismustheorie der *Grenzboten*," *Orbis Litterarum* 39 (1984): 38–53; here p. 45.

20. I would agree with critics like Michael Schneider who contend that Jewish business in the novel is supposed to represent a deviation from the bourgeois norm, an unfortunate consequence of a certain stage of capitalism. But I think that in ignoring the passages in which the German-Jewish dichotomy collapses, such critics fail to note an important, albeit unintended, subtext in this work. Michael Schneider, *Geschichte als Gestalt: Gustav Freytags Roman "Soll und Haben"* (Stuttgart: Hans-Dieter Heinz, 1980).

21. See Stockinger, pp. 182–97.

22. Jeffrey L. Sammons likewise notes a collapse of "Freytag's socio-ethical structure." Although he views it chiefly in literary terms, I think he is correct in seeing it as "paradigmatic for the dilemmas of the bourgeois intellectual of mid-nineteenth-

century Germany." Jeffrey L. Sammons, "The Evaluation of Freytag's *Soll und Haben*," *German Life and Letters* 22 (1968–69): 315–24; here p. 321.

23. This is the important point made by E. McInnes in "'Die Poesie des Geschäfts': Social Analysis and Polemic in Freytag's *Soll und Haben*," *Formen realistischer Erzählkunst: Festschrift für Charlotte Jolles*, ed. Jörge Thunecke (Nottingham: Sherwood Press, 1979), pp. 99–107.

24. For a description of this success, see T. E. Carter, "Freytag's *Soll und Haben*: A Liberal National Manifesto as Best-Seller," *German Life and Letters* 21 (1967–68): 320–29.

25. Parenthetical citations refer to Wilhelm Raabe, *Der Hungerpastor*, ed. Hermann Pongs, in *Sämtliche Werke*, ed. Karl Hoppe, vol. 6 (Freiburg: Hermann Klemm, 1953). I have consulted the abridged translation of *The Hunger Pastor* by Muriel Almon in volume XI of *The German Classics: Masterpieces of German Literature* (New York: German Publication Society, 1914), pp. 353–540.

26. Although the similarities are evident, as far as I can tell, Raabe scholarship has tended to play them down. Typical in this regard is Hermann Pongs, who feels that only the "larger framework" is similar to that of Freytag's novel. Hermann Pongs, *Wilhelm Raabe: Leben und Werk* (Heidelberg: Quelle & Meyer, 1953), pp. 214–15. Because of its proximity to *Soll und Haben* and its blatant stereotypes, one can understand why Raabe scholars are uncomfortable. That this work has been perhaps Raabe's most popular over the years is further cause for distress, and in this regard one is forced to agree with Barker Fairly's judgment: "We put this work down with the regrettable thought that *Der Hungerpastor* would hardly be alive today if the names were distributed differently and the bad youth were called Hans Unwirrsch and the good boy Moses Freudenstein." Barker Fairly, *Wilhelm Raabe: Eine Deutung seiner Romane* (München: Beck, 1961), p. 164.

27. I am ignoring here, of course, differences in form and in narrative technique. Even in this novel, which is not Raabe's finest performance by any means, he clearly shows that he is a more skillful and engaging writer than Freytag.

28. Raabe's anti-Semitism has been a controversial topic. Although he himself was obviously not anti-Jewish, it is difficult to deny that this novel is. Still, he has had apologists for his work, the most recent of whom is Horst Denkler, who, like Schwitzgebel, attributes the Jewish characterization to a fidelity to reality. This argument is at best extremely naïve. Indeed, one of the points of this study is to show that there is no reality waiting to be captured, that realism, the movement identified with depicting social reality, is much more complex and contradictory than the mirror metaphor usually associated with it. Raabe may have even thought that he was simply describing reality, but it is precisely the intersubjectively determined structures of perception and portrayal that are significant for the realist enterprise. See Horst Denkler, "Das 'wirckliche Juda' und der 'Renegat,'" *German Quarterly* 60 (1987): 5–18; and my reply to Denkler, "Raabe's Impartiality: A Reply to Horst Denkler," *German Quarterly* 60 (1987): 617–22. A more sober and balanced account of "Raabe and the Jews" may be found in the recent monograph by Jeffrey Sammons, *Wilhelm Raabe: The Fiction of the Alternative Community* (Princeton, N.J.: Princeton University Press, 1987), pp. 73–87. In general, Sammon's book takes on the rather formidable task of establishing Raabe as a major German and European writer of the late nineteenth century. Denkler's last two book-length publications, the first of which contains the apology for anti-Semitism, undertake a similar task for a German audience. See Horst Denkler, *Neues über Wilhelm Raabe:*

Zehn Annäherungsversuche an einen verkannten Schriftsteller (Tübingen: Niemeyer, 1988); and *Wilhelm Raabe: Legende, Leben, Literatur* (Tübingen: Niemeyer, 1989).

29. A strange episode in *Der Hungerpastor* reinforces the—perhaps unconscious—anti-Semitism. When Hans travels to Grunzenow for the first time, he witnesses a Jew being beaten (364). Later, when he is taking his beloved Fränzchen to his village paradise, we read: "Today it was only pleasurable [*vergnüglich*] to show Fränzchen the spot on which, during his first trip to Grunzenow, the wagon got stuck in the mud and where the enraged farmer driving the team had once beat up the Jew and then wanted to collar the servant of God, the candidate Hans Unwirrsch" (419). It is rather odd that Raabe has the kindly Hans derive pleasure from recalling and relating another's misfortunes. It seems that the Jew is worth little more than an animal in this passage—unless we ascribe the association of amusement and the beating of the Jew to a syntactical oversight on Raabe's part.

30. Pierre Angel has also seen that Moses resembles the Jewish businessman despite his occupation: "D'alleurs, dans l'esprit de Raabe, Moïse n'incarne-t-il pas plutôt que le judaïsme qu'il a renié, les aspects negatifs de la civilisation moderne axée sur la recherche du profit?" Pierre Angel, *Le Personnage juif dans le roman allemand (1855–1915): La racine littéraire de l'antisémetisme Outre-Rhin* (Montreal: Didier, 1973), p. 33.

31. This "revolutionary" aspect of the bourgeoisie is continuously stressed by Karl Marx, most prominently, perhaps, in the first section of the *Communist Manifesto*: "The bourgeoisie cannot exist without continuously revolutionizing the instruments of production, and thus the relations of production, and thus the entire social relations." *Marx Engels Werke*, vol. 4 (Berlin: Dietz Verlag, 1974), p. 465.

32. Parenthetical citations refer to vol. 12 of Gottfried Keller's *Sämtliche Werke*, ed. Carl Helbling (Bern: Benteli, 1943). Translations are my own.

33. Walter Benjamin, *Schriften*, vol 1, ed. Th. W. Adorno and Gretel Adorno (Frankfurt: Suhrkamp, 1955), p. 498.

34. The naiveté that Adorno finds in the novel seems to stem from his identifying Martin's economic perspective with Keller's own. See Theodor Adorno, "Über epische Naivetät," *Noten zur Literatur* (Frankfurt: Suhrkamp, 1974), pp. 34–40, esp. 36. In my view what makes the novel interesting in terms of ideology and character is precisely Keller's inability to subscribe to the "petty-bourgeois" notions that he formerly harbored—for example, at the time of the composition of *Die Leute von Selwyla*—and that Martin still espouses.

35. See Margarete Merkel-Nipperdey, *Gottfried Kellers "Martin Salander": Untersuchungen zur Struktur des Zeitromans* (Göttingen: Vandenhoeck & Ruprecht, 1959), p. 94.

36. "He knew how to talk to and to confuse large and small creditors in such a way that they could not become decisive" (74).

37. For a discussion of the structuring principle of the novel, see Dieter Kafitz, *Figurenkonstellation als Mittel der Wirklichkeitserfassung* (Kronberg: Athenäum, 1978), pp. 65–90.

38. The term "poetic realism" continues to be popular among scholars of German literature, despite the oxymoron, as a designation for the period and for the style used in that period. Although I prefer Martini's term "bourgeois realism," Roy C. Cowen has a point when he argues that the best authors of "bourgeois realism," Keller, Storm, Fontane, Meyer, and Raabe, can be viewed as a subgroup of "poetic realists." In this

case, of course, the term forfeits any literary-historical value and becomes evaluative in nature. See Roy C. Cowen, *Der Poetische Realismus: Kommentar zu einer Epoche* (Munich: Winkler, 1985), esp. pp. 9–31. The most useful book on the topic in English is Clifford Albrecht Bernd's *German Poetic Realism* (Boston: Twayne, 1981).

39. Otto Ludwig, *Werke*, ed. Arthur Eloesser (Berlin: Bong & Co., n.d.), vol. 2 (part 4), pp. 183–84.

40. See Wolfgang Preisendanz, "Voraussetzungen des poetischen Realismus in der deutschen Erzählkunst des 19. Jahrhunderts," *Wege des Realismus: Zur Poetik und Erzählkunst im 19. Jahrhundert* (München: Fink, 1977), pp. 68–91.

41. Ludwig, p. 182.

42. These are the identical sentiments Freytag himself expresses in the *Grenzboten* 12 (1853): 77–80, 157–60. He criticizes contemporary fiction for seeing the poetic in contrast with reality, affirming the poeticity of work and practical life.

43. The phrase is found in Bernd Bräutigam, "Candide im Comptoir: Zur Bedeutung der Poesie in Gustav Freytags 'Soll und Haben,'" *Germanisch-romanische Monatsschrift* 35 (1985): 395–411; here p. 403.

44. For a discussion of the anti-Semitism latent in even this seemingly positive Jewish figure, see Mark H. Gelber, "An Alternative Reading of the Role of the Jewish Scholar in Gustav Freytag's *Soll und Haben*," *Germanic Review* 58 (1983): 83–88.

45. See, for example, J. M. Ritchie, "The Place of 'Martin Salander' in Gottfried Keller's Evolution as Prose Writer," *Modern Language Review* 52 (1957): 214–22; and Bernd Neumann, *Gottfried Keller: Eine Einführung in sein Werk* (Königstein/Ts.: Athenäum, 1982), pp. 266–302.

46. Gerhard Kaiser, *Gottfried Keller: Das gedichtete Leben* (Frankfurt: Insel, 1981), p. 588.

47. Keller himself saw that his novel was lacking the former poetic element. In a conversation reported by Adolf Vögtlin, referring to *Martin Salander*, he supposedly said: "It is not beautiful! There is too little poetry in it!" (531). *Gottfried Keller: Dichter über ihre Dichtung*, ed. Klaus Jeziorkowski ([München]: Heimeran, [1969]), p. 531.

48. Hegel, 14: 222.

CHAPTER EIGHT

1. This is certainly the reason that realism has always received so much support from Marxist critics. Though it purports to show simply what is actually happening, by doing this it exposes the most blatant societal abuses. This was, of course, Karl Marx's and Friedrich Engels's rationale for favoring realism over tendentious literature, and their views were followed, with slight modification by Franz Mehring and Georg Lukács. What this view ignores, and what I have been trying to show, is that these texts also possess an ideological function, and that this function is frequently more problematic and ultimately more conservative than critics have cared to admit.

2. Indeed, in some senses one could contend that the crisis in poetic imagination and representation reached a climax in the naturalist movement, on the one hand, and in the aestheticism of *Jugendstil*, on the other. Each of these movements exaggerates one half of the uneasy concept of poetic realism.

3. Arno Holz, *Die Kunst: Ihr Wesen und ihre Gesetze* (Berlin: Wilhelm Issleib, 1891), p. 115.

4. Ibid., p. 117.

5. Ibid., p. 122.

6. See Ulrich Fülleborn, "Form und Sinn der 'Aufzeichnungen des Malte Laurids Brigge': Rilkes Prosabuch und der moderne Roman," *Deutsche Romantheorien: Beiträge zu einer historischen Poetik des Romans in Deutschland*, ed. Reinhold Grimm (Frankfurt: Athenäum, 1968), pp. 251–73.

7. Parenthetical citations refer to Rainer Maria Rilke, *Werke*, vol. 5 (Frankfurt: Insel, 1965). I have consulted the translation by M. D. Herder Norton, *The Notebooks of Malte Laurids Brigge* (New York: Norton, 1949).

8. See Judith Ryan, "Hypothetisches Erzählen: Zur Funktion von Phantasie und Einbildung in Rilkes 'Malte Laurids Brigge,'" *Jahrbuch der deutschen Schillergesellschaft* (1971): 341–74; here p. 344.

9. Sigmund Freud, "Das Unheimliche," *Psychologische Schriften*, Studienausgabe, vol. 4 (Frankfurt: Fischer, 1982), pp. 241–74; here p. 244.

10. See Idris Parry, "Malte's Hand," *German Life and Letters* 11 (1957): 1–12; and Frederic C. Tubach, "The Image of the Hand in Rilke's Poetry," *PMLA* 76 (1961): 240–46.

11. The connections between the two are reinforced in the mirror episode when Malte again notices his hand: "My hand, over which the lace cuff fell and fell again, was anything but my usual hand" (204). Similar to the earlier experience under the table are both the recognition of, and the alienation from, his own hand.

12. In contrast to my view, Ernst Fedor Hoffmann, in "Zum dichterischen Verfahren in Rilkes 'Aufzeichnungen des Malte Laurids Brigge,'" *Deutsche Vierteljahrsschrift* 42 (1968): 202–30, sees a progression away from the fantastic from the hand to the mirror episode (p. 227). In my opinion he thus makes too much of the uncanniness of the former and ignores this same quality in the latter.

13. The actual circumstances contradict this meaning. Christine is obviously not in the gallery, but Erik has also stated she is not in the mirror.

14. According to Small's commentary, these six tapestries were hung in the Cluny Museum in Paris. Five represented the senses; the other belongs to another grouping. William Small, *Rilke—Kommentar zu den Aufzeichnungen des Malte Laurids Brigge* (Chapel Hill: University of North Carolina Press, 1983), p. 38. M. D. Herter Norton claims that the sixth represents "the summation of all that man requires of the fair sex." See Rainer Maria Rilke, *The Notebooks of Malte Laurids Brigge*, trans. M. D. Herter Norton (New York: Norton, 1949), p. 225.

15. See Ryan, pp. 362–63. Ryan's essay contains the best analysis of the complex narrative techniques and of the relationship between text and reality.

16. In the poem "Das Einhorn" in *Neue Gedichte*, Rilke calls the unicorn "das niegeglaubte / das weiße Tier." Rilke, *Werke*, 2: 262.

17. Ibid., p. 509. (*Sonette an Orpheus*, Part 2, IV)

18. Ibid. The translation is by M. D. Herter Norton, *Sonnets to Orpheus* (New York: Norton, 1942), p. 77.

19. See Fülleborn, p. 261.

20. "We found that if everything happened naturally that would always be the most fantastic" (199).

21. Although the novel was first published posthumously in 1925, Kafka worked on it in 1914 and 1915. In a recent study Stephen D. Dowden examines *Der Prozeß* as a pivotal work in Kafka's oeuvre. Dowden claims that this novel "demarcates his

turn towards self-reflexive irony" and discusses the work in part as it relates to realist aesthetics. See Stephen D. Dowden, *Sympathy for the Abyss: A Study in the Novel of German Modernism: Kafka, Broch, Musil, and Thomas Mann* (Tübingen: Niemeyer, 1986), esp. pp. 94–134.

22. Heinz Politzer, *Franz Kafka: Parable and Paradox*, rev. and exp. ed. (Ithaca, N.Y.: Cornell University Press, 1966), p. 206.

23. Parenthetical notations refer to Franz Kafka, *Der Prozeß* (Frankfurt: Fischer, 1983). I have consulted the standard translation by Willa and Edwin Muir, as revised and adapted by E. M. Butler (New York: Random House, 1964).

24. See, for example, Wilhelm Emrich, *Franz Kafka* (Bonn: Athenäum, 1958), pp. 285–97; and H. Uyttersprot, *Eine neue Ordnung der Werke Kafkas?: Zur Struktur von "Der Prozess" und "Amerika"* (Antwerpen: C. de Vries-Brouwers, 1957), pp. 54–60.

25. An exception here is Walter H. Sokel in "The Three Endings of Joseph K. and the Role of Art in *The Trial*," *The Kafka Debate: New Perspectives for Our Time*, ed. Angel Flores (New York: Gordian Press, 1977), pp. 335–53. In contrast to my view, Sokel attributes a more active function to art in Kafka's universe. He sees art as "myth-making" (p. 347); I see it as myth-affirming.

26. Most critics, of course, starting with Herbert Tauber's book *Franz Kafka: Eine Deutung seiner Werke* (Zürich: Oprecht, 1941), have concentrated on the three possibilities of acquittal. My own view is that these are of no more help for K. than any other information he receives, and that the portions of the conversation that deal with art are much more important for an understanding of K.'s predicament and the workings of the court.

27. Malcolm Pasley, "Two Literary Sources of Kafka's *Der Prozess*," *Forum for Modern Language Studies* 3 (1967): 142–47.

28. Freud's analysis is based on a careful examination of the position of the right hand and the tablets. See Sigmund Freud, "Der Moses des Michelangelo," *Studienausgabe*, vol. 10 (Frankfurt: Fischer, 1982), pp. 195–220.

29. For an opposing view see Laurence Arthur Rickels, "The Iconic Imagination: Pictorial Signs in Lessing, Keller, and Kafka," Ph.D. diss., Princeton University, 1981, pp. 216–26. Rickels is one of the first to pay careful attention to Titorelli's paintings, and he analyzes them as serial repetitions of a nonexisting original. His aesthetics are thus a kind of pictorial representation of the juridical alternatives he provides to K., since they entail the indefinite postponement of a verdict. Neither painting nor the legal procedure ever reaches a conclusion or emanates from an identifiable source.

INDEX

251

INDEX